THE JOURNAL OF
ARNOLD BENNETT

**

FACSIMILE PAGES FROM THE JOURNAL AT DIFFERENT PERIODS

THE JOURNAL OF

ARNOLD BENNETT

1911–1920

* *

NEW YORK

THE VIKING PRESS

MCMXXXII

THE JOURNAL

1911–1914

1911

Friday, January 6th. Paris.

After several days' delay owing to indisposition, I began to write *Hilda Lessways* yesterday afternoon; only 400 words. Today, 1100 words. It seems to be a goodish beginning.

On Wednesday the Godebskis[1] came for dinner, and Simon, Châteaubriant, and Fargue came afterwards. I got from the last all details necessary for my preface to the English translation of *Marie-Claire*.

The *Chronicle* asked me to resume my articles at 5 guineas a col. I asked for six.

Thursday, January 12th.

I went to see Lee Matthews[2] and B. de Zoete at Hotel St. James Sunday afternoon. Discussion of play prospects.

Monday.

B. de Zoete and Violet Hunt came for lunch. Calvo[3] for dinner. F. M. Hueffer[4] and V. Hunt came after dinner, and stayed till 12.15. He smoked 4 of my cigars and took away another 2 to smoke at his hotel. He

---

[1] Cepa Godebski, a painter of considerable repute in Paris, was an intimate friend of Arnold Bennett.
[2] An intimate friend, member of the Stage Society.
[3] Cipa Calvocoressi, music critic and lecturer, and a close friend of Arnold Bennett.
[4] Ford Madox Hueffer, who did not change his name to Ford Madox Ford until 1919. Violet Hunt, the novelist and author of racy memoirs, collaborated in 1915 with Mr. Hueffer to write *Zeppelin Nights*.

told us Conrad had first idea of writing through seeing a "Pseudonym" at the bookstall at Vevey Station. He chose English in preference to French because, whereas there were plenty of stylists in French, there were none in English.

Wednesday.

Today I received cable from Brentano's saying that *Buried Alive* was "going strong," and asking permission to reprint in U.S.A. instead of buying Tauchnitz sheets.

I finished third chapter of *Hilda Lessways*. Usual doubts as to whether the thing is any good.

Friday, January 20th.

Impossible to keep this journal while I am beginning *Hilda Lessways,* and either going out or receiving, every night and Sunday afternoons. The stuff is slowly improving. I had not been able to even read, until I received H. G. Wells's *The New Machiavelli.* This book makes a deep impression on me, and even causes me to examine my own career, and to wonder whether I have not arrived at a parting of the ways therein, and what I ought to decide to do after the book—after *Hilda* is finished. London or Paris?

Sunday, January 22nd.

Friday night, visit with Châteaubriant to Romain Rolland. Found him in a holland-covered room, disguised bed in one corner. Tea at 9.45. Sister, spinster aged 35. Bright, slightly masculine. Mother, an aged body, proud of children, shrewd, came in later. Romain Rolland, arm in sling; large face, pale, calm, kindly, thoughtful, rather taciturn. Giving a marked impression of an absolutely honest artist, and a fine soul. Considerable resemblance to Marcel Schwob [1]; but bigger and more blond. No particular talk. But an impression of rightness, respectability in every sense, conscientiousness, and protestantism (intellectually).

---

[1] Marcel Schwob (pseudonym: Loyson-Bridet), general writer and bibliographer, had been an intimate friend of Arnold Bennett until his death in February 1905.

January 31st.

I went to see the historic Durand Ruel collection. The furniture of the abode was startlingly different, in quality and taste, from the pictures. All the furniture might have been bought at the Bon Marché. The table in the dining-room was covered with the chequered cloth so prevalent in small French households. (In this room was a still life of Monet.) The doors, however, were all beautifully painted in panels. Aged and young domestics moved about. There was a peculiar close smell—no, not peculiar, because it permeates thousands of Paris homes.

From the front windows was seen a fine view of St.-Lazare Station, with whiffs of steam transpiring from the vast edifice. The visitors while I was there included two Englishmen; one very well dressed, though his socks were behind the times and he had rouged his nostrils; some Americans, and four doll-like Japanese. Certainly the chief languages spoken were American and Japanese. The "great" Renoir (the man and woman in the H box of a theatre) hung in the study. It was rather thrilling to see this illustrious work for the first time, as it were, in the flesh. There were Monets of all periods, and the latest period was not the best. A magnificent Cézanne landscape and a few other Cézannes; Manet, Dégas, Sisley, Boudin—all notable. Yes, a collection very limited in scope, but fully worthy of its reputation. Only it wants hanging. It simply hasn't a chance where it is. The place is far too small, and the contrast between the pictures and the furniture altogether too disconcerting. Still, the pictures exist, and they are proof that a man can possess marvellous taste in a fine art, while remaining quite insensitive in an applied art.

Afterwards I called in on a painter in Montmartre, and learned to my astonishment that it was precisely he who had painted Durand Ruel's doors. 70 doors had been ordered.

The painter told me how Durand Ruel had bought Renoirs for 20 years without selling. The "great" Renoir had been sold at Angers for 400 francs, after a commissioning amateur had refused to give Renoir 1500 francs for it. The amateur had said, "Yes, it's very good, of course, but it isn't what I expected from you." (They always talk like that—these commissioning amateurs.) Then Durand Ruel bought it. And now he has refused 125,000 francs for it. In my friend's studio I was told how dealers who specialize in modern pictures really make their money. A "lord" wants to dispose of, say, a Rubens on the quiet. It comes mysteriously to the dealer, who puts it in a private room and shows it only to a very few favoured young painters, who pronounce upon it. Soon afterwards it disappears for an unknown destination. The dealer is vastly enriched, and he goes on specializing in modern pictures.

Wednesday, February 15th.

I got as far as the death of Mrs. Lessways in *Hilda Lessways* on Sunday afternoon, and sent off the stuff as a specimen to Pinker yesterday. 33,000 words. During this time I haven't had sufficient courage to keep a journal. I suspect that I have been working too hard for 5 weeks regularly. I feel it like an uncomfortable physical sensation all over the top of my head. A very quick sweating walk of half an hour will clear it off, but this may lead, and does lead, to the neuralgia of fatigue and insomnia and so on, and I have to build myself up again with foods.

Yesterday I signed the contract with Vedrenne and Eadie for *The Honeymoon* at the Royalty Theatre.[1]

Sunday, February 26th.

Reviews of *The Card*[2] much too kind on the whole. 6 on the first day, 6 or 8 on the second. Dixon Scott's in *Manchester Guardian* one of the best I ever had, and no effusiveness either.

I did practically no work between Monday and Saturday, but 3500 words on these 2 days. In between, I was mysteriously ill. I hope to finish the second part of *Hilda* a week today. But *tant pis* if I can't. News of edition of *Sacred and Profane Love*[3] with my water-colour cover arrived from United States on Wednesday, together with figures showing that Doran had sold about 35,000 copies of my various books (in about 8

---

[1] J. E. Vedrenne and Dennis Eadie managed the Royalty Theatre together in 1911.
[2] Just published in London. Its American title was *Denry the Audacious*.
[3] *Sacred and Profane Love* was published in England in 1905. The American edition was called *The Book of Carlotta*, Bennett's original title for it.

months, I think). This does not include Dutton's books nor Brentano's editions of *Buried Alive*.

Wednesday, March 1st.

Dinner last night at Maurice Ravel's. He played us extracts from the proofs of his new ballet, *Daphnis et Chloë,* and I was much pleased.

This morning I found that W. D. Howells had devoted the whole of the "Easy Chair" in March *Harper's Magazine* to me; very friendly. So I sat down and wrote to W. D. Howells.

Tuesday, March 7th.

Last week appeared March *Bookman,* being an "Arnold Bennett number," with a pretty good article by F. G. Bellamy. I got six different letters about different businesses from Doran yesterday.

Monday, April 10th.

We left Paris on Friday morning. On Wednesday night I saw Copeau's adaptation of *Les Frères Karamazov* at the Théâtre des Arts, and it was very good. It finished at 12.55 A.M.

April 21st.

London. Palace Theatre. Pavlova dancing the dying swan. Feather falls off her dress. Two silent Englishmen. One says, "Moulting." That is all they say.

We got to London at 4 P.M. Friday, and I came straight down to Burslem.[1] On previous visits I have never made adequate notes, but this time I am doing a little better.

Sunday, April 23rd.

I lost my note-book of the Potteries, and only began a new one 2 or 3 days before I left. On Tuesday the 11th I went to Manchester to stay with Mair till Thursday. I met the usual fine crowd, and also Stanley Hough-

---

[1] The town in Staffordshire where the Bennett family lived. It was the Bursley of the *Five Towns* stories.

ton,[1] who impressed me; and Irene Rooke,[2] whom I liked; and, in particular, a certain Hughes, of Sherratt & Hughes, the largest booksellers in Manchester, who told me he had sold 950 copies of *Clayhanger,* and over 400 of the cheap edition of *The Old Wives' Tale* in 3 weeks (I think).

M.[3] came to the Potteries on Thursday. On Saturday we went down Sneyd deep pit, and on Monday to Rode Heath. We came to London on Tuesday, and Marguerite went direct to Pinner. I came to 2 Whitehall Court, and what with the Authors' Club, and the N.L.C.[4] next door, and a fine bedroom on the 7th story, I ought to be comfortable. I took up *Hilda Lessways* again on Thursday afternoon, and shall finish reading what I have written this morning. Better than I expected. At the Authors' Club, I have met Morley Roberts, Charles Marriott, and Charles Garvice.[5] Some of the men seem to waste 3 hours in gossip every afternoon.

Saturday, April 29th.

Lunch with Massingham at Devonshire Club. Afterwards Shorter [6] and Robertson Nicoll [7] joined us, and then Lewis Hind.[8] When Shorter said he would willingly tell me the name of a young artist of genius whom he had found, only for the moment he could not recall it, everybody laughed, and Nicoll said to me, "There's much more in Shorter than you think!" Roars of laughter. It was a good *rosserie* for Shorter. They stayed till nearly four, and then Massingham and I made an arrangement for articles for the *Nation.*

M. and I dined at Romano's and then went to the Tivoli. Harry Lauder was, as I expected, very common and under the mark.

---

[1] A playwright of the Manchester school, who died in 1913.

[2] At that time playing in Miss Horniman's company at the Gaiety Theatre, Manchester.

[3] The first Mrs. Arnold Bennett, *née* Marguerite Soulié. She is referred to by this initial almost always in the Journals.

[4] The National Liberal Club.

[5] Three veteran novelists. Roberts was then 53 years old and had already published nearly fifty books. Marriott, born in 1869, published *The Romance of the Rhine* in 1911. Garvice's romances, including such works as *A Coronet of Shame* and *Where Love Leads,* enjoyed tremendous popularity in England and America.

[6] Clement Shorter, the eminent authority on the Brontë sisters, published that year an edition of *The Complete Poems of Emily Brontë.*

[7] Sir W. Robertson Nicoll edited the *British Weekly* and wrote for it under the pseudonym of "Claudius Clear."

[8] C. Lewis Hind published his work on *The Post Impressionists* in 1911.

Thursday, May 4th.

Worked all right in the morning. Josiah Wedgwood[1] lunched with me at Authors' Club. I saw Vedrenne at 5 P.M. (also Eadie), and learnt that *The Honeymoon* probably could not be produced owing to impossibility of getting either Irene Vanbrugh[2] or Alex. Carlisle in London, and uncertainty of Doris Keane in New York. However, they had cabled to the latter.

Wednesday, May 10th.

Wells came in to take me out to lunch at N.L.C. I didn't go. Mrs. Wells was lunching with Marguerite on ground floor. We dined alone at Grand Hotel Grill, and afterwards I went to N.L.C. Nothing there except food for thought. Yesterday Mrs. Belloc Lowndes[3] lunch at Sesame —Mrs. Aria, James Douglas, Seccombe, etc. An American came to tea. Dinner at the Gourmets with Waring. Lord Howard de Walden also came. A nice intelligent boy, very well used to things and people. We all went to *Fanny's First Play* (poor) and then saw Lillah McCarthy[4] afterwards, and I finished up with Waring at Authors' Club.

Friday, May 12th.

Scott-James[5] for lunch yesterday. He seemed to be a severer and better critic than I had thought. Granville-Barker came in while I was writing for *M'chester S. Chronicle*. He said he had never made any money out of his plays except as books.

Monday, May 15th.

Saturday night Rickards[6] dined with us at Café Royal. Afterwards we saw George Moore, and later, at the M——, a fine selection of *souteneurs*.

---

[1] England's most notable exponent of the single tax, and author of *Essays and Adventures of a Labour M.P.*
[2] The actress, wife of Dion Boucicault.
[3] Wife of Frederick Lowndes of *The Times* and sister of Hilaire Belloc. She is the author of several novels.
[4] The actress, then wife of H. Granville-Barker.
[5] R. A. Scott-James, at that time literary editor of the *Daily News*.
[6] Edwin Rickards, of the architectural firm of Lanchester and Rickards, was one of Bennett's oldest friends.

Lowndes came for lunch today, and Austin Harrison for tea. Then Authors' Club banquet to Tree, Courtney in chair. The most appalling orgy of insincere sentimentality. I left at ten, utterly disgusted and exhausted.

Monday, May 22nd.

A long day of work in the Club library yesterday. At 7.15 I walked up to Pagani's. Dined with Austin Harrison there; other guest, May Sinclair, and the Howard Joneses. Mrs. Jones extremely beautiful. An American with no accent. Jones from Potteries. After midnight Harrison, May S., and I went off in a taxi. I dropped Harrison at Davies St. and took May S. to her studio in Edwards Sq. I rather liked this prim virgin. Great sense. She said she lived absolutely alone—not even a servant.

Wednesday, May 24th.

I finished the 5th part of *Hilda* yesterday morning. Yesterday, lunch with Mrs. Lowndes at Sesame. Maurice Hewlett, just like a boy, impulsive and exaggerated and quite grey. I liked him at once.

Thursday, May 25th.

Mozart, Strauss concert. 3 P.M. Old man with St. Vitus next to us. He stood some time at door with young girl in charge, waiting for first piece to finish. She armed him with difficulty to seat. F.C.B. helped him to sit down. Long thin legs. Knees that stuck out to next seat. Both hands trembling violently nearly all the time. Kept his head down. Took him about a minute to lift up one hand to his face to move his specs. Peculiarly smooth reddish skin of hands. The girl put programme in his hands. He could read it, in spite of shaking. Handkerchief stuck in waistcoat. She wiped his moustache for him. She took his gloves off, and afterwards put them on. He never looked up the whole time. Once, not being comfortable, he had to be lifted and re-sat, and at intervals he stood up, holding on the front seat. All his movements very slow and trembling. Once when hand on knee it did not tremble. Lips, and especially upper lip with moustache, trembling all the time. We left her arranging him for departure.

Saturday, May 27th.

44 today. Yesterday for a change we lunched alone and dined alone. Dined at Savoy Grill Room. The only good service I have come across this time in London, outside clubs. Performance of *Nan* at Little Theatre in the afternoon. Splendid.

Monday, May 29th.

Dined with Larbaud at the Cecil, and the rest of the evening at Whitehall Court. We met Wheeler by accident at Appenrodt's, and he told us all about his difficulties with the production of Reinhardt's *Œdipus,* and how Lafayette, who had promised to find all the money, was burned to death the day before the contracts were to be signed.

Tuesday, June 6th.

Week-end, Friday to Tuesday, with Atkins at Brightlingsea. One of the times of my life. Perfect weather; a most pleasant house, brains, and two days of yachting.

Thursday, June 8th.

Tuesday, Florence [1] and Rickards to dinner. R. and M. and I went to *Playboy of the Western World.* Splendid, but I was too tired to appreciate it properly. Yesterday, Irving Brock of *N. Y. Times* came to see me; an argumentative person, but I rather liked him. Dinner at Albemarle Club as guests of May Sinclair.

Friday, June 9th.

Lunch with T. B. Wells, one of the editors of *Harper's,* and Pinker. Vague talk of his buying my American impressions. Pinker had sold my next humorous serial to the Hearst combination for £2000, all serial

---

[1] Arnold Bennett's sister.

rights. This means at least £3000 for the novel, or 1s. a word. I was justly elated.

Knoblock dined with me at the Club, and we settled the main outlines of our play.[1] Today I wrote him putting our terms in writing.

Saturday, June 10th.

I wrote the last chapter but one of *Hilda* yesterday. Contract with *Harper's* laid down for serial rights of 6 articles on the United States for £800.

Sunday, June 11th.

Reflections at Piccadilly Circus upon my article thereon for the *Nation*. Rideing, editor-in-chief of *Youth's Companion,* came for lunch, and told me with a grin the funniest things about its editorial policy. Sexual love is banned. At most, at the end of a story, it may appear that a girl is beginning to care slightly for a lad.

Wednesday, June 14th.

On Tuesday morning I finished *Hilda Lessways,* which is exactly 100,000 words—a curiously good forecast. Yesterday afternoon, tea at Lady Ottoline Morrell's. I re-read *Hilda* and put in chapter headings after dinner.

Saturday, July 1st. Fontainebleau.

I finished *Just at a Venture,* story for *The Odd Volume,* on Thursday; and last of *Life in London* series for the *Nation* today. Frank Vernon came to see me yesterday afternoon. He said Marie Tempest wanted to play in *Honeymoon,* in co-operation with Vedrenne, and wanted her first entrance made much later in the first act. I declined to alter the play. He said I was right. At best, even if the thing comes off the date of production will be changed.

---

[1] This was *Milestones,* by Arnold Bennett and Edward Knoblock, not produced until March 5, 1912, at the Royalty Theatre.

Saturday, July 8th.

I began to write my little book on Xmas,[1] on Wednesday last. On Thursday I went to see the Wellses[2] at Pont de l'Arche. I came back yesterday, and found myself in a railway accident at Mantes, 6 wounded.

There had already been a breakdown in a tunnel. Officials said that a *rotule* of an *attaché* had got broken. It was repaired, and we jolted onwards at, I should say, about 30 or 35 kilometres an hour. Then just after we passed Mantes station there was a really terrific jolting. I knew after four or five jolts that one coach at any rate had left the metals.

I was in a sort of large Pullmanesque compartment at the back of a first-class coach, two or three coaches from the engine. The windows broke. The corridor door sailed into the compartment. My stick flew out of the rack. The table smashed itself. I clung hard to the arms of my seat, and fell against an arm-chair in front of me. There was a noise of splintering, and there were various other noises. An old woman lay on the floor crying. I wondered, "Shall I remain unharmed until the thing stops?" Immense tension of waiting for the final stoppage. Equilibrium at last, and I was unhurt.

I couldn't get out at first. Then some one opened the door. I soothed the old woman. I took my eyeglasses off and put them in their case. I found my hat (under some débris) and my stick. My bag had remained in the rack. I left the train with my belongings, but I had forgotten all about the book I was reading, *L'Ève Future*. This book was all that I lost. Two wounded women were ahead, lying out on the grass at the side of the track.

Up above, from street bordering the cutting, crowds of people were gazing curiously, as at a show. One woman asked if she could do anything, and some one said, "A doctor." I walked round to the other side of train, and a minor official asked me and others to go back. *"Ce n'est pas pour vous commander, mais . . ."* We obeyed. Two coaches lay on their side. One of them was unwheeled, and partly sticking in ground.

---

[1] *The Feast of St. Friend*, published in October 1911.
[2] Mr. and Mrs. T. B. Wells.

No sound came from an overturned 2nd-class coach, though there were people in it.

Presently some men began lifting helpless passengers on to cushions which had been laid on the ground. I had no desire of any sort to help. I argued incompassionately that it was the incompetent railway company's affair. I held my bag and stick and I looked around. I didn't want to see any more wounded nor to be any more *impressionné* than I could help. My recollection of appearances quickly became vague. I remember the face of one wounded woman was all over coal dust. We had shaved a short goods train standing on the next line, and the tender of the train was against our coach. A young American said that it was sticking into our coach, but I don't think it was. He said that the front part of our coach was entirely telescoped, but it wasn't entirely telescoped. It was, however, all smashed up. My chief impression is of a total wreck brought about in a few seconds.

I walked off up line towards station and met various groups of employees running towards train. At last two came with a stretcher or ambulance. I passed out of the station into the *place,* and a collector feebly asked me for my ticket, which I didn't give. I went straight to a garage and demanded an auto for Paris. But all autos had been taken off to the scene of the accident. Having been promised one in due course, I waited some time and then had a wash and took tea. I couldn't help eating and drinking quickly. Then I was told that two Americans wanted an auto. I said that they might share the one promised to me. Agreed. At last my auto came. The price was 100 francs. A Frenchman came up who wanted to get to Paris quickly (he had not been in the accident), I gave him a place for 20 frs. making a mistake in thus dividing 100 by 4. This detail shows I really was upset under my superficial calmness. We went off at 5.50.

Friday, July 21st.

Everything neglected in the way of notes, while writing *The Feast of St. Friend*. I did it in 12 working days, and finished on Wednesday.

The Honeymoon arranged for with Marie Tempest and Lillah McCarthy anxious to buy *The Great Adventure*.

Monday, July 31st.

The Dorans came on Wednesday last and left this morning. *Séjour agréable pour tout le monde.* Doran showed great optimism about future sale of my books, and was quite ready to offer £1500 on account of a new novel to be written in 1914.

Sunday, August 13th.

I began to write *The Family* (tentative title of play in collaboration with Edward Knoblock) on August 1st. I had finished the first act on August 6th. He revised it (but slightly) and on Friday the 11th he read it in our kiosk to the Mairs, Alice Kauser, and her brother, Ed. Sheldon, and me.

I read the draft of what I had done of the 2nd Act. *Succès très vif.* I shall finish the 2nd Act on Wednesday, and count to have the whole play finished on the 29th. I write a scene of the play each morning, and Knoblock comes in most afternoons for tea, to go through what I have done.

I didn't alter at all his construction of the 1st Act, but I have immensely improved his construction of the 2nd, and I shall entirely reconstruct the 3rd. His revision consists chiefly of rearranging the dialogue here and there, and shortening. Whenever he adds a phrase of his own it is heavy and uncolloquial, and has to be altered. Still, he knows the stage, and his help is valuable. Also the original idea of the play was his, and the skeleton his. Nevertheless I do not in the least regret the collaboration. It will have occupied me less than a month.

Saturday, August 19th.

Finished 2nd Act of *The Family* on Wednesday, and I began to write the third this morning. I have found two good titles for this play: *The Man with the Scythe,* and *The Milestones,* or *Milestones.* The latter will probably be used.

I have been reading *Tom Jones* for about a year. I finished it the other night. It is equal to its reputation; consistently interesting. There is no dull chapter. But he makes the hero too good. He seems to think that so long as Tom goes in for a little miscellaneous fornication he will be saved from priggishness. I doubt if this is so, especially at the end, where Tom's angelicalness upon the misfortunes of Blifil is really a bit thick.

Wednesday, August 30th.

On Thursday, 24th, I finished the play, which we finally decided to call *Milestones* (my title). Knoblock finished the revision of the last act on either Friday or Saturday, and it was sent to the typewriters on Monday.

I leave for London tomorrow morning, and do not mean to live at Avon any more.

October 7th. Lusitania.

The Honeymoon produced at the Royalty last night. Lukewarm. Supper at Marie Tempest's afterwards. Home at 2 A.M. I had finished packing at 10 A.M. Left at 11.15 for Euston.

My fatigue had been slowly increasing for a fortnight, and this morning, after about 3 hours' sleep only, I was just at the end of my tether.

2nd class crowd afar off.

Much waiting and crying for them.

None for us.

We left at 5.40, landing-stage; then anchored in river to wait for tide.

Hire of 4s. for deck chair. Must be some remnant of an ancient custom.

Gent at dining-table: "I wonder how many souls we have on board."

Strong also on the indecency of the Russian ballets, which, however, he much admired.

Curious recurrent moaning sound at night, apparently of wind in ventilators, or something.

Sunday, October 8th. At sea.

Strange noises through the night. Tappings. Waiting for the dawn to come, forgetting that there could be no dawn. The dawn was the turning on of the electric lights in the corridor.

Barbers. An American shave 1s. Very elaborate, and I felt I was in

America. Tipping downwards of chair, putting you at his mercy. A very clean shave. Dropping a bit of powder on towel, and then rubbing it in. Then hot damp towel, and very elaborate rubbing dry. He then wanted to do my hair, but I told him it was not my style to have my hair too rough.

Walk on navigating deck, where all the ventilators were secretly whirring, and two engineers arguing about a valve. Steering places hidden off. Top steering place deserted, so that it seemed as if the ship was steering herself. I look down a shaft like a coalpit (into depths of ship), which is lighted at stages by electricity, and there is a great draught *up* it. What it was for I didn't know. Enormous amount of covered-in machinery on top deck, but I could actually *see* one fan whirring.

Lovely morning. Rippled sea as we leave Ireland. Dining-saloon for breakfast. Size of it shown by sudden perceptions that features of people in opposite corner were blurred by distance. But the great sensation of this part of the ship is that of waiters and parlourmaid persons walking rather quickly long distances in straight lines, bearing plates often. They must walk very many miles in a day. A blue and white nurse-looking person approaches out of the distance, and gets clearer, and as she passes you see two rampant lions on her breast—*the sign of the Cunard*.

Humility of people waiting till they are served. It would want some pluck to make a row in this place, the stewards are so self-respecting.

Going out on to starboard deck (on this floor), I am startled to see it crowded. Steerage passengers. This is their playground. I walked round the forward part of the ship and saw their dining-rooms, kitchens, and broad staircases leading to different sections of berths. I had a glimpse of one berth; it seemed all right. All along deck here and there were entrances to paradises forbidden to them. Netting hung down from deck above gave sense of being cooped up. Certainly they were very close together. A certain natural brazenness about some of them—girls, who would not give and take to me in passing.

I discovered vast parts of the ship whose existence I had not imaginatively preconceived.

Monday, October 9th.

7 A.M.

Ragged sky. Black water all round horizon. Nothing in sight. Moon not set. Full moon.

Again, sense of unsuspected populations. This sense helped by a mysterious ringing of a bell in distant part of ship, calling some unknown population to its meal.

Inspection of ship with Mr. A——, Chief Steward.

3rd Class. Inoculation for smallpox. Fares £7.

Men watching girls, and girls then watching men. "Having their sweet revenge," said A. Another of his great phrases was "No time like the present."

1st Class. Kitchens. All this steerage was another world mysteriously opened. We went back into a still unknown part of our world.

Roasting ovens. Intense heat. Revolving spits.

Special orders primed on a board with hours marked; then I heard a man call out, "Baked potatoes for 4 at 8 o'clock. Extra order."

Fire. In 1st class kitchens, a table of posts for every man. I noticed a list of about 30 or 40 stewards "to control passengers."

52 cooks for 1st and 2nd class.

The baking goes on day and night, never stops.

Dough-mixing by electricity.

Potato-peeling machine.

Egg-boiling machine. 1 minute, 2, 3, etc. Automatically lifted out when done.

Firemen's kitchen.

Special menu for leading firemen. 12 leading firemen. Meal served every 4 hours (goes down by lift) night and day. 110 firemen on each watch.

Every member of crew has a bunk.

In each store dept. (wine, grocery, etc.) in the depths of it, a quiet, generally nervous man, keeping accounts on a green cloth.

The second class was like 1st class on a small scale. Less space. Had we not been in 1st class it would have seemed spacious and magnificent. Many obviously well-to-do men in smoke-room. Fine view over stern of ship.

Purser at dinner.

He said he knew practically the whole of the professional gamblers. Once 2 got on unawares. At night when smoking-room full, he got carpenter in, who prominently took down all warning notices of gamblers and prominently put up new ones underlined with red ink. Still, they won 40 dollars off a man, who, however, refused to pay.

Forbes-Robertson, Knoblock, Burton, and me in lounge after dinner. Got talking of theft of "Mona Lisa," and then each told tales of thefts— marble mantelpieces out of Russell Square, etc. Italy; pictures rotting from damp through neglect in Venetian churches, and so on, until one had the idea that the whole art world was undermined and everything going or gone.

Bit of wind at 11 P.M. Looking through porthole of hall of E deck. Waves swishing by. Hopeless position of any one overboard. Suddenly a wave bangs up against porthole with a smash, and you draw your face away startled.

Visiting ship with Chief Officer.

Chart Room. "Holy of Holies." Brass and mahogany effect. Dodge for detecting and putting out fires in inaccessible holes. Fan to draw out smoke, and steam attachment to drown it. All same pipes. 4 or 500 feet of piping at least.

Sounding tubes (?) wire draws out water from a tube. Even the wire so drawn in by an electric motor. It can be done at full speed.

Bridge. 75 ft. above sea. The house was carried away and wheel carried away once by a wave—one wave. One dent, made by glass, left in wood, to commemorate the day.

Telegraphs. Telephones. Private telephone for chart room that does not go through Exchange.

Subterranean signalling. A bell sounds through it like tapping a pencil on wood. Nantucket bell heard *16 miles off*.

Down below, forward of steerage, capstan gear.

The cables will each break only at 265 tons. That is, they could hold in suspension 26 10-ton trucks of coal. The capstan gear is so strong that it will break the cable if it is overwound.

Imagine 265 tons of M.P.'s dropped into the sea.

Well may all this powerful machinery be encaged, just like wild beasts in a menagerie.

7 different steering gears. The last by a hand wheel almost direct. Auxiliary engines, etc. We went down 2 or 3 stories from lowest passenger deck and saw the tremendous gear actually at work, slowly and apparently capriciously moving to and fro at intervals in obedience to sailor on bridge 5 or 600 feet away and 70 feet higher up.

Up and down steel ladders. Climbing over moving chain (like a bike chain) of steering-gear, through stray jets of steam, in a forest of greasy machinery, guarded by steel rails, grease on floor: all apparently working alone under electric lights, but here and there a man in brown doing nothing in particular. Dials everywhere showing pressures, etc.

Up a flight to dynamo room.

Machines revolving 1200 to the minute.

Then to stokehold. Vast. Terrible. 190 colossal furnaces, opened and fed every 10 minutes, and coal flung in. Mouths of furnaces seemed to me very high for coal to be flung into them. This effect was like that of a coal mine with the addition of hell.

This was the most impressive part of this ship. It stretched away with occasional electric lights into infinite distance. 1000 tons of coal a day. Finest coal. Very hot. An inferno, theatrical. Above, confectioners making *petits fours,* and the lifts going for 1st-class passengers.

Invited into Captain's room. He showed us his photograph after being invested C.B. by King.

Talk of Royal Family. The Englishman's reverence for his old institutions, of all kinds, and his secret sentimentality (according to F.R. the

King was fine fellow, and the Queen a woman of really unusual brain-power) comes out all over the ship the whole time.

Marvellous after-sunset exactly ahead, as we came out. Sea like slightly uneasy oil.

Previously, at dinner, the purser on his Airedale terrier, Paddy. So comprehending that when his wife and he wanted to say something they did not want the dog to understand, they had to spell out the important word, instead of pronouncing it.

Dr. Hutchinson introduced himself to me in smoke-room, as being a great admirer. He began to talk about his biological researches and travels and theories, and kept on—very interestingly, and never referred to my work at all.

He said that the progress of sanitation in Naples (where up to a few years ago there were no privies at all) was very much hindered by the fact that a company paid the corporation 300,000 francs a year for the right to remove human excrement. Another company pays 100,000 for right to remove dog excrement. (Same thing in Constantinople, Aleppo, etc.) Dog excrement sent to U.S.A. for preparing of kid gloves, etc. Nothing like it for that.

Wednesday, October 11th.

Impossible to round the forward part of the boat deck without a struggle. The variations of temp. and the differences between temp. of sea and air are quite remarkable.

At 2.30 we passed the *Baltic;* which left L'pool on Thursday, 2 days before us. When I looked again at 3.30 she was out of sight.

Thursday, October 12th.

Up at 5.35. Entire ship's company seemed to be at work. I asked for tea, and got it at once, with apologies for it being Ceylon instead of China, as the storekeeper was not up.

L.W., the little, well-dressed wealthy traveller (with valet and house-keeper) who gave us a most appetizing account of Yucatan, with the most beautiful women in the world.

Subdued excitement as to hour of landing tonight, and conflicting prophecies. Turning up of people never seen before.

At 5 P.M. ship supposed to dock at 9 P.M. Continued appearances of people never seen before. Also, although 4 hours yet to pass, men in hats and town overcoats, instead of caps, etc., women in large hats, which seem extraordinarily large and grotesque. General excitement.

Montague Glass introduced himself.

Friday, October 13th.

Last night. Taking pilot and (?) health officers aboard. But perhaps they were ship's officers. First we saw some coloured lights which we took for something on land. It proved to be a ship, and then it proved of course to be the pilot-boat. We had been burning flares.

Doran and two press men came into saloon off revenue cutter. Only I didn't know they had come off revenue cutter, and I didn't know Doran had done a great feat in getting there. I was interviewed by 2 journalists apparently on behalf of the crowd. This was while ship was manœuvring into dock. And at last we went on shore, after I had been interviewed by 3 other people. Irvin Cobb was part of our group.

Called at 2 hotels (free lunch-counter, etc.) and had time at the N.Y. Central to go to Hotel Belmont, which was our second hotel. I had had views of Broadway, 14th Street, 5th Avenue, etc. Lots of sky signs. Roads up. Not very many people, but a sensation of grandness, immensity, lights, heights. Streets full of holes. The Elevated, on a forest of pillars. Cable cars long and noisy, but fewer at that time of night.

We got into a long train, smoker—rather shabby, and exactly at 11.19 left the station. I had a lot of evening papers, a wilderness to me. We crossed the Harlem, saw the old ship canal, and then skirted the Hudson. Very blue arc-lights. Through the town a regular succession of lightning glimpses of long streets at right angles to the track.

Cobb said you could see N.Y. and get a good idea of it. I said, "But what about the home life of people to learn?" He said, "There is none. It's a half-way house. Constant coming and going, and changing of centres and so on. Only one man in 3 is American born." He indicated a whole vast quarter as we passed—probably several miles—which he described as nothing but apartment houses and bedrooms. . . . Arrival at Yonkers. Station being reconstructed. All wood stairs, etc. A buggy, on remarkably thin wheels, and 2 horses, brown and white, ill-groomed, waited for us. And we seemed to drive a very long way. Through an Italian quarter. We passed through a district full of remains of decorations of Christopher Columbus Day, which was yesterday. At last, after sundry hills and dales, into an obviously residential quarter. Here roads all interminably winding curves. Then the house.

Today, walk down to Yonkers with Mrs. D.

Young men and maids coming from high school.

Station wagons—thin wheels.

Ice wagon—"Danger."

One or two old Colonial houses.

A "tinder" boarding-house, all wood, rather nice.

Outdoor boot-blacking stands.

Roast chestnuts.

Beautiful Hudson, gasometer, and sugar refinery.

Strangeness of hearing *English* in this strange place.

Badness of tram lines at intersections.

Saturday, October 14th.

Going down change at 155th on to Elevated.

No crush. First view of baseball ground.

The effect of millions of staircased windows of apartment houses, with glimpses every now and then of complicated lines of washing.

Street after street, dirty streets, untidy, littered.

Baseball game. Giants v. Athletics, N.Y. v. Phila.

Again cigarettes, chewing-gum, programmes.

Cheers for kid practising, sharp sort of cheers.

Advertisements round arena.

Drive through Central Park, and then past Carnegie etc. houses.

Pitcher lifting left leg high. Tip on right toe.

Applause for a run. First red man near to me in joy.

Members of audience being turned out.

The catching seemed to be quite certain,

As rare as a woman in a ball match.

As difficult as to make a first base.

The eagles on top of stand.

The yellow ushers against the dark mass.

The blue men against a red-bordered mat, N.Y. police.

The blue purple shadow gradually creeping up to the sign,

"The 3-dollar hat with the 5-dollar look."

A 2-base hit is the height of applause, real applause.

Chewing-gum.

Combined movements of jaws.

Obstinacy of chewing gum at *end*.

The pitcher is the idol of the affair, as may be seen when he comes in to strike.

The hunchback mascot of Philadelphia.

I was told afterwards that the real 1st-class stroke of the game was a player jumping instead of *sliding* on to a base. Had he slid he would have been touched. Welter of autos and torn paper afterwards.

Sunday, October 15th.

The friendships between American men seem to be more charming than between English. They call each other more by their Xtian names, and are softer to each other. "A very dear friend of mine" is a frequently heard phrase. (Messmore Kendall & J.H.D.) They are more caressing with their voices.

One of the greatest sights in America: Irvin Cobb like an Indian god sitting at the shinery opposite Park Hill Station having his shoes shined. And they *were* very well shined, too.

The flexibility of arrangements for business and social affairs. Ingenuity expended in getting things to fit in for comfort, etc.

Sunday morning. Auto trip into N.Y.

The sheer Italian beauty of vista of Fifth Avenue.

Gigantic fine cornices, etc.

All N.Y. packed in. 2 steps from Wall Street is Syria and Greece. In and out of Chinatown in a moment.

My *intense* fatigue afterwards.

Interminability of Broadway.

Tuesday, October 17th.

Doran and I took 3.34 Congressional Limited from Pennsylvania Station to Washington. This station is very impressive. Silence. Not crowded.

Trains a mere incident in it, hidden away like a secret shame. Tunnel under Hudson. Very neat, regular, and well lighted: seen from observation car. Noise from steel. Jolting of smoking-car. General jolting when brakes put on.

Electric sign sticking up high as we passed through Baltimore in the dark: "Baltimore, the electric city."

Arrival at fine station at Washington.

Apparently a long drive to Shoreham Hotel, across avenue after avenue. Still, all the air of a provincial town. Had to get out of bed to extinguish final light, otherwise good hotel.

Congress chamber.

Old Congress chamber is a sort of rule-chamber. Its astounding collection of ugly statues. Whispering point, where Adams fell. I was exhausted after this. Declined to visit Library of Congress. Saw Washington monument. Phallic. Appalling. A national catastrophe—only equalled by Albert Memorial. Tiny doll-like people waiting to go into it.

Sub-guide said, pointing to a portrait in oils: "Henry Clay—quite a good statesman," in a bland, unconsciously patronizing way. Guide also said of picture, "Although painted in 1865, notice the flesh tints are quite fresh."

General effect of Washington. A plantation of public edifices amid a rather unkempt undergrowth of streets. Pennsylvania Avenue the great street. Cheapness of its buildings (old private houses turned into business) as the thoroughfare approaches the Capitol.

The White House very nice architecture. Rather small. Distinguished.

Overflow of Capitol into huge buildings at either side rather to front of Capitol. Dome too big for sub-structure. The wings rather fine.

Badness of saddle of mutton at bkfst. Finger bowls after every damn snack.

Wednesday, October 18th.

Met Macrae in big hall. We had bkfst. in station restaurant. Open 6 A.M. to midnight. Kids in certain parties. High chairs for kids. One party, husband (who had probably come to meet after their absence from home), wife, and 2 children. Youngest kid slept. Other, boy about 5, sat up in chair. Great calm gaiety, a delightful scene—mother particularly.

Heavy rain.

Thursday, October 19th.

Lunch at Harper's, with chief members of staff including Major Lee,[1] under presidency of Colonel George Harvey.[2] I liked Harvey. Quiet, ruminative, accustomed to power, and so on. Good laugh. Good story. But a sinister-looking person, rather. T. B. Wells had come to fetch me in taxi. Very heavy rain. We called at Brevoort-Lafayette for Frank Craig, who is to illustrate my articles, and for whom Wells had an inordinate admiration. I thought he said, "Clean, wholesome," which is just what Craig is. The clean young governing-class Englishman to perfection. I liked him much, but I doubt his views in art.

Lunch was at Lawyers' Club, in a private room thereof. Rex Beach, one of the best sellers, there. Nice athletic youngish man. Then I was taken to Harper's office—two Elevateds—and shown over it. Old-style building for America.[3]

---

[1] Albert Lee had been editor of *Harper's Round Table* in 1895-9 and editor of *Harper's Weekly* in 1901-2, but at this time he was managing editor of *Collier's Weekly*.

[2] He was president of Harper & Bros., 1900-15. In 1921-3 he was Ambassador Extraordinary and Plenipotentiary to Great Britain.

[3] The Harper's offices were then in Franklin Square. They were not moved to their present location on East 33rd Street until about ten years later.

Humorous serial sold for £2000 to Phillips.

Then to Waldorf, where a room had been obtained, and to bed for ¾ hours after a bath. Considering I had had only one hour's sleep at most in night on train, I was doing pretty well.

Still heavy rain off and on. We drove to Republic Theatre (Belasco) to see *The Woman* by William C. De Mille. Telephone girl play. Melodrama plot. Essentially childish. Nevertheless, in spite of too much talk in 1st act, I was not really bored. It appealed to the child in me.

Guggenheim pointed out to me at theatre.

Looked like a little grocer.

Pirie MacDonald, 10 A.M.

Photographer of men.

Electric blue light.

Shirt and belt.

Gesture of triumph with bulb at end of tube.

Squeezing tube harder and harder as he makes the exposure. Boyish gestures.

"Not *at* my eyes. *Into* my eyes. That's it. Just a little more challenge. A *little* more. That's it. Don't wink. We'll try again. I'll just play *round that spot*.

"D'ye know, I feel kind of guilty." Then history of yarn. English path. Late. "I was thinking of that this morning. I got up thinking about that, instead of about A.B." Then, as I was going: "Don't expect anything mighty grand. What I've been trying to do this morning is A.B. as I've seen him in his books. I may be wrong in my interpretation, just as you may be in your interpretation of a person."

P.M.: "I want you to dash your head round."

Me: "I was afraid of moving my head too far."

P.M.: "Don't be afraid. This place is yours. If you want to spew on the floor we've got people who'll clean it up.

"I've made money so that I can take *you* this morning and tell a 100-dollar client to go to the devil; that's what I've made money for.

"Joy isn't a contortion. It's something right deep down. Put your back against the chair. Get your back right against it—like an Englishman, that's it."

He told Doran, on bringing proofs, that if he hadn't read my pocket philosophies he couldn't have got such a good portrait.

Friday, October 20th.

Lunch, with Paul Reynolds and Whyham (*Metropolitan Mag.*) at Players' Club. Pictures and playbills at Club. General frank air of good fellowship at principal central table. Interviews, including 2 good ones from *Tribune.*

Then Doran took me to *New York Times* Building, where almost 1st person I met in editorial office was Brock, who had come to see me in London. We were shot up to top, about 27 stories altogether. View of New York. Yellow and blue lights. View of bridges. Feeling on top of being on top of a great cathedral (about 350 feet high, I suppose); solidity of parapets. But Metropolitan tower looked much higher. Steamers moving about on river. Fine wet wind.

Then down to see George Buchanan Fyfe on 16th floor. Curious three-cornered room. "City" editor. Stopped his leader to talk to us for 15 minutes. Sharp "Williamson" sort of man. Feeling of him being in an eyrie. All rest of staff without coat or waistcoat—belted. Then down 4 stories below ground to see machine room. Blue corpse light, as outside Paris opera. Rolls of paper being arranged on their steel angles. (Cf. Brock writing story of aviator's fatal fall, 20 stories above.)

Then to low dancing hall—an old man, really old, probably official of house, dancing with a young girl. 35 cents entrance. Mineral water. Small band. Rather shabby Montmartre. Doran didn't know how it was arranged with police. All the women were tarts. We stayed 10 minutes. Bed at 1.10.

Miss Gurney and Mrs. Doran for tea. Then I went to Altman's store and McCreery's store with Mrs. D. Marvellous white effect of former. Shop girls not so prosperous-looking and rather sloppy, but a few were pretty, and one had the mien of Marie Tempest with a waist too thin. . . .

Miss Gurney said women were not as well turned out here as in London.

Saturday, October 21st.

The Dorans dined with me last night at Louis Martin's. Café de l'Opéra, the place where only morning dress was allowed and it failed. Pruger used to have it. It is now an ordinary restaurant. Very glittering, with scenery painted on some walls, and the wall opposite street all mirror. Friezes of bulls (Egyptian character of decoration) and other animals. Strange statuary.

Then to Astor Theatre, where Henry B. Harris presents *The Arab,* a play of the Orient, by Edgar Selwyn.

Afterwards Mr. and Mrs. Edgar Selwyn (Margaret Mayo) invited us and Mr. and Mrs. Crosby Gaige to supper at Knickerbocker. Another lofty large restaurant. Food quite good. Both Selwyn and wife agreeable. She a smiling little thing, with a cute eye. She told me she had 4 companies playing *Baby Mine* in America, and that each of them brought in more than London. Gaige put in that one week's royalties at San Francisco brought in more than 8 in London, where play was a success. Selwyn said American theatres held more. His held 1800 dollars per performance and it was a smallish one. They played to 16,000 or 15,000 dollars a week on road, and in N.Y. Actors got more. He played in *Arizona* in London, and one American actor had to leave. They got an English one at 1/6th his screw.

Journeyed by Elevated (change at 155th) and N.Y. and Putnam R.R. to Yonkers. Talk about the sadness and raggedness of this. Occasional ship. Brokendown wooden houses. Sloppy planks. One house had drifted out into Hudson River and sunk. Mrs. D. said that really terrible crimes were committed here. Sight of 2 or 3 pleasant young children on stoop of a wooden house. Sloppy ends of cars.

All this in fine driving rain.

Monday, October 23rd.

Walked up 5th Avenue in bright warm sunshine at 12.45. The skyscraper coming at fairly regular intervals (apparently) seems to divide length of street and so aid perspective. But buildings are so big that they deceive you as to their nearness. Fine blue sky and general feel. Cornices of architecture again. Otherwise nothing very special. This walk, though hurried, was very pleasant.

Lunch with Mrs. Ullman [1] at Arts Club. Mr. and Mrs. May Wilson Preston, Mr. and Mrs. Day, Mr. and Mrs. Doran, and me. May W. P. was in great form. When Alice said something cutting about George, May said, "Now you're making a noise like a wife." She was one of the liveliest and wittiest women, if not the most so, I have met in N.Y.

Tuesday, October 24th.

It is only 17 days since I left London, and it feels more like 17 weeks.

Dinner with Mr. and Mrs. James Clark and Mrs. Adelaide Ames and the Dorans at Rector's. During dinner a pianist played a ballade of Chopin's. Never heard such a thing in a restaurant before.

To the Playhouse, managed by Wm. A. Brady. *Bought and Paid For,* a play in 4 acts by George Broadhurst. This is the best new Anglo-Saxon play I've seen for a long time. Perfectly simple story of a poor telephone girl marrying a wealthy man who turns to drink: with her comic sister and extremely comic brother-in-law. These were the only necessary characters. The rest were servants, including a fine Japanese servant. The brother-in-law was colossal. Splendidly drawn comic character. Whenever the author might have excusably gone wrong, whenever the thing was really difficult, he came out well. The reconciliation at the end was excellent. The drunken scene in second half of 2nd act, with its clear suggestion—both there and at beginning of 3rd act—that the husband outraged the wife sexually while drunk—was very excellently unpleasant. In short, I really enjoyed this play. The story was interesting and the sense of character very strong indeed.

Upton Sinclair. A brief chat. Not a bad sort of chap, I thought.

---

[1] The former Alice Woods. She and her husband, George Ullman, were great Paris friends of Arnold Bennett.

For the doorman, the Waldorf is simply a place where the doors revolve 18 hours a day or more.

Wednesday, October 25th.

Last night. Rhodes,[1] dramatist, came in with Knoblock for tea. Mrs. Adelaide Ames and her friend (heralded as beautiful, Gibsonish). Mrs. Glaesner came for tea, too. Knoblock dined with me and Rhodes (societyish dramatist) at Café Martin, and then I took them to Wallach's to see George Arliss in Louis N. Parker's *Disraeli*. Doran joined us. An awfully tedious play. English players. Just the Louis Parker artificial drivel. We left after 1st act. We came to the Waldorf bar. Went to bed before 12. Rhodes wanted to take me on to the Guinnesses in Washington Square; I wouldn't go.

Bad night.

I had breakfast in bed. Very well served on table brought in. Soft-boiled eggs. Difficulty of breaking them into glass. Appointment with Björkman[2] at 11 and with Arthur Hooley[3] at 11.30. Björkman too talkative. An analytic and probably uncreative brain, but very decent.

I said, "A good book is interesting. A book that isn't interesting isn't good."

Arthur Hooley said instantly, "Could you say that of a man?"

At 2.30, Lingley called in his auto to take me to Columbia University. 20 minutes' drive.

Classes chiefly closed at 3 when we got there. We were met on steps by Dean Keppel. Proved himself more and more pleasant as interview and inspection went on. Showed me the leaf in looseleaf book of information about each student.

Took us to modern history laboratory, where I saw a Chinese tabulating history of world day by day.

---

[1] Harrison Rhodes's *Ruggles of Red Gap* was produced in 1915.
[2] Edwin Björkman's book *Gleams* appeared in 1911. He is best known for his translations from the Scandinavian, including the plays of Strindberg.
[3] Before 1908, when Hooley came to America, he had collaborated with Bennett in writing plays which were never produced. Hooley wrote under the pseudonym of Charles Vale.

Then to political laboratory. Same kind of thing, but not yet quite in working order. All vast rooms; well equipped. Then to see 2 chambers. 3 dollars a week. Simple, quite large enough. Photographs on shelves, etc. Sofa bed. Very nice in adolescent way. Met hunchback contributor [1] to *Atlantic Monthly*. This man had to pay his way—got 25 dollars a month from Keppel for certain editorial work.

Loyalty of men together who join in a certain year. They will club up years afterwards for a contribution to University. Such as a flagstaff, or marble seat.

Then to the gymnasium, basket-ball and baths (naked) under that.

Then to Horace Mann school. Grey-haired ladies knocking about corridors. Started originally as school for teachers to learn to teach in.

Tea at Faculty Club. Talk with young Professor (Walker?) [2] of English who taught Shakespeare, chiefly by making youths read the plays. He said they read them for story.

Also visit to Thorndike, head of English department in University. Grey-haired young-looking jolly man, who made us sit down and gave us cigarettes.

I came away pretty nearly dead. Impressions. Size. Groupings of buildings. Richness where richness advisable, as in libraries and chapel. Manual work of kids of 10 in model houses, and reinforced concrete. Ferns, etc., in Horace Mann School.

Drive home by Riverside Drive. 1st U.S.A. warships with patent wirework masts that are said to be indestructible.

Drive back to Waldorf. Wait at top of 5th Avenue (Plaza corner) and watch crowd going home. Richness. Tiffany's by night. A dazzling and lovely building.

University Club, glorious buildings.

Traffic. Policemen with coating of dust on blue coats.

Impression of youth and hope and inspiringness.

---

[1] Randolph Bourne. He was also on the staff of the *New Republic* from its inception.
[2] Possibly Professor Charles William Wallace, noted Shakespeare authority.

Thursday, October 26th.

New York (or Yonkers). Young people coming out of school or college. Confident. Defiant. Phrase: "These *invaders* of *our* time, *our* earth."

October 27th. Boston.

Blotting-paper in U.S.A. is darker and thicker. Blue and green, till you aren't sure what it is.

Corrigan came for breakfast. Went out with him to see booksellers.

Jordan Marsh the principal. Pitman, head of book department. Largest booksellers in town. Young Jordan (a grandson) absolutely English—manner, accent; rather aristocratic. Complete counter given to my works.

Visited 7 other stores. Lauriat—bluffer, nice assistants. De Wolfe. Narrow, noisy, curly streets. Business character of England. So much so that nothing struck me as queer or curious the whole morning—except the size of everything. Jordan Marsh's probably bigger than Harrod's.

Excursion to Cambridge, and Harvard with Basil King,[1] who came to fetch us and insisted on us taking tram. King said every one did it and we must do it. Remember underground tram station and gradual emergence, *very uncomfortable.* View across from Charles River. Strange idea of building an island and putting cathedral on it. Town of Cambridge, rather slatternly. Then we came to residential part.

House of Lowell. *First thrill.*

House of Longfellow. Kids of town had bought plot of ground in front so as to assure him from being built in.

Long walk with stalwart Basil King. Ex-parson. He said major vices did not exist in this community of professors, writers, and professional men.

A.B.: "No adultery?"

B.K.: "None.

"Extraordinary state of intimacy we live in," he said. "But we live for social service—for each other."

---

[1] His *The Street Called Straight* was published in 1912.

Then Professor Schofield took us in charge in a fine motor car. Brief visit to University. Saying: "You can always tell a Harvard man, but you can't tell him much."

October 28th. Boston.

Library. The Puvis de Chavannes (blue going so well with marble) are the most beautiful things in America.

Yesterday. Pre-revolutionary homes still occupied by same families at Cambridge.

Auto drive—continuation after Public Library. Parks. Fenlike park. Skirting Brookline—richest per capita. Mrs. Jack Gardner's [1] house with a screen to cut off school.

Women chauffeurs.

Pleasure roads only.

Yacht clubhouse overlooking old harbour. 4-masted schooner.

Boston is a circular city, repeated ad infinitum.

Harbour, 6-masters.

Then vast wool warehouses.

"Coffee and spices."

Then circular streets. Elevated. Tram cars.

Fearful racket.

To Boston Yacht Club; in an old warehouse.

Low ceilings—great beams.

Extreme and splendid nauticality of this club.

Wheel of *Spray* in which the regretted Slocum wafted himself round the world.

Huge square porthole (faced with arm-chairs with great wide arms), across which ships are continually passing.

"Best thing about Boston is 5 o'clock train to New York." (Thomson.)

I had no glimpse of real Bostonians, "old Back Bay folks" who gravitate between Beacon St. and State St. and Somerset Club and never go beyond. Confusing New England with the created universe.

---

[1] Mrs. John L. Gardner was the owner of one of the finest private art galleries in the world.

Navy Yard. *Constitution,* built 1799.

Roomy, much metal.

Then into Italian quarter, curving tram-liney streets, cobbled; Italian signs up and down, and so gradually into business quarter, which I saw yesterday with Corrigan (all previous part of morning so different from this).

Legend of Paul Revere floating like a mist through Italian streets.

Paul Revere's signal church spire, by Wren. (Closed [?] because only 6 in congregation.)

Old State House. Beautiful building. Massacre close by. Lion and unicorn on roof.

Boston is finished, complete.

Sunday, October 29th.

Lunch with Rideings at Brandon Hall on way to Brookline or at Brookline. He came to fetch me. Fine morning. He grumbled at everything.

"This is the most snobbish place in the world. There is no real democracy. First thing people do is to show you their family tree and prove that they came over in the *Mayflower.* Very dear. . . . I would accept 1/3rd less salary to live in England," etc.

Tuesday, October 31st.

Dinner at Margaretta Deland's [1] on Sunday night. Mrs. Deland was extremely sympathetic. Note her hands, strong and decided.

We left Boston by 9 A.M. train. Invited by telephone to lunch at George Day's, treasurer of Yale (at New Haven). Horrible railway station at New Haven. Drove up in a sort of funeral carriage. Nice wooden quaint house. G. Day a very quiet and patriotic sort of man (had chucked banking to do this). Tales told of his saying at football of a member of opposing team in game he was watching, "Kill him, I can't stand his red stockings coming up the field." President Hadley and his wife came to lunch. President Hadley a remarkable man. Extremely nervous laugh

---

[1] Her novel, *The Iron Woman,* was published that year.

(very like Lanchester). Greatest authority in America on railway economics. Speaks Latin. Lectures in German at Berlin. Tells funny stories and remembers all sorts of punning rhymes. His wife excellent. I didn't see university, except drive round, and yet here I got the best idea I have had of university spirit, fine.

Character of American men in lips more than in anything else. Sticking out and holes beneath. Strange outlines formed by lips.

New York. The incapacity of Americans to deal with street traffic is shown in everything—from elevated to absence of refuges even in main thoroughfares.

Wednesday, November 1st.

To dinner last night at Waldorf: Doran, Knoblock, E. Sheldon, and Hopwood, a dramatist (author of *Nobody's Widow*). This was Hallowe'en. Kid's parties, etc., and general appearance of festivities in hotels.

Then to Hippodrome, where Hopwood had obtained a box. A vast, ingenious, striking and impressive, and grossly inartistic spectacle, *Around the World*, "conceived" by Arthur Voeglin. We just missed the *clou*—the sandstorm in the desert. But we saw the forest fire, and noted particularly the realism of the clouds in the yacht scene in Honolulu harbour. The Irish scene was prodigiously idiotic. The final tableau: waterfall, electric bulbs all over it, and girls behind that in bowers of light, a great tank in front, out of which came a golden barge, swans, and real people. Nobody knew how it was done. Hero the "eccentric millionaire," of course.

Thursday, November 2nd.

Lunch at Harvard Club. 15 men. Sisson and Lingley hosts.

The Return of Peter Grimm, by David Belasco, in 3 acts, at Belasco Theatre, 44th Street.

I should soon get tired of Belasco's productions. Can see same style in this as in *The Woman*. Nice, agreeable, ingenious. Fundamentally impossible and unconvincing. All the ghost business infinitely too solid. Still, a great cleverness about the whole thing.

Theatre only built 5 years, but very fussy, dim, old-fashioned architecture. A fashionable audience. Only you couldn't see it. Place full.

Dinner at Delmonico's. Nothing particular. A rather swagger crowd.

We called afterwards at the Lambs Club to find Tarkington. Wasn't in. The Lambs was like what one would have expected the Lambs to be. We then went to the Princeton Club, and found Tark. Rather round-shouldered and ripe.

Friday, November 3rd.

Messmore Kendall's lunch.

Judge Gary (steel trust president) on my right. Slow to talk. Rather dull. But very wise and upright. Said he was making 75,000 dollars a year as a lawyer when he chucked law. Said up to 6 years ago J. P. Morgan had never spoken in public—that after, for 1st time, he had said just 6 words in public, he told Gary that he had been obliged to hold on to a chair.

Advanced and good, fair, honest views on women's suffrage.

Kendall on my left, and then Dan Guggenheim, eldest (?) of 6 or 9 brothers—anyhow chief of them. They never took same steamer or train. A short, merry man. I liked him very much. Very frank. He was U.S. envoy to coronation of George V. President of Smelting and Refining Company. Head of Alaska and Yukon explorations.

R. W. Chambers.

Colonel Braden, the great copper man.

Very agreeable lunch.

I forgot to put down Mr. Cahan, editor of the Yiddish *Forward,* Socialist. A Russian Jew, very enthusiastic for literature, and for any work. Urged me to go and dine with him one night. This man seemed to know as much about art as anybody I've met. And he assured me, what I'd previously heard, that my stuff and art generally was better understood on the East Side than anywhere in N.Y.

Saturday, November 4th. Waldorf.

7.45. Business men—the humanity beneath. A man said, "I'm just going to get a bromo-seltzer."

Thus giving the whole show away.

Postal Telegraph. Girl coming behind her counter in hat and cloak, and turning on her counter lights and opening up her shop.

Luggage men sitting in a group under stairs and discussing their affairs.

Princeton.

Man conducting the "official yell."

Quarterback calling numbers.

Adams said there was a Glee Club concert last night that was delightful. Contortions of enthusiasts. Artistic amenity in contrast to this bloody barbarity.

Reserve men waiting in pairs under red rugs. Whole crowd rising up and sitting down at points of play.

Nassau Club. Confusion.

Princeton Inn. Confusion.

After freshman game met Booth Tarkington at Nassau Club. Drink in dining-room. He said he had been drinking beer with undergraduates late, and then couldn't sleep owing to men singing Chinese songs all night in corridor.

Auto back to club and then to field.

Coloured effect of hats on stands, heaps of violet colour.

Harvard opposite to us.

Cheer-leaders with megaphones.

Standing up and sitting down. At high moments standing on seats.

Accident at start. Man led off amid cheers.

Several minor accidents.

Naïve and barbaric! Merely an outlet for enthusiasm.

Touch and goal scored.

Left at half time.

Sunday, November 5th. New York.

Cobb on interviews:

You gather that an extremely brilliant young man or woman has been interviewed by a very commonplace stranger. Confused in her presence. She picks him up on an absurdity, with a brilliant inspiration. Then another "brilliant inspiration" and so on.

If interviewers had achieved the excellence of American oysters, American journalism would be better than it is. They don't come with prepared questions and are ignorant. No one knew less of my books than they did. They want you to write their interviews for them. Women so infernally badly dressed.

"It is so pitifully easy to be flippant."

Tuesday, November 7th.

Dinner last night given by the Dutch Treat Club at Keen's Chop House. Over 100. Wallace Irwin gave a good skit on "How to Live in New York on 48 Hours a Day."

In a few words I said I would thank him in print.

I walked down to 34th Street to waterside offices of Italian lines; saw *Duca degli Abruzzi* half ready to go. A lot of people on board and a line of 3rd-class passengers waiting outside shed for admittance. Nothing but Italian spoken all round me. This swift transition from 5th Avenue is very picturesque.

Declension of streets sets in immediately after Broadway. 6th Avenue is atrociously paved.

After 7th the declension is frank.

10th and 11th are appalling, atrocious, and some of the sidewalks staggering—unworthy of the suburbs of a small provincial town.

Trains allowed to shunt over 10th and 11th Avenues. Extraordinary.

This was election day. I saw the sinister but genial fellows bearing openly the insignia of Tammany. Don't, please, think that Tammany is a disease that happens to have attacked N.Y. It is as much an expression of N.Y. character as the barber's (remember my shave this morning at Waldorf), the pavements, the fineness, the interest in education, etc., etc.

Thorough badness of barbers.

Dinner at Sherry's. Robert H. Davies, Franklin Adams, Doran, and I.

Davies told how he interviewed Li Hung Chang for W. R. Hearst. Hearst, on it being pointed out to him that bribery would be necessary to get round the whole crowd of Dutch waiters at Waldorf (where he had a suite), said he would give 1000 dollars for the expenses of the interview. Davies went straight to the head underling and gave him 500 dollars in cash, simply to say whenever asked, "Who is the greatest journalist in N.Y.?" that Davies was the greatest journalist in N.Y. Said Davies to underling, "When you've been asked this question and fallen down in a fit, rise up and breathe the sacred name, and keep on breathing it." Ultimately, after a week, Chang sent for Davies. And Davies entered his suite, "with my shoes in my hand." He interviewed him through an interpreter. At the end Davies said: "I asked his Excellency if he spoke English; he answered in English, 'No.' Asked if he was rich, he said, '600,000,000 dollars today; nothing tomorrow. All I have is at the mercy of the State.'" He was very curious about rich men in America. Later he sent for Davies as a private man and spoke to him in English. He asked if Davies was married, and Davies said he wasn't because he couldn't afford to be. He then said: "Get money. Get a wife. Get a home. Get children."

Wednesday, November 8th.

C. called. Talked very interestingly. X., who I said had seemed to me, positively, an honest man. He denied it. Told me, what he said was notorious, X. had committed adultery with a girl and had two children by her. Then his wife had died, and he had thrown her over for the "large florid creature" now his wife. Girl had only got her rights through a lawyer. Still he admitted that X. was honester, and had the new sense of right and wrong to a greater extent, than any of his rivals. But he had done all the usual bad things. He said there were two people in each big trust man—the head of the vast corporation, and the private individual. He said X., like others, by the force of his character and his autocratic spirit, had killed really efficient co-operation round about him, and that the other best men had left, because no room for them.

Lunch at Aldine Club, given by Phillips of *American*. Miss Marbury, Miss Anne Morgan, Miss Ida Tarbell.

These three women all extremely interesting; all different, yet intimate, calling each other by Christian names, coming together on a purely personal basis just like men.

Elisabeth Marbury. A very business woman. Fat. Human. Kindly. Shrewd. Very shrewd, and downright in her remarks.

Anne Morgan. Handsome, complexion going. Apparently doing nothing, but interested in everything. Art, for instance, (and art dealing) and reform. Knew France and Germany well. Spoke firmly and efficiently. Showed us her beautiful new enamel cigarette case, with her monogram worked regularly into all the crossing lines of it. A peculiar accent. Evidently an energetic woman. Again, efficient. Good judge of human qualities, and wide in interests. At 10 to 3, I said, "It's 10 to 3; I must go." "Yes," she said quietly, "I must be going soon. We're going down to Washington by the 3.30."

Ida M. Tarbell. The most wistful and inviting of these 3 spinsters. A very nice kind face, of a woman aged by hard work, by various sympathies, and by human experiences. A sort of appealing face, and yet firm and wise. When asked to go down to Washington with Anne and Bessie, she said, "I've only just come back (where from ?), and I haven't been at my desk for 4 or 5 days." Just like a man. One imagined her desk.

Miss Hale's report on immorality of Boston. Her visit unawares to house of assignation.

Saturday, November 11th.

Last night. Dinner at Mrs. Edgar Selwyn's. Then Geo. M. Cohan's theatre.

The Little Millionaire, written, largely composed, and produced by G.M.C., who takes the principal part and who built the theatre. He has in particular a voice, but he is a good dancer. Man about 35 probably, slim, and looks on stage what he probably is—a mixture of shrewdness and good nature.

Brings his family into show. Both his father and mother have principal parts, and he is ingenious enough to make them marry at the end. The last curtain is he and his father doing a *pas de deux*.

A N.Y. institution, apparently beloved.

Plot of piece quite clear. In 3 acts. "The Action of Act II will not be interrupted by musical numbers." The second act is beautifully constructed, and dramatically effective, and full of invention of all kinds. No salacity in the piece at all.

Sunday, November 12th.

Yesterday. Abraham Cahan came to fetch me for lunch. Mr. Cahan at Café Boulevard (2nd Ave.), "Art Nouveau" in dining-halls. Mrs. Cahan a little, fatigued-voiced, Russian woman. Unable any more to go to Russia owing to warrant being out for her spouse (owing to spy's revelations). Long talk on literature. Home by surface car. Cahan said: "Russians talk a great deal more than English. They like talking, and I'm going to talk." He did.

Why is not N.Y. the real America? It seems real enough. Is it more material than, say, Paris, or Hamburg or London? What's up with it, anyhow?

Why are the few artistic people in America so internecine?

Art will come unconsciously, and it will be jeered at.

Monday, November 13th. Twentieth Century Limited.

Telephone, typist, library, papers. All this is typical.

Began by running fairly smoothly.

Along the Hudson. Ugly general effect.

Stop in the mysterious electric-signed city of Albany. Crossing Hudson. River steamer with several stories.

Watched changing of enormous engines.

Before Syracuse 10 P.M. night train running through night. Mysterious habitations, stations, and hints of strange life.

Authority of train men compared to English guards. More like naval officers.

"Syracuse bids you welcome." Electric sign on probably town hall.

Tuesday, November 14th.

Night a series of short dozes.

Rang for tea at 7.45 (N.Y. time) and attendant said no dining-car till Elkhart, 1½ hours off, and that engine had broken down at Cleveland, and train was 2 hours late. I got up 1½ hours later and went out of compartment and asked one of head-men and was informed train 2 h. 10 m. late. Train full of hungry passengers. I had felt our car chilly. Found observation car damn chilly, and everybody complaining, and attendants excusing.

Before all this, fine steamy view of Toledo, at about 7 A.M., with river and chimneys various shades of grey and black.

Line quite straight for innumerable miles. Slight coating of snow. Flat.

2 dining-cars for breakfast. Nevertheless a queue, women and men waiting 20 minutes at door.

Arrived Chicago. 10.45 (1 h. 50 ms. late.)

Blackstone Hotel. Taylor (Frank Adams of Chicago *Tribune*) for lunch.

Opening of Art Institute.

Mobbed by women.

Woman: "I'm a regular Bennett fan."

Autograph hunter who followed me round and was always staring right in front of me.

Reporter who on being refused an interview at once said, "Well, can I follow you round, and take down any observations you make?"

Female reporter afterwards who called me "my dear man."

Met Thomas Nelson Page and his wife.

Scene from my window. Morning. Michigan Boulevard. Sound of

trains puffing. Skyscrapers with ledges of snow. All roads chiefly snow-covered. Frost. Procession of autos. Many snow-covered flat roofs of lower buildings. Illinois Central Station apparently in front. Grey, dirty bituminous region. Can't keep hands or linen clean.

Barometer lower than it has been during my stay in U.S.A.

Wednesday, November 15th.

Rottenness of female interview in Hearst paper *Chicago Examiner*. Next reporter told me the Hearst paper had mercilessly guyed all best men in Chicago.

Man who telephoned to Doran, "Tell Mr. Bennett he stinks." This would probably happen in no other city in the world. I might say, "Chicago is the city in which this happened to me." But I won't.

Lunch Chicago Press Club. I applied for foreign membership. Douglas Mallock in chair (editor of *The Lumberman*). Two members made speeches as "Mr. B. would have spoken if he had spoken."

Number of doctors. Two said that my books, *Human Machine* and *How to Live on 24 Hours a Day,* were regularly prescribed to patients. One said that they had "changed his whole life." Number of autograph hunters.

On the way, in cab in which they fetched me, Goble and another member expressed sorrow and disgust of club at interview with me in *Examiner* today.

Chicago city of superlatives.

Biggest store, bookshop, press club, post.

Reynolds Club (students).

Commons (replica of Oxford).

Fine twilight effect on magnificent boulevards.

Then reception at Mrs. Judson's.[1] She looked after me grandly. Tea. Told girls not to talk till I had had tea.

Then stood in corner of drawing-room, and procession of faculty and wives filed past me, and I joked with each.

Nice, unassuming large house.

---

[1] Wife of Harry Pratt Judson, then President of the University of Chicago.

Drive home with Hutchinson to Blackstone.

Half an hour to prepare to go in Ross's auto to dine at his house in Evanston.

Drive out to Evanston. Long gas-lit roads. Very smooth and straight on the whole, but with half-made bumpy intervals.

Entire company interested in children.

Talking of kids, I must not forget 2 stories of Cobb's. Elizabeth Cobb, when her parents began to spell: "Too damn much education here for me." And of another girl, when her parents began to whisper: "What's the good of being educated, anyway? When I've learnt to spell, you whisper."

November 16th.

Floyd Dell, successor to Francis Hackett, of *Chicago Evening Post* (literary), called to see me.

Hamlin Garland came to take me to lunch at the Cliff Dwellers.

Charles Hutchinson, the banker, and originator of Art Institute and all sorts of municipal stuff, had found time to come during morning and arrange flowers; on principal table. Many handshakers and autographs. Talks with architects and musicians. Then Garland, with his two brothers-in-law, Taft [1] (sculptor) and Browne [1] (painter), and Jensen (a Dane, head of parks section), took me in auto to make circuit of boulevards round city.

Fine internal "landscape" gardening. Enormous completeness of everything, and fine upkeep of everything on boulevards.

River. They turned its course towards Mississippi, so as to get rid of sewage. This is most remarkable thing I have come across, spectacularly.

Smell of stockyards.

Taft's studio. Colony created by him after 20 years' dreaming. A dreamy timid man. Several young sculptors and sculptresses said to have great talent, at work on vast municipal sculptures (such as groups and bridge near University). Sense of enormous protracted detailed labour in these undertakings.

---

[1] Hamlin Garland and Charles Francis Browne had each married a sister of Lorado Taft.

Dinner at C. L. Hutchinson's.

Ayer and wife (collector, etc., aged 70), Burnham (architect), Miss Monroe,[1] Mr. and Mrs. Ryerson. President and Mrs. Judson.

Some good and many bad pictures.

A crowd of younger ones came in afterwards.

General impression of shallowness left after seeing all these people. As if one had come to the end of them at once.

Yet Hutchinson's idea of hospitality, and of how to look after a sought-for visitor and how to leave him alone, is unequalled by any one else's in U.S.A. so far.

Spectacular effect of their municipal spirit (born in '71). Curious wistful quality in their constantly expressed inspiration after "The City Beautiful."

Letter (probably falsely) signed "Jack London" of abuse about interview with me in the *Examiner*.

Home at 11.30.

Wet street view of Michigan Boulevard with flood of yellow reflections and the 2 long lines of lights, punctuated by red globes showing crossings.

Chicago is full of public spirit.

Friday, November 17th.

Maurice Browne called 9.20.

Prim little professional Englishman. Very nice. Gloomy about art in States.

Went to Sears Roebuck & Co. in their auto. Got on very well with Murkland, head of book and China dept.

8 million dollars business last month.

Over 7000 employees. Over 4000 women. 5½ millions of large catalogues sold. Big bill-typing room. 600 clickers.

Gradually on to car-yard, where cars being filled up. This yard of cars sent out full every day.

But most interesting thing was glimpses of real life of these outlying communities everywhere, as seen in ugly common simple stuff they

---

[1] Miss Monroe's magazine, *Poetry*, did not begin to be published until October 1912.

ordered. Thousands of cheap violins. In one basket ready for packing, all sorts of little cooking utensils and two mugs (fearfully ugly) labelled "Father" and "Mother." 4-cent curling-iron. Most startling realistic glimpses of home life. All the life (cheap music, chairs, etc.) of these communities and separate farms could be deduced from this establishment.

Concert of Thomas orchestra in Mrs. Hutchinson's box. Good. Piano (bad) coming up through floor. Bauer pianist.

Then to Little Room in a studio in Fine Arts Building.

Met Jane Addams at Little Room. A middle-aged benevolent creature.

Dinner given by Herbert Kaufman. Very nice table in handsome private room.

Mr. and Mrs. Medill McCormick. She daughter of Mark Hanna.

Mrs. Cobb, daughter of Governor of Ohio.

John McCutcheon, who does a cartoon every day for *Tribune*.

McCormick (young man retired on account of nervous breakdown) is a good radical and well up in English politics.

"Ruth," he said suddenly to his wife, in tone of commanding suggestion. And they went and the party broke up at once. 10.10. I was glad. I was just going to break it up myself.

Saturday, November 18th. Indianapolis.

Set out for Indianapolis this morning at 9.47.

Sort of accommodation train.

Chiefly flattish country (with welcome breaks), yellow stubble land. Occasionally a dark muddy river. Single track (after once clear out of industrial Chicago, which seemed to be one vast shunting yard). Stopped at little towns. At very little ones. A group of men and a woman. Man holding gun and shot rabbits, and dog leaping up at it. Wooden houses with concrete narrow walks and grass on either side. Fat little German girl (daughter of house) cleaning windows.

Arrived Indianapolis 3 (12 minutes late, about). Maple trees in all streets. Monuments to sailors and soldiers. Dome of State House.

State fair ground outside town. Said to be same in all State capitals.

Dinner. Tark,[1] Doran, Craig, me.

Reception at night. About 40 people. Meredith Nicholson.[2] Senator and Mrs. Beveridge (very beautiful, with a soft, and probably Washingtonian, voice); also wife of ex-President Harrison. Numerous provincially dressed girls and women. One débutante almost the only person who wasn't shy. She had made her début yesterday evening and gone to bed at 2 o'clock. Said she slept very well.

Punch in study made by 2 Japanese boys from University Club.

Sunday, November 19th.

Lunch of ten people at Tark's, including Meredith Nicholson and Tark's father.

Afterwards in auto to pay several calls, including one on James Whitcomb Riley. Fine old man, recovering from paralysis. Red face, yellow teeth, right hand affected, sitting in corner in easy chair. Fire. Mid-Victorian feel. An old friend near him. Talk about a picture of a literary star of good order. Here it was, and in a literary town. Why say there is no American literature? Riley has infectious laugh. Told funny tales of his tragic adventures in lecturing tours, and how he slept on two boxes, one a little higher than the other, covered with papers. Inquired about Lucas. "Tell me about Lucas." Then talked about my books. "I didn't mean to talk about them, to talk 'shop,' but I couldn't help it." Women talking in another room.

Monday, November 20th.

Indianapolis just beginning to spend money. Malaria is gone. Just beginning to be sure that Indians aren't coming and that there'll be plenty of wood. Even now it's rather daring to buy a picture. Formerly you could spend money only on a house, because that was solid and could be sold. And of course you had to have wallpapers and stove.

And now gradually to Art Institute with loan collections, and ripping aquarelles by Winslow Homer.

---

[1] Booth Tarkington.
[2] His *A Hoosier Chronicle* appeared the next year.

Wednesday, November 22nd. Philadelphia.

Took train for Philadelphia Monday at 7.05 P.M. and arrived at Phil. promptly at 3.30, about. Had a drawing-room to myself, but slept little. Row in other part of carriage between conductor and a passenger in middle of night.

Geo. Hellman looked me up in Bellevue Stratford Hotel, and took me to a bookseller (Dr. Rosenbach) where there were some 1-class MSS., Caxtons, and W. de Lourdes. Also old English MS.

Dinner: Corrigan, Craig, Hellman, and me. Last night opera. *La Gioconda.* Caruso.

Malignant ugliness of house. If any spark of artistic feeling in Philadelphia, the place would have been ripped to pieces.

Enormous place. Crammed. But very wealthy and a few very fine dresses.

In train, Corrigan's criticism that *à la carte* service in American trains much better than *table d'hôte* service on European trains.

Bad service at breakfast. "Right away." This is one of the most deceitful phrases in the U.S. language.

Visit to Wanamaker's. Largest organ. Wireless between N.Y. and Philadelphia establishments. Mrs. Hall, book-buyer, said that *How to Live* had eminently stimulated sales for all books mentioned in it—for example, Krehbiel's *How to Listen to Music.*

Lunch at Bellevue Stratford given by G. H. Lorimer of *Saturday Evening Post.* Sam Blythe and Irvin Cobb principal talkers. Racy tales and slang, politics, and murders.

Crossed ferry to 23rd Street. Wonderful view of N.Y. as if on a hill, topped by tower. Mrs. Schiff's auto, with English servant, waiting. She took me to Waldorf, where I soon found Doran. Dined with him and Mrs. Doran. Then I went to elder Mrs. Schiff's box at opera, where were elder Mrs. Schiff, Mr. and Mrs. Mortimer Schiff, the Hellmans, and a Schiff cousin from Frankfort.

Faust, with Geraldine Farrar and unknowns. A lifeless performance. Fine house. Plenty of pearls. I was in the "horseshoe" (W. C. Whitney's box next door).

The open boxes at Metropolitan Opera give the women's dresses a better chance than in London. There is apparently less talking than in London.

Thursday, November 30th..

The Dorans, T. B. Wells, Inglish, John Macrae, Davies, and May Preston came to see me off; not to mention several reporters and photographers. The *Lusitania* left at 9.30 A.M., having been delayed half an hour waiting for the mails. I met the Forbeses on board about 11, and Edgar Selwyn at lunch. Mrs. Selwyn much later. These two had gone to bed at 2.15. Either they or the Forbeses had received a lot of fruit and flowers, and Forbes had installed a supply of champagne at the foot of the table, in ice. I helped to consume everything except the flowers. I had, nevertheless, previously sworn neither to drink nor smoke on board. But having drunk, I thought I might as well buy the best cigar and the oldest brandy on the ship; which I did, and stood liqueurs round. This was after dinner.

I was overcome by sleepiness both before and after lunch and also before dinner; the air gave me a headache. I was very gloomy, spent all afternoon alone and had tea alone, and wondered what the hell was the matter with life anyway. I was all right after I had tasted champagne again.

We spent the whole evening in talking shop, Edgar Selwyn being the quietest. Boat rolled, always. In the middle of the night she rolled so much that she overthrew my red clock. Also fiddles on the tables, last night at dinner. Quite unnecessary, but it is probably a dodge to convince passengers that they are good sailors. No fiddles on at breakfast this morning, when they were necessary and crockery was rattling and crashing about all over the place. The Selwyns and the Forbeses had parting gifts which they displayed, but I also had a parting gift, which I did not display. It was an article for desk use, in silver, heavy and elaborate, engraved with my name, and the card on it bore the following words: "Thank you for all the delightful things you have written and are going to write during the coming year." George [1] will think he can guess the woman it came from at first guess. He couldn't. But he might guess it in three, perhaps. And I had five letters from other ladies, chiefly hating *Hilda Lessways,* but nevertheless all rustling with flattery.

Friday, December 1st.

A general feeling of cold on the ship—no doubt the contrast with N.Y. hotels and houses. But the *Lusitania* is an English ship, and you know it. However, the head dining-room steward is apparently a Frenchman. We had a Thanksgiving dinner last night, and the Frenchman had menus specially printed for our table. Thus, although dyspeptic, I had to eat something of all his dinner, though it irked me to do so.

First gleams of sunshine this morning, after snow and rain. Not caring to read any books that I had, I got *L'Anneau d'Améthyste* out of the library.

Saturday, December 2nd.

Following gale, overtaking us. I began to construct a 1-act play for ship use, and this put me off going to sleep last night, and then I was kept awake by rolling and noises connected therewith. Hence, bad night. Read a lot of *Sanine.* Insincere, voluptuous stuff.

Went out at 10.30. High seas. Whole surface of sea white with long marmoreal lines of foam. Through the mistiness the waves on the horizon looked as high as mountains; or high as a distant range of hills. Curious that distant waves should seem so much higher than those close to. Ship rolling enormously, and her prow yawing about. Yet forward, sheltered by deck-houses from following gale, one had no sensation that the boat was moving forward. Walking backward, from stem to stern, the following gale struck one sharply in the face, though one was running away from it at about 30 miles an hour.

Big squall gradually overtook us. All sunshine clouded out for 15 minutes and snow came down almost horizontally, and much faster than

---

[1] George Doran.

the ship in the same direction. The wind blew spray fiercely off the water in clouds. The screws half raced from time to time.

From newspaper: Annual Meeting of Children's Aid Society. "Bad food, excitement, noise have favoured development of St. Vitus's dance among young children. Poor food, little sleep, and long hours of confining work, have had effect on older children.

"In 3 months during summer over 1000 boys taken up for rowdyism in public places and conveyances.

"During year 8125 homeless boys sought shelter in our homes—a record!"

While waiting in barber's shop, read Jane Addams on *A New Conscience and an Ancient Evil*. Dept.-store girls spending their whole evening in *bathing their feet* and going with men because they were just "sick."

15,000 dept.-store girls in Chicago downtown.

Sunday, December 3rd.

Still rough sea and following gale, and creaking and noises all night. Not yet one good night's rest on this steamer.

Mr. and Mrs. Compton Mackenzie had tea with me. She is a beautiful young woman.

Concert in aid of Seamen's charities last night. Half of it done by Harry Lauder.

I read most of Artzibashev's *Sanine*, skipping. Mostly clever, *naïf*, and dull. Some of the salacious parts are pretty good. But how infantile, these Russians!

Monday, December 4th.

Following gale all yesterday, and the ship yawing about before it. This morning, moderation, and wind from the south. Supposed to get to Fishguard at 8.30 tonight, and Liverpool 8 A.M. tomorrow. I gave my dinner-party last night. Each of the others—the Forbeses, Mr. and Mrs. Selwyn—had given a dinner. I had a chill again. But last night I slept well for the first time on this voyage. These big ships, it seems, are difficult to steer, hence the yawing, and hence the comparatively slow runs.

Friday, December 8th.

Arrived Fishguard 9.30 P.M. Monday. *Standard* man came off to interview me. I gave him all he wanted. Arrived L'pool Monday 8.15. Got to Burslem for lunch. Saw Mater.

Arrived in Paris Thursday at 6.30 P.M., nearly 2 hours late. Very seasick indeed. *Descendu avec M. au Meurice.*

Total expenses of American tour to this morning £252 5s. 8d.

1912

January 6th. Cannes, Hôtel Californie.

Georges d'Espagnat came for lunch yesterday; we drove to Maugin's—he with us—and we deposited him at station at 4.15. He had come from Renoir's villa at Cagnes. He reported how Renoir's pictures 15 years ago were admitted by dealers to be unsaleable. Now the slightest sketch fetches 4 or 5000 frcs. And pictures which formerly had a theoretical price of 5000 frs. sell for 70 or 80,000. Dealers came down from Paris while D'Espagnat was at Renoir's, and bought and paid for everything that Renoir would let them take away. He has been a terrific worker, and in spite of very large sales, still has 2 or 300 pictures to be disposed of. He now lives luxuriously. Formerly *dans la dèche,* D'Espagnat had known him rent splendid houses in which he could not put furniture. He is 71, and scarcely able to move a limb. Cannot rise without help. Has to be carried about. Yet manages to paint, even large canvases. He said to D'Espagnat that were it not for ill health, old age would be a very happy time, as it has all sorts of pleasures special to itself. Although so old, he has a son aged only about ten. This child came as a surprise, and Renoir was furious.

I finished the first three of my *Harper's* articles on U.S.A. yesterday.

Hundredth performance of *The Honeymoon* last night.

Accounts for provincial performances of *W.T.P.W.* and *C. & C.*[1] show

---

[1] Respectively *What the Public Wants* and *Cupid and Common Sense.*

that those plays are playing to better money now in provinces than ever they did.

Thursday, January 18th.

Yesterday I finished the fifth article of the *Harper's* series. And today I turned towards the construction of the sequel to *The Card*[1] for the *American Magazine.* It is only between two spells of work that I can find time for unimportant correspondence, notes, etc. My days are always absolutely full; without counting that I have had three abscesses, two together, as a result of a chill in December. The last one is not yet gone, quite.

I am now in the full swing of my ordinary day; writing, reading a lot of newspapers and several books at once. I bought Whymper's *Scrambles among the Alps* and Stendhal's *Vie de Napoléon* and began reading them together, and immediately felt that I had got hold of two rattling good things. These, with a more or less daily instalment of Sorel's *L'Europe et la Révolution Française,* keep me busy.

Tuesday, January 23rd.

The other day a *vendeuse* and an *essayeuse* came up from the Maison de Blanc, with a *robe d'intérieur* for M. and another for Mrs. Selwyn. A porter of the Maison de Blanc carried the box. The general tableau—the two *employées,* young and agreeable, but certainly not *vierges,* with soft, liquid, persuasive voices, speaking chiefly English; the frothy garments lying all about on chairs and in the box, Selwyn, Alcock, and me loung-ing on chairs, and M. and Mrs. S. playing the mannequin, and the porter waiting outside in the dark corridor—this tableau produced a great effect on me. Expensive garments rather—and I felt that for my own personal tastes, I would as soon earn money in order to have such a tableau at my disposition, as for a lot of other seemingly more important and amusing purposes. A fine sensuality about it. There was something in the spec-tacle of the two *employées* waiting passive and silent for a few moments from time to time while we talked.

---

[1] The American edition was called *Denry the Audacious.* The sequel was *The Regent,* published in 1913.

Weather still very bad indeed. Heavy rain stopped a projected drive this afternoon. We did, however, yesterday make our auto-*canot* excursion to Les Îles Lérins without getting wet. Seaward tower on Île Saint-Honorat, quite striking. On grass by this was an old shepherd tending brown sheep. One of these sheep had 3 tufts of old wool left on the back, making her look like a kind of miniature triple dromedary. Marguerite asked the shepherd what it was for. He replied: *"Oh, madame, c'est seulement un peu de vanité."* He was quite simple, and answered simply, but he was evidently a bit of a character.

Saturday, January 27th.

Yesterday we went to Monte Carlo. Tables more tedious than ever. We came home by the Corniche. It began to rain. Brakes got hot and we had to stop. At Nice it was raining well. Twice or three times the driver lost his way.

I began my sixth American article for *Harper's* on Thursday. The two letters that T. B. Wells had written me show that *Harper's* do not at all appreciate these articles. But they probably will do when they have appeared in book form and people have begun to talk about them.

Read in a gulp *He Who Passed*,[1] sent to me by J. B. Pinker. Second- or third-rate; and a very poor end; but nevertheless containing a goodish picture of theatrical life in U.S.A.

On Saturday we drove to Napoule. And the colour was more wonderful than I ever remember seeing it anywhere, even at Fenayrols-les-Bains. The fields were all pools, and all the pools were full of sky and cloud. The view of Grasse was enchanting.

Tuesday, February 6th.

On January 31st I began an attack of *gastro-entérite*. Very decidedly ill on Wednesday afternoon. Full development of attack on Thursday. Doctor on Thursday and Friday. I got up for a few minutes yesterday morning and more in the afternoon. Not yet achieved complete disappearance of symptoms. While ill, I read Dostoievsky's *Le Sous-Sol,* which is great.

---

[1] It had just appeared anonymously.

Larbaud, who calls to see me nearly every day, prefers it to anything else of Dostoievsky's. Also Dostoievsky's unfinished *Le Crocodile*. Good.

Last night I listened to first act of Selwyn's new play, and the criticism on it was united—good beginning, and imperfect end. I ought to have begun my humorous novel on Thursday last, and I have not yet begun it. But on Sunday night I decided on the title *The Regent*. I read a lot of *The Oxford Book of English Verse,* just bought, with great satisfaction.

Sunday, February 11th.

Pinker came Thursday night. Friday we did little, but drove out. Saturday we went out in auto for the day, to Grasse, Gourdon, Gorges du Loup, Tourette, Vence, Antibes. On Thursday, by chance, we saw hydro-aeroplane in action at Juan les Pins. Very agreeable to see. I get better every day but do not propose to begin work again till Wednesday.

Friday, February 16th.

On Monday we all went and deposited Pinker with the Williamsons[1] at Monte Carlo. We lunched with them at Ciro's. On Tuesday, M. and I motored over to Grasse to have tea with the Galsworthys, and the interview was very agreeable.

On Wednesday morning at 7 A.M. as programmed a week ago, I began *The Regent*. By noon this morning I had written 4500 words of it.

Yesterday afternoon Mrs. Julia Frankau (Frank Danby) called to make my acquaintance, and produced a very agreeable impression indeed on us and on the Selwyns. A thorough London type; very chic, extremely capable and alert, of wide ideas, and of a sympathetic nature. She must have a full life, with a large family and her literary work, of which latter, by the way, she said about twenty times—really—that she was ashamed.

Tuesday, February 20th.

Yesterday the Frank Harrises called and took us to Saint-Raphael for lunch. He said: "God when he was young had a liking for the Jews. But when he was old he had a senile weakness for the English."

---

[1] C. N. and A. M. Williamson are known chiefly for their detective stories.

Thursday, February 29th.

This morning I had passed the 20,000-word mark of *The Regent*. It is going along with great ease. Pinker returned from Monte Carlo here on Tuesday, and the Williamsons came yesterday, when Selwyn and I gave a most admirable luncheon at the Casino restaurant. In the evening the whole band of us dined with Mrs. Frankau.

Monday, March 4th.

Coal strike began last Friday.[1]

Said Mrs. Frankau, who with Sydney Pawling came for tea yesterday: "Of course I'm feudal. I'd batten them down. I'd make them work. They *should* work. I'd force them down."

A man stopped me on the stairs the other noon, and asked me my opinion about Kipling's neologisms. He had been reading an article in *The Times*. I referred him to Wordsworth. He understood. Staggering, to find any Englishman in a cosmopolitan grand hotel with even a faint curiosity about the processes of literature. Such a thing never happened to me before.

Wednesday, March 6th.

Milestones by me and Knoblock produced at Royalty last night. I had four telegrams today, all agreed as to its immense success, if only the coal strike won't upset it.

Battle of Flowers yesterday. The most interesting people were the flower-venders. 3 frs. the *panier*, without the *panier!* Quarrelling and grumbling about ticket-holders all the time: "*Vous avez le No. 1. Eh bien, le No. 1 est pris. Vous pouvez vous mettre là. Qu'est-ce que ça fait?*"

Five sisters (secretly bored) in carriage, all dressed alike. American imitation of a rowboat. Mother as a sailor. Habit of thinly dressed women standing up in carriages all the time and exposing themselves. Rapacity of two young shop girls or something who placed themselves in the wrong

---

[1] The general coal strike of 1912 actually began on February 26 and lasted until April 6.

seats in front of us and snatched in the most shameless manner at all the bouquets that were thrown our way. They worried us to death. Astonishing the joy one took in a really pretty woman in white, when there happened to be one.

Larbaud brought André Gide in at 5.30. And we kept them to dinner and had a great evening that finished at 10 P.M.

I wasn't so well today.

Saturday, March 23rd.

I finished the first part of *The Regent* on Tuesday and wrote *Clay in the Hands of the Potter* for *Youth's Companion* (Boston) on Wednesday, and sent it off on Thursday. The Selwyns came over for lunch on Thursday. On Friday we went to Monte Carlo, and had lunch with them —Mary Moore, Charles Wyndham,[1] and H. B. Harris (N.Y. theatrical manager) being of the party. At the Hermitage. Food not so startlingly good as rumour says. Beautiful view of the harbour and yachts from the Selwyns' bedroom. Selwyn was still worrying me to write a play on *The Card*. We went and came home by train.

Coming up to hotel in omnibus, an oldish sea-captainish sort of man said to a youngish red-haired woman that miners had refused the terms of the Minimum Wages Bill. "But of course they refuse everything!" said she scornfully. I must have a strike in my continental novel. It is very funny that all the English inhabitants of grand hotels should be furious because miners insist on a minimum of 5s. per day for men and 2s. per day for boys.

Good Friday, April 5th.

Knoblock and sister came last Saturday. On Wednesday we excursioned to Monte Carlo, and lost about 500 frs. between us, I having played to amuse Gertrude Knoblock. I was ill yesterday through too much smoking (immediately) and did nothing, and very little today. Two chapters of *The Regent* remain to be done.

---

[1] Mary Moore and Sir Charles Wyndham were the joint proprietors of the Wyndham Theatre. They were married in 1916.

Thursday, April 11th.

Today at 3.30 I finished *The Regent*, 78,200 words, written in two months less three days. So far this year, I have written:

Four articles of *Your American States* (two last year, 10,000) for *Harper's* 22,000
Clay in the Hands of the Potter for *Youth's Companion* . . 2,200
The Regent 78,200

102,400

This morning the Knoblocks departed in an auto for Paris. They picked up Walpole and Anderson at the station.

By the way, at the Princess's Restaurant, I saw Lord X. He looked a vulgar and damned scoundrel. Not his fault, of course.

I have read Walpole's new novel, *The Prelude to Adventure;* satisfactory—and am to try to arrange a contract for him with Doran.

Wednesday, April 17th. Paris.

We left Hôtel Californie, Cannes, at 7.50 on Monday morning and got to the Hôtel du Rhin, Paris, at 11.45 at night. Flat in this hotel, 2 bedrooms, servant's bedroom, bathroom, sitting-room, and *débarras,* for 50 frs. a day, all included (*troisième*), but no central heating.

Saturday, April 20th.

Wednesday night *Le Petit Café* by Tristan Bernard at Palais Royal. Excellent, and well played. Yesterday the Selwyns and Calvo came to lunch. Only their anxiety to meet us here and hear the rest of my comic novel prevented them from going home with the H. B. Harrises on the *Titanic.*[1]

Tuesday, April 23rd.

Sunday at Fontainebleau, packing up books.

I told Selwyn I would turn *The Murder of the Mandarin* into a one-act play.

---

[1] The White Star liner *Titanic* had gone down with 1513 souls on board, April 15.

Finished reading *Quentin Durward* last night. A few goodish scenes, but on the whole mediocre and careless. I made a few notes as to it at the back of the *édition* Nelson.

Monday, April 29th.

Left Paris and got to Newhaven yesterday. Drove car for the first time this morning round about Newhaven.

Went over to Brighton to see the Sharpes.[1] Newspaper man in street talking to Oswald Sheppard (Bonnot[2] killed yesterday): "I wish I'd been in Paris yesterday. I could have made a bit o' money. When Crippen did it, I made £3 before 5 o'clock. Nobody got no change that day. . . . Now they mucked up this *Titanic* disaster for us. They put on the bills 'Titanic sunk.' That was no use to us. They ought to have put 'Hundreds drowned.' Then we should have made a bit."

Sunday, May 5th. London.

I came from Newhaven to London yesterday morning in the car, and drove it myself as far as Putney Hill, 62 miles, in under 4 hours.

May 29th.

John Burns, National Liberal Club.

He did not smoke. The first thing he said was, "We must talk about Federation"; then he immediately changed the subject to the strike. He talked most of the time leaning back in a chair and looking round sharply if he thought any other person in the smoking-room was observing him. Often he left out his "h's" on purpose. When he had told me that he had read all that I had written, obviously a lie, and I said that I could not understand how the busy public men had the time to do all they appeared to do, he said that public men soon began to cultivate a special faculty.

He said, socially speaking, England is the laboratory of the world. At the present time all the new movements are initiated here; untrue! He

---

[1] A family of musicians, old friends of Bennett.
[2] A notorious Paris bandit who was killed after the siege of his house by the police.

said, "I get more letters about my town planning and housing scheme from the United States than I do from England." He then, after quickly asking me about New York and Chicago, went on to describe his own adventures in New York, Chicago, and Denver. He explained how the editor of the *Chicago Record & Herald* came out thirty miles from Chicago to obtain his impressions of the city before he had arrived, and when he declined, became angry. Afterwards he saw this man in Chicago and made his celebrated epigram that Chicago was "a pocket edition of Hell," or, if the newspaperman preferred it, "Hell was a pocket edition of Chicago." This man worked up such an agitation against Burns that when the time came for him to speak on "The Duties of Citizenship" at a very large meeting in Chicago, not a single member of his committee dared to appear on the platform. However, he came on alone and little by little won the enthusiastic sympathy of the audience. As he did so he said that he could hear the members of the committee coming, one by one, behind him on to the platform. All this made a very good story, but he must have told it a great number of times, and have gradually arranged the details for his own glory. He said that his little epigram about Chicago had been appropriated by Choate, and that Choate had stolen more of his things than any other man in the world.

He then described how in the strike at the docks, either last year or the year before, he was sent down by the Prime Minister to try to persuade the men to obey the leaders. He took a lot of matches out of the match stand and arranged them in two squares. He said:

"Well, there were 5000 military in this square and 15,000 workmen in the square next door. And there was only a gravel path of about twenty feet between the two. The Socialists were walking round the outskirts of the crowd, pointing to the soldiers, who could plainly be seen, and the guns, and things looked very threatening indeed. I regard this as the greatest crisis that I have ever been through. I remembered my old cry, and in a voice of thunder I shouted out, 'A gangway, lads,' and they made enough room for me to go into the centre and stand on the cart. I talked to them and called for three cheers for the leaders, and so on, and so on, and I could see their old-time affection for me returning," etc., etc. These were the exact phrases he used. He was not exactly conceited, but vain in a rather ingenuous way. He spoke freely of the conceit of other people.

As we walked home, passing through Downing Street, a young boyish-faced man in evening dress, carrying a bag, came out of the Prime Minister's house. Burns called across the road and then went to meet him in the middle of the road and spoke to him for a minute or two. Practically all the illumination came from a small gas lamp over the Prime Minister's door. This was Mr. Asquith's secretary. He seemed to be to me an exceedingly ordinary and good-natured young man.

As we passed along the front of Wellington Barracks, Burns began to explain how the moral conditions of the soldier had improved during the last twenty or twenty-five years. He said, "There, in spite of all their faults, are 8000 of the very finest infantry in the world."

As one soldier after another came walking along in the gloom, he seemed to be able to tell at a glance from the medal strips, even in the dark, what campaigns they had been through. He remarked how they were all walking perfectly straight and how twenty-five years ago not one of them would have been able to walk straight, or, perhaps, even to walk at all. This is a specimen of his picturesque way of stating things.

Tuesday, October 1st.

Hospital for Incurables. West Hill.

What must be feelings of patient as he drives into entrance of this Hospital and sees the big sign, "Hospital for Incurables"?

Thursday, October 3rd.

Granville-Barker's *A Winter's Tale* at Savoy. Quite half the words incomprehensible. Esmé Beringer alone was clear. No music. Impossibility of seeing whole of stage from front row of dress circle, near middle, without leaning on the balustrade. Scarcely ever possible to distinguish blank verse. Revels in last act agreeable. Very little good acting—except Whitby's Autolycus and Esmé's Paulina. Lillah [1] fairish in last scene,

---

[1] Lillah McCarthy played Hermione.

when she could be statuesque. The text was given almost integrally, and one perceived portions of dullness which might have been cut with advantage. General impression of a simple, good, impossible plot with lofty emotion in it—delectable enough after *Bunty*. But the beauty of detail nearly all lost. From such a performance no one could divine that this is a late play of Shakespeare. Wilkinson's setting unimportant. Many of Rothenstein's wild-cat costumes were merely idiotic. A few, imitative, might pass.

October 6th.

Boer War.

Mrs. S.'s story, gathered in S. Africa, of Kitchener suddenly appearing in ball-room of Mt. Nelson Hotel, where officers sent down by Roberts as worse than useless were dancing with prostitutes, etc.: "Gentlemen, your train leaves in ¾ hour. You will be there. So shall I." Some of them had to turn up in dress clothes. K.'s idea was that they should at any rate do *some* kind of work, so he drove them out of there. . . . She said that of one cargo of 319 nurses that went out, 300 were dead in 2½ months, owing to idiotic hygienic arrangements and general stupidity. I doubt the figures.

October 7th.

Beecham at rehearsal. A player said, "You said you'd beat 4 in that bar, sir, but you're only beating two." Beecham: "You're thinking of another bar." A voice: "Four ale bar." Roars of laughter.

When Henry Wood conducts, he changes three times a day. Perspiration. It drops out of the back of his flannel jacket, having penetrated it. Always takes his waistcoat off. Cedric [1] spoke very highly of his extraordinary energy. Often stays up till 2 or 3 or all night, reading scores. On a Wednesday, in midst of Birmingham Festival rehearsals, he said: "Energy! You shall see next Monday—I shall have some sleep on Sunday night. Wait and see me on Monday."

---

[1] Cedric Sharpe, the well-known 'cellist.

October 8th.

2nd Post-Impressionist Exhibition. Self-satisfied smiles of most people as they entered. One large woman of ruling classes with a large voice and *face-à-mains,* in front of a mediocre picture: "Now no one will ever persuade me that the man who painted that was serious. He was just pulling our legs." Self-satisfied smiles all over the place all the time. One reason of the popularity of these shows is that they give the grossly inartistic leisured class an opportunity to feel artistically superior. A slight undercurrent of appreciation here and there. A woman to whom a young man pointed out a pencil drawing by Matisse said, "That's what I call beautiful." (It was.)

I met Frank Harris. He was prepared on principle to admire everything, though there was a large proportion of absolutely uninteresting work. When I said I had seen much better Picassos than there were there he hardened at once. "I find it all interesting," he said grimly. The photograph room, where photos of Gauguin, Van Gogh, etc. were supposed to be on sale, was in charge of an ignorant young ass who had all the worst qualities, from the languishing drawl to the *non possumus* attitude, of the English salesman.

October 10th.

Dinner. Talking about women's suffrage, some one said that it would come when the majority wanted it, and George Moore said: "The majority never *wants* anything. I don't think the majority even want to breathe." He talked in this pseudo-effective strain nearly all the night— probably nervousness as usual. About half a dozen times he repeated that for *The Winter's Tale* Barker had made the stage "look like a public lavatory." He said he liked farces and preferred *Charley's Aunt* to Barker's *Winter's Tale.* And he thought *Lady Windermere's Fan* was "a charming and fine comedy." Which it is not. Not until somebody said that *The Importance of Being Earnest* is the finest farce of modern times (which it is) did he think at all of Wilde's only good play. He liked Becque, and he thought Ibsen's dialogue unequalled and that it would probably not be beaten by anybody hereafter. But he regarded the theatre generally as a clumsy and infantile art, in which he was quite right. "You've made a very great deal of money," he said to me politely. I told him that that wasn't my fault, and I couldn't help it. Whereupon he emerged from his *gaffe* with a certain grace by saying with a serious air that he wished *he* could do it.

Pawling came and interrupted us with a tale about the Luard murder, explaining that only one ring had been taken from Mrs. Luard, and that that ring contained a stone taken from an Indian idol, that old Luard received many letters accusing him of having killed his wife, and that he then committed suicide; and now that Luard *fils* had telegraphed to England from India that the jewel was mysteriously back on the idol in the temple! ! ! "Strange, isn't it," he said, "that there was an Indian exhibition that year?" I asked if this remarkable story was in the papers. He said enigmatically that it would not be "allowed" to get into the papers for several days yet, and that the Government had ordered an inquiry. He thoroughly believed the tale; he hugged it and loved it. He always has some such tale to tell. And yet if one told him he was ingenuous he would be astounded.

October 12th.

Tate Gallery. Crowds. A class of girls. Many couples, who simply used the place as they would a park in summer. One couple stood right up against Steer's "Music Room" (which I went specially to see) for about a minute, and then retired saying it looked queer. This picture still seems as good as I first thought it was. What's the difference between a lot of Post-Impressionism and Turner's "Interior at Petworth," a picture I never remarked before, but one of the finest pieces of rich colour in the world? Very little difference in method of seeing and treatment. Note the dinginess and dirtiness of Turner's paint-box in a glass case. Inconceivable almost that those pictures came out of it.

Tuesday, October 15th.

Today I began a new novel—the serial for *Harper's*. Since April I have written naught but 4 articles—two for *Harper's* and two for the *Strand*. I did practically nothing in London and in Brighton. We shall probably be here until we go to our new-old house—Comarques. Thorpe-le-Soken [1] —at the end of next January. In the meantime I have made a lot of notes which are being typewritten daily by a succession of secretaries. I began secretaries again in May, and am already at my third.

October 21st.

Romano's. This restaurant is quite different at lunch from dinner. Groups of theatrical people entering; mutually known, a few actresses, pretty and vapid. On the whole the most ingenuous crowd of people to be seen in any restaurant in London. Waiting bad. Tables too close together as usual.

F.H. told me more fully than ever before the story of Oscar and *Mr. and Mrs. Daventry*.[2] He said he gave Oscar £50 for the screen scene and £50 for the whole scenario. He never got the scenario, though he paid for it. Oscar was to have written the first act. Mrs. Pat [3] insisted on F.H.'s writing the first act. F.H. refused as it had been allotted to Oscar. Then Oscar refused. So F.H. did it. F.H. then found out that Oscar had sold the screen scene and the scenario to Leonard Smithers, and the latter showed him the whole MS. of scenario signed by Oscar. F.H., after saying to Smithers that he didn't want the scenario and that in any case he owed him nothing, promised £50 in any case and £100 if play succeeded well. He said he hadn't a cent at that time. Smithers got the money from F.H. in tens and twenties. F.H. gradually found out that Oscar had sold the screen scene and scenario to eleven different people. When taxed with this by F.H., Oscar didn't deny it. He merely said, "The fact is, Frank, by writing this play and getting it produced you're taking away one of my sources of income!" Later Oscar asked for another £150. He badgered F.H. till he got it. He then said: "Frank, you've

---

[1] A Georgian mansion in Essex bought by Bennett. It was named after a Huguenot family who settled there.

[2] Frank Harris's *Mr. and Mrs. Daventry* was produced at the Royalty Theatre in October 1900.

[3] Mrs. Patrick Campbell, the actress.

paid me £250 for the screen scene from *The School for Scandal;* and you're a very poor man of business." Thus F. H.'s version.

F.H. said that Oscar was most brilliant as a talker during his last days in Paris. He had listened to him for five or six hours together, saying nothing but "Go on, Oscar. Go on."

F.H. stuck me out that *Lady Windermere's Fan* was good. Indeed, he said it was one of the six best comedies in English!

October 28th.

Politics at Reform Club. Lunch with Methuen, Spender, and Mac-Kinnon Wood.[1] Latter got into Cabinet within 5 years of entering Parliament. Scotch. Broad, heavy; no perceptible Scotch accent. Same agreeable self-satisfaction as other prominent Liberal politicians in the marked inequality between two Front Benches. He said: "What sort of a show do you think they'd have (with Balfour absent) if they introduced Tariff Reform Bill? *We* should have the time of our lives." Also like other Liberal politicians, he expressed the most absolute confidence in Asquith's efficiency. Nobody seemed to think that Tariff Reform Bill ever would be introduced. MacKinnon Wood regularly said nothing when he had nothing to say. The unwillingness of everybody to discuss the details of the Balkan War [2] was astonishing to me.

Wednesday, November 6th.

Day before yesterday, after having written about 6000 words of new novel, I decided to begin it again, in a somewhat different key, but with exactly the same construction. And I did begin it again, and at once felt easier in my mind. I also decided that I would not make a fine MS. of it. The regularity of the lines and handwriting does not seem to accord with style in which this novel is to be written. A freer style than before— a little more capricious and swinging.

I had to interrupt the work last week but one to do an article of reminiscences for the *Metropolitan* and the *Strand,* and again on Sunday to

---

[1] M.P. for St. Rollox Division, and Secretary for Scotland in the Asquith Cabinet.
[2] The First Balkan War had broken out on October 15.

review Allan Monkhouse's new novel, *Dying Fires,* for the *Manchester Guardian*. This last is a good book.

Also I have begun to order a new library of music, through Sharpe, and the first noble batch of stuff came today. More in a few days.

Tuesday, November 19th.

Last week appeared in *La Grande Revue* the opening instalment of Maurice Lanoire's translation of *Sacred and Profane Love*. This is the first of my serious novels to appear in French. The first serious story was *The Matador* in *La Nouvelle Revue Française* in August.

Today I heard from Pinker that he had bought back from Constable's their rights in *The Truth about an Author* for £40. It was issued about ten years ago, and the financial result of the English publication to me is thus, so far, a loss of at least £30.

Walford Davies's Phrases in Conducting a Rehearsal

Must be all dubious.

I want a savage staccato.

Nice and limpid.

Nice and stormy.

Nice and gusty.

Nice and manifold.

Weep, Mr. Parker, weep. (Mr. Parker weeps.) That's jolly.

Press that "A" home.

Don't handicap the crescendo.

It's not a bee's wedding, it's something elemental.

Gentlemen of the first fiddles.

Try it slurred, a sort of dot and carry two.

Not a wind you can cut with a knife, you must come and die.

This echo is so teasing.

Sorry to tease you.

An intimate 'cello solo.

Sixth desk forward, please. (Somebody in the orchestra, "Sign please.")

Sigh and die.

Can we court that better?

Now, side-drum, assert yourself.

Everybody must be shadowy together.

I want it mostly music.

That regular rum-tum which you do so ideally.

Let the pizzicato act as a sort of springboard to the passage.

A freshness inside the piano.

A sudden exquisite hush.

December 31st.

A material year. Largely occupied with intestinal failure and worldly success. By Chetham Strode's direct treatment of massage and vibration I am now almost cured of intestinal caprices, but I shall ever be feeble in that quarter.

All my five later plays have been performed this year. About 1155 pfces altogether. I received (less agents' commissions) about £16,000 during the year, which may be called success by any worldly-minded author. It is apparently about as much as I had earned during all the previous part of my life. And I bought a car and a yacht, and arranged to buy a house.

We came to Paris to finish the year, after I had written one quarter of my serial story for *Harper's*.[1] This gave me the chance to heighten the plane of the rest of the novel. We stay at the Hôtel du Rhin, and pay 50 frs. a day for a fine ground-floor flat. Most exhausting holiday, in spite of the extreme excellence of the food in this hotel.

Gold scarce in Paris, on account of Balkan War and on account of fear of a big war in the spring. Nearly all change given in silver.

I wrote comparatively few words during the year. About as follows: *The Regent*, 80,000. *Those United States*,[2] 35,000. *Harper's* serial, 25,000. Articles, 20,000. Total, 160,000, without counting Yacht Log, Journal, and a fair quantity of notes. Possibly 200,000 in all. But then between April 1st and October 1st I did practically nothing.

---

[1] *The Price of Love*, published in book form in 1914.
[2] Published in America as *Your United States*.

1913

January 6th.

Henry James at Pinker's. Very slow talker. Beautiful French. Expressed stupefaction when I said I knew nothing about the middle class, and said the next time he saw me he would have recovered from the stupefaction, and the discussion might proceed. Said there was too much to say about everything—and that was the thing most felt by one such as he, not entirely without—er—er—er—er—perceptions. When I said I lay awake at nights sometimes thinking of the things I had left out of my novels, he said that all my stuff was crammed, and that when the stuff was crammed nothing more could be put in, and so it was all right. He spoke with feeling about his recent illness. "I have been very ill." Said he was now settled down in Cheyne Walk, and had one or two faithful dependable servants, and so on. An old man, waning, but with the persistent youthfulness that all old bachelors have.

January 28th.

Political debate between G. B. Shaw and Hilaire Belloc as to connection between private property and servitude. At Queen's Hall.

Went with Vaughan. Crammed, at concert prices. Not a seat unsold. Shaw very pale with white hair, and straight. His wife beside him. Effect too conjugal for a man at work. Sidney and Beatrice Webb next to them. Effect also too conjugal here. Maurice Baring supporting Belloc, both very shabby. Maurice with loose brown boots and creased socks.

They spoke thus: Belloc 30 mins., Shaw 30, Belloc 20, Shaw 20, Belloc 10, Shaw 10. Time was kept to three minutes. Belloc's first was pretty good. Shaw's first was a first-class performance, couldn't have been better; the perfection of public speaking (not oratory); not a word wrong. But then afterwards the impression that it was a gladiatorial show or circus performance gained on one, and at the end was a sense of disappointment, as the affair degenerated into a mere rivalry in scoring. Still I have never seen Shaw emotional before, as he was then. Curious trick of audience, as of all audiences, of applauding sentiments with which they were already familiar, and receiving anything relatively new in silence.

January 29th.

First production of *Rosenkavalier* in England.

Covent Garden. Began at 8.20 (20 minutes late) and finished at midnight, with many cuts. Then 30 minutes' wait nearly, for motor in procession of motors. The thing was certainly not understood by stalls and grand circle. What its reception was in the amphitheatre and gallery I was too far to judge. First act received quite coldly. Ovation as usual at end—and an explosive sort of shout when Thomas Beecham came to bow. The beauty and symmetry of the book came out even more clearly than on reading it. An entirely false idea of this opera so far in England. Not sensual, nor perverse, nor depraved. It is simply the story of a young man providing a tragedy for an ageing woman by ceasing to love her, and an ecstatic joy for a young woman by beginning to love her. All the main theme is treated with gravity and beauty. The horse-play, and the character of Ochs, and the 18th-century colour is incidental. It seemed to Rickards, F. Lanchester, Walpole, and me to be a work of the first order.

January 30th.

Courting.[1] Tonight sheets of rain, strong wind. I put on overshoes and

---

[1] This incident made an impression on Arnold Bennett; he frequently mentioned it subsequently and worked it into the courting of Elsie and Jo in *Riceyman Steps*.

mackintosh to go to the corner of the street to the post. Several times lately about 10 P.M. I have noticed a couple that stand under the big tree at the corner next to the pillar-box, shielded by the tree-trunk from the lamplight. They stand motionless, with hands nearly meeting round each other's backs, tightly clasped. They were there tonight. The man was holding an umbrella over them. Can't see what sort of people they are. In the first place I don't like to intrude and in the second place the shade is so dark.

Tuesday, April 1st.

On Tuesday, February 25th, I came to live at Comarques, Thorpe-le-Soken. Marguerite came on the previous day. But the last carpet was only put down (on the stairs) on Saturday last. Even now fenders and fire-irons are not complete. And we find that we could do with many more small pieces of ornamental furniture to finish off the appearance of the rooms. However, the house is done.

On Monday, March 3rd, we went to London (Berkeley Hotel) for the dinner to celebrate Mrs. Atkins's [1] recovery, and for the anniversary of *Milestones,* and for rehearsals of *The Great Adventure.* After being very lively at the Atkins dinner at the Café Royal on Monday, Marguerite fell ill. No sleep. No sleep for two nights. I had Farrar,[2] and then two nurses. One of them, an Irishwoman, lively, who broke most things she touched, came up with us to Comarques on Monday, March 10th, and stayed about a week. The *Milestones* anniversary supper was a great success except for the absence of Marguerite.

Great Adventure produced at Kingsway on Tuesday, March 25th. M. said it was the most successful 1st night of mine she had been at. But she's been to so few. It finished at 11.40 and thus made the critics cross.

Knoblock told me about a fortnight ago that in discussing terms of French contract for *Milestones* with Lucien Guitry he said, to shelter himself behind me as regards certain conditions, "M. *Bennett est très*

---

[1] Muriel Atkins, wife of J. B. Atkins, editor of the *Spectator.*
[2] Bennett's doctor and life-long friend.

autoritaire," whereupon Guitry said, "*Quelle belle chose, l'autorité: mais —pourtant . . . !*"

We went to London on Saturday last, and I saw my first public performance of *The Great Adventure*. House held £125. Barrie with an adopted son on either side was there and he never laughed. C. K. Shorter in a box opposite roared nearly all the time. Wish Wynne a genius. I formed the opinion that there was a goodish run in the play.

Thursday, April 3rd.

Hugh de Sélincourt came in the afternoon, and left yesterday afternoon. His face is getting more and more strikingly bizarre in its line, and his hair much greyer. He said Coleridge's *Ode to Dejection* was one of the supreme things. He was convinced that both Lord and Lady Northcliffe were "dead keen" on his work, and that satellites in the *Mail* office were up against him. Anyhow he had received two autograph letters from Northcliffe, and Lady Northcliffe, in response to a long telegram from its parents, had been to see the baby Bridget. At present De S. gets £100 down and 15 per cent royalty, and he has published seven books. These details will be precious in 50 years.

Unable to resume my novel yet, though I am now on the very edge of doing so.

Friday, April 4th.

Yesterday morning I wrote a complete 1500-word article, *Phenomena at Covent Garden,* for the *New Statesman*—a gift to the Webbs, due to the skilful fascinations of Beatrice Webb. I was tired after it. I read Coleridge's *Ode to Dejection,* and liked it, but didn't think it one of the supreme things in the language. . . . Another of an intermittent series of bad nights, so that I couldn't resume novel this morning as I meant to do.

Receipts of *Great Adventure* at Kingsway mounting up. Which inspirited me somewhat.

Monday, April 7th.

Last week, being in need of an inspirational bucking-up, I dropped *War and Peace* and read Balzac's *Curé de Tours* and *Pierrette*. Latter better than Saintsbury says it is. Balzac was an ignorant and a crude man, often childish in his philosophizing. But if he had been properly educated and influenced he would have been a great social philosopher. His *aperçus* are often astounding. And his vitality is terrific. He made *War and Peace* seem very tame. He is full of inspiring and agreeable ornament. Nothing of the kind in Tolstoy. All a flat recital. Often dull, unless you give yourself to it. But if you do, he is never dull. Some of Tolstoy's long descriptions (such as of the wolf-hunt on Count Ilza's estate) are extremely beautiful. Natasha is the most beautiful character—anyhow up to p. 700 or so, where I now am.

Monday, April 14th.

Advance of age. I now sit down to brush my hair and put my collar and tie on. I also take a decided pleasure in forming habits, and re-forming old ones connected with the furniture from Fontainebleau, whose little peculiarities of locks and knobs, etc., I recognize again with positive satisfaction. The pleasure of doing a thing in the same way at the same time every day, and savouring it, should be noted.

I am now at close on p. 1000 of *War and Peace*. Curious, the episode of Lavrushka the valet, and Napoleon, in which he takes a historical incident, and feigns that as recounted in history it is all wrong, and gives you what he alleges to be the real truth. Even in this early book his theory of war is already fairly complete and obvious.

Wednesday, April 16th.

Fourteen hundred words yesterday. And passed p. 1100 of *War and Peace*. The description of Borodino is excellent. And as for the French entry into Moscow, it is interesting to compare the account by a French sergeant (I forget the name) published last year or so—2 years ago perhaps.

Monday, April 21st.

We went to London on Thursday, I for dinner of Omar Khayyam Club. Interview with Pinker, who lunched with me, and told me privately of his scheme for increasing dramatist's royalties according to length of run. This at Reform Club.

Exhibition of Max Beerbohm's cartoons at Leicester Galleries. Crowd. I was at once recognized—with a certain lack of politeness—by two men. I was ill all day. Probably liver—anyhow pains in back—very mysterious and disconcerting. Bad night. Same illness on Friday complicated by dyspepsia. I went to Leicester Galleries and bought my caricature. Then to Agnew Galleries to see alleged finest collection of water-colours by Turner ever got together. I thought both the Blue and the Red Righi rather overpraised, and I preferred the "Scarborough" picture—marvellous microscope figures of women in foreground. A few loud-voiced English upper classes patronizingly present. This show superb, but still I left it with slight disappointment—a flat feeling, a suspicion of prettiness and academicism. Lunch alone at Reform. Ill.

Thursday, April 24th.

Finished *War and Peace* on Tuesday. The last part of the Epilogue is full of good ideas the Johnny can't work out, and of course, in the phrase of critics, would have been better left out. So it would; only Tolstoy couldn't leave it out. It was what he wrote the book for. The first part of the Epilogue is as good as anything. All that domesticity is superbly rendered, with a natural and yet ruthless veracity. The battle of Borodino is fine. The Rostov family is fine. And many of the "set" descriptions of Russian life—such as the wolf-hunting on the Rostov estate. Terrific book. I wanted to write one of the same dimensions. And the final thrills of it *did* inspire me to a good basic scheme for the foundations of the third *Clayhanger*.[1]

I am just finishing instalment three of the *Harper's* serial (out of 8). It is sound, but not brilliant. Returns of *Great Adventure* at Kingsway going up. Over £150 a night now. Could scarcely be better.

---

[1] *These Twain*, not published until 1916.

The *Velsa*[1] arrived at Brightlingsea from Ostend yesterday. We drove to Harwich yesterday afternoon and saw the Gothenburg steamer. I wanted to go on it but wasn't sure what country Gothenburg is in.

Began to read correspondence of Flaubert yesterday. Letters at age of 9 and 10 are remarkable.

Finished Sitwell's *Cannibals of Finance* yesterday. A naïve and rather impressive book, confirming one's view of the autocracy that rules U.S.A.

Finished also the Webbs' book on highways.[2] This is an absolutely efficient work.

Friday, April 25th.

Yesterday we went over to see the *Velsa* in Brightlingsea creek. Lovely weather, but bar. falling quickly and wind S.E. She looked superb in every way, except inside the engine case. Entirely Dutch crew, of whom two cannot speak any English at all. I liked the aspect of the cook, but it was impossible to communicate any ideas to him direct. We got home at six o'clock; we forgot the dog on the land, absolutely; but he was collected by the harbour-master and saved for us.

Dreadful worry over third instalment of *Harper's* serial. It is an infernal nuisance writing scenes which you know all through are only sound instead of being fine. Health imperfect.

I now notice one or two devoted heads among critics who lose no opportunity of going for me both tooth and nail. And it is astonishing how this small minority of criticism, convinced though one may be that it is obviously wrong-headed, and perhaps malicious or prejudiced, has a capacity for annoying the successful person surfeited with money and laudation.

Tuesday, April 29th.

Ill for last 3 days. Perfectly laid aside by a sort of chill effect yesterday. Began to read Flaubert's correspondence all through the other day.

---

[1] A Dutch yacht, lying anchored in the Thames off Richmond when Bennett bought her. She had an auxiliary engine and could navigate by sea or canal.
[2] *Bibliography of Road-Making and Roads in the United Kingdom.*

Much of it is as depressing as the rest is inspiring. The letters to Madame X are the most terrible, and must have been terrible to receive. This sentence (Vol. I, p. 107) shows the *maladif* quality of Flaubert very well: *"Un amour normal, régulier, nourri et solide, me sortirait trop hors de moi, me troublerait, je rentrerais dans la vie active, dans la vérité physique, dans le sens commun enfin, et c'est ce que m'a été nuisible toutes les fois que j'ai voulu le tenter."* Also his declared habit of cutting himself off absolutely from the world in order to have peace! What a mad scheme for a novelist! It is this kind of thing in Flaubert that stopped him from being in the first rank.

Friday, May 2nd. On board Velsa *in Harwich Harbour.*

The W.'s with infant and nurse came on Tuesday. Almost at once, in my study, W. began to tell me a dramatic story of a shindy with his wife over her Uncle Joe. The latter wrote to W. as to his mistress; W. left the letter lying about, and Dorothy picked it up, and learnt that Uncle Joe had a mistress. Horror! Hysteria even! She would not listen to anything. She would not admit his right to have a mistress, nor that it was no business of hers. She wrote a long letter to Uncle Joe belabouring him, and ultimately W. allowed this letter to be posted. And U.J. committed the folly of replying to it in an apologetic tone. It seems she has still not got over it. She told W. she would have preferred to be deceived. She has naturally much changed since becoming a mother. She is the young mother and nothing else, and her outlook on everything is deeply influenced by the relation of everything to the infant. She has a somewhat worn expression, anxious, and even slightly hysterical. Her outlines have all changed; and her face is thinner. She is yet full of the shock of being a mother.

Saturday, May 31st.

J.C. came yesterday to make an oil sketch of me. When I went into the drawing-room he said, "I knew you couldn't like me to make all that journey alone." He had brought his chief model with him. Damned cheek, I thought it. But a beautiful girl—especially lips and main lines of body. In C. all that I didn't like physically was his sloping shoulders. But then Swinburne had them. But a very little of this kind of young man goes a long way with me. His ignorance of everything except just his work is too trying. Can't dress; can't dress his hair, can't even look dignified except in the face, which he keeps clean-shaven. Has read practically nothing, and has seen very little. Comes into a 1700 A.D. house and asks you whether you have built it! And so on. Fastened on to a tiny reproduction of a nude by Cranach, and said it was the most beautiful thing "in your house." He wants taking seriously in hand by an expert for about 5 years and merely educating. He seemed a strong man, and did a good sketch of me.

Wednesday, June 4th.

Still unable to do my work. *Une espèce de rechute.* Very bad headache on Monday. But I have amused myself with D'Aurevilly's *Une Vieille Maîtresse*—admirable romanticism. The Granville-Barkers came for the week-end, and made one or two efforts to get my new play. We went to Flatford Mill on Sunday afternoon. Very luscious and English. The finest of the sort.

Saturday, June 21st.

Vedrenne and Eadie came up to lunch yesterday, in order to angle for my next play. However, they were agreeable, and did not angle too much.

Today I began the last of the nine articles for the *Metropolitan Magazine* and wrote 1800 words before one o'clock. Quite unable to work yesterday, through being wakened up again, in the middle of the night (2.38) by a banging door.

Knoblock comes today for the week-end.

Friday, June 27th.

Went to London on Tuesday for Cedric's concert and returned yesterday. At the concert I seemed to see every one I had ever known up to the age of thirty. Vast air of a family party about it. Simultaneous carrying of two similar bouquets by two attendants up the two aisles to Evelyn Jennings after her first group of songs. Probably most of the friends were nervous.

In the afternoon, just after our arrival, we saw the King and President Poincaré pass,[1] two lonely men, one red and gold, the other black and white and bald, along the empty road, with soldiers and policemen dividing them from a thin crowd.

Wednesday morning, David Rice accosted me in Bond St. Hadn't seen him for at least 15 years. He cursed the British tradesmen. So did I. On Thursday morning I went into a swagger West End hosier's to buy a necktie. I said "Good morning" on entering. *Vendeur* was a man of 50 at least. Through sheer social clumsiness and heaviness he made no response, didn't even smile. It was not that he meant to be impolite. He thawed before I had bought two neckties, and gloomily saluted me as I went out. Many of the shops in this district are being cleaned and garnished at 10 A.M.

At lunch on Thursday, 3 Amazons in silk toppers in grill-room, with two men. Very quiet and nice. Contrast to bevies of American girls on previous day, couldn't even use knives and forks properly. But well dressed—good hats.

Saturday, June 28th.

I went to launch of *Velsa* at 5, but she was already gone. So I put off in a rowboat and waited for her to return. The new engine was pulling her along at a fine speed. Good sensation in boarding her, in Brightlingsea reach. Guest and two other fitters on board. The cockpit in a fearful mess.

E. V. Lucas came, and after dinner went to bed with a cold.

Wednesday, July 2nd.

Lucas left on Monday night. We drove him to Colchester. Progress made with three of his plays.

I read through first half of *Harper's* novel yesterday and found it *très*

---

[1] The newly-elected President of the French Republic, paying an official visit to England.

convenable. Some things in it jolly good. But now I want to write an entirely different sort of novel—as regards construction and manner and material.

Friday, July 25th.

Returned from yacht Monday afternoon. I wrote over 5000 words of *Harper's* novel in 3 days up to last night. Health about 95 out of a possible 100. Yacht waiting at Harwich for a favourable wind to go to Denmark. N.E. again this morning. I went out for a walk, and at Landermere I asked a bargeman on a barge in what direction wind was. He said due E. and stuck to it, though he must have known it was N.E. "Due east according to our flag. It may have northered out a bit since this morning, but not much." He gazed idly up at our flag. "I wish it wasn't, I want to get out o' here. How long do I think it'll last? I think it'll last for 2 or 3 days. I hope it won't. If it keeps on I shall get my rigging down and poke her out—over these pleasant flats." A nice humorous card. But still I don't understand why he should stick to his error about wind.

Wednesday, July 30th.

H. G. Wells and wife and Mrs. Byng (future neighbour) [1] came yesterday for lunch and tea. I beat H.G. at tennis; he played in bare feet.

Friday, August 29th.

Yesterday I returned from my cruise in the Baltic round about Denmark. I kept the log, but made no general observations in it. What strikes me now most as regards Denmark is the charm, beauty, and independence of the women. They go about freely, sit in cafés together, smoke without self-consciousness. They seem decidedly more independent than Englishwomen. The men have charm of manner, especially of voice and tone. The race is evidently receptive, and it must be beneficially influenced by the attractiveness of its women. On the other hand, Den-

---

[1] Wife of General Julian Byng, created first Baron of Vimy in 1919. Mrs. Byng, *née* Marie Evelyn Mareton, was at this time engaged on her first novel, *Barriers*.

mark struck both Rickards and me as being an unimportant and dull little country. Its villages were simply naught. They had nothing, except a material sufficiency—no beauty, no evidence of ancient traditions. The landscape also was practically everywhere negligible.

Admirable voyage home, though we *did* have to sleep in the saloon. Fine food on the *J. C. La Cour* (2000 tons). Smooth sea. Sunshine. Heat. Favourable wind. But about 20 miles or so of fog after we left Eshey on Wednesday evening. The boat *empesté* by a gang of English girls— probably clerks in some large establishment—doubtless quite decent in their own line. But terribly *gauche,* ungraceful, and unfeminine and *mal ficelées* by comparison with the Danish.

Today I began the reading of Lavisse and Rambaud's *Histoire Générale*,[1] an enterprise less enormous than the writing of it, but still enormous.

Sunday, August 31st.

Read through the third quarter of the *Harper's* serial this morning. It seemed goodish. But there is no doubt in my mind now that I want to change to another sort of novel—much more autobiographical than I have yet written. The first and third part of *The Glimpse* contained a lot of essentially autobiographical stuff, and *Clayhanger* something of me as a boy. But I want to write more immediately autobiographical work. The third *Clayhanger* must be quite different from *Clayhanger* and *Hilda.* I think I am now beginning to be anxious to write the 3rd *Clayhanger,* but there is a play, also two stories, to come in front of it.

A Reverend Falconer called yesterday and tapped Marguerite for a sub- scription for his orphanage. He showed a list of subscriptions from people in neighbourhood, and there was no subscription on it of less than £1. So Marguerite gave £1. Naturally. The psychology of charity be- comes clear. It is fairly certain that the Rev. F. does get and accept sub- scriptions of less than £1, but he keeps them out of his show-list. That there might be disadvantages in an orphanage directed by a Church of

---

[1] *L'Histoire Générale du IVe Siècle jusqu'à nos Jours* by Ernest Lavisse and Alfred Rambaud.

England parson had not occurred to M. She saw that people in the neighbourhood had given, and none less than £1; so she gave £1. This afternoon a band passes along the road, with several collectors. Quick! Sixpence for the band! (Gabrielle says, *"On demande des sous."* That is enough.) What the band is, what the subscription is for, nobody has the least idea.

Friday, September 5th.

Richard Pryce came on Wednesday and before night he had read to us his play founded on *Helen with the High Hand,*[1] which was all right in essentials. He worked on a few minor alterations yesterday.

By yesterday evening I had written 3400 words of *Harper's* novel in three days. By means of sharp exercise and perspiration I about cured.my liver in 6 days, despite a N.E. wind.

Sunday, September 7th.

The extreme inventiveness of some dreams is remarkable. I dreamt last night that I had to rush every few minutes to see Russian trains come into a tube station, as I was expecting a friend from Russia, I think. Between two trains, I strolled off the platform on to a bridge over a canal, on which were ships whose immense and very ornate bowsprits came up as high as the bridge. Turning another way, I saw a very muddy road, and in this road a little acrobat (one of a troupe) was performing. He was 8 or 9 years of age. The greasy road was a very difficult take-off, but he had to do a double somersault with such a take-off, and he did it, two complete revolutions, with only a slight slip on his back on alighting. He then lay on his back in the mud to do another trick, and I then noticed that he was smoking a thick strong cigar, puffing away at it all the time. He was forced by his brutal persecutors to smoke this awful cigar all the time, and to keep puffing at it continuously. A tremendous refinement of cruelty. Even as I write my gorge rises at the memory of the cigar in his small mouth. He clenched his small hands to prepare for the spring from his back. He did this several times, and then I woke

---

[1] This appeared in 1914 under the same title.

up. I can't imagine what led to this dream, unless it was my physical exercises daily and a fairly strong cigar at night.

Tuesday, September 9th.

Yesterday was a proper sort of day for my trade. 400 words before breakfast. After breakfast, newspapers, cigar. Then 800 words. Then dictation of letters. A few Muller exercises. A quarter of an hour in garden. A section of Lavisse's *Histoire Générale*. Lunch. Flaubert's correspondence. Sleep. Early tea. In car with Marriott[1] to Landermere to make a watercolour—4 to 6 o'clock. Car came back to fetch our things. We walked home. Over 2 miles, mostly uphill and over rough ground, in 29 minutes. Profuse perspiration. Change. Bath. Dinner. Champagne. Cigar. Coffee. Bed at 10 P.M. and a very fairish night. Absolutely no time at all cut to waste between 7 A.M. and 7.30 P.M., when we dine. I can always do more work when I have many other things on hand, and when I am following a programme that is rather a tight fit for the day.

Wednesday, September 10th.

W. W. Ellsworth, president of the Century Company, came to lunch yesterday. Man of 60. Deaf. Carrying an apparatus like a camera with him for hearing. Liked A. C. Benson, and so on. It was understood he took 6 yachting articles for £1000, and engaged Rickards to illustrate. The most interesting thing he said was after he had looked round the grounds, and I questioned him as to his own home. "Yes. I have a very beautiful country home. I can only go down to it for week-ends, but the rest of the time I spend in my N.Y. flat and I'm quite comfortable. Every member of my family has a particular and tender regard for our home. We've had it for forty years. There's one place in the gardens enclosed by four trees, and plenty of other trees round about. We've had three weddings there and four funerals." I rather liked this. It would be impossible in England. I also liked his attitude to Minetta[2] when I

---

[1] Frederick Marriott, the artist, was an early friend of Bennett's.
[2] Child of the Marriotts, who were guests in the house at this time.

held her to him to say good-bye before she went to bed after lunch. First he kissed her hand, and when she was told to kiss him he said, evidently moved, "May I really?" He must be somewhat sentimental in business where money is not concerned. Very pleased with his new editor, Yard. He told one or two mildly bawdy stories, including cne of a studious farmer who announced to a lady (Ellsworth's sister-in-law) that he always gave names to his animals from books, and that the bull she had just bought from him was called Sir Galahad. He said that Jack London had gone into the ranch business, had a payroll of 2000 dollars a month, and had bought a stallion for 2500 dollars and expected the Century Company to pay increased advances to pay for all this, and sent them abusive telegrams when they didn't.

Sunday, September 28th.

To Marguerite's golf club yesterday. We went there through a street of villas, with tennis-lawns rather close fitted, etc. Excellent imitation of suburbs of London, and cleaner. Golf club. House the most miserable architecture, with no proper place for autos to drive up to, though plenty of autos, and so far as I knew, no accommodation for chauffeurs. Whole place too small. Men's rooms (lords at ease therein). Common tea room (devilish cold in winter) and women's quarters. Course beautiful. Shut off from sea by a natural sea wall. Some gestures of men in playing a ball superb in ease, laxity, and strength. Women following a couple of men about who were playing. Doubtless wives or lovers, etc. Immense sense of space. Also great sense of a vast organization. But no artistic sense. The architecture, I repeat, miserable, piffling, mean. And a rotten little 3-cornered flag flying "F.G.C." instead of a superb standard floating in the breeze. The women in white or gay colours were not unattractive in the mass, and some were beautiful, and quite a few pretty. Certain matrons also very agreeable.

Thursday, October 2nd.

Finished *Harper's* serial, *The Price of Love*, at 12.15 on Monday last, in a state of some exhaustion.

Thursday, October 16th. Antwerp.

Last night we drove to Harwich, took G.E.R. steamer *Vienna,* and arrived at Antwerp at 8.15 A.M. today. Grand Hotel. Room and bathroom, both large. 20 frs. Old-fashioned and ugly; but seemingly good. Dreadful ride in hotel omnibus over cobbled roads from quay to hotel. We drove out at 10 A.M. in closed cab, round boulevards to Musée Plantin, where I searched for a particular room whose details I thought I had remembered for 16 years, and couldn't find—indeed was about convinced that such a room had never existed.

Friday, October 17th.

Last night in lounge of Grand Hotel Antwerp. Old-fashioned decoration. Old-fashioned lettering over door (Fumoir, Restaurant), once considered, no doubt, the latest fashionable form of lettering. Plush ornamented doors with glass doorknobs. There is something poignantly pathetic about such decoration, still dignified, but pitied, where once it inspired perhaps almost awe.

This morning absolutely perfect October weather. Musée Royal. Very fine old masters. Modern side rotten. Market place. Endless time on chimes from 11.30 to 11.41. We went into cathedral—and the carillon started again for 11.45. Big pictures in cathedral veiled in green. *Loucheness* of ecclesiastical attendants. Market afoot in market place.

After lunch we visited port. Finest thing in Antwerp. We were first struck by little *brasseries* along good main street, each with a little *grue,* aproned and *nu-tête,* sitting outside sewing, to attract; they must be extraordinarily attractive to sailors. Scores of these places. Glimpses of streets *encore plus louches.* Immense impression of *travail.* 30 miles of quays. New basins still being constructed. Bridge from one road to another opened for passage of steamer. Much traffic held up on both sides. By the time it is closed again, hundreds of workmen collected, and dozens of heavy wagons. Some men chewing monstrous lumps of bread. Red Star liner *Lapland* had arrived from U.S.A. Long processions of returned emigrants therefrom; some stupid, some full of character. One procession solely men (with a long *camion* in middle full of their handbags), another both of men and women; all had little round discs on breast.

I saw one steamer move out (scraping her side all the way) and a larger one come into a basin with 4 tugs. Immense area of port. Superb view of Antwerp with spires from one spot, over blue water. Magnificent sunset; all masts and derricks gradually became black and silhouetted. Drove back to town, passing through 2 streets full of *cafés concerts*. Same effect of silhouette against superb red and orange. Port full of grain and wood.

Sunday, October 19th. Brussels.

We came to Brussels yesterday. Journey 28 min. M. indisposed. At Gare du Nord scarcity of porters, and very bad and unwilling work because tips are put into a common fund. It takes one man's time to watch what the men receive. A non-porter said to me, *"Les porteurs sont trop fainéants pour venir ici"* (i.e., to the far end of the platform when the train stopped).

I walked out alone, and was astonished at the liveliness and richness of this small town. I dined alone at Restaurant du Helder, and it made much the same impression on me as 17 years ago. Good, but not good enough. Too dear. Still, a discreet place, with good service. A fat middle-aged man came in with a *grue*. *Grue* very vulgar. She turned her head away from the *grosse* brute most of the time, and sneered a lot. The efforts of the man to be gay and natural were rather good. She was just another of those who are content to take money which they are too careless to earn.

While here we had news of the production of *The Great Adventure* in New York on Thursday last—ten days late. It does not seem to have been a very *éclatant* success.

Wednesday, October 22nd.

Drove about. Admirable lunch at Restaurant Étoile. Then Musée Royal, old masters. Satisfactory. Then Palais de Glace. Tearoom *gratuit*. Many *gentilles petites femmes*. Ideas for *Don Juan*. Dined in hotel at night. Not good. Then Donnay's *Les Éclaireuses* at Théâtre du Parc. First two acts *passablement amusants*. Third feeble. Fourth rotten. False throughout, with too many idiotic *jeux de mots,* but impression of first two acts agreeable though mediocre. This suffragette play is supposed to be very advanced. *C'est déjà vieux jeu.* Oldish couple behind us who told a friend that they had not brought their daughter, who was just about to be married, as they feared it might unsettle her. Brussels public very stolid and uncomprehending.

Thursday, October 23rd. Paris.

Arrived in Paris at 5.15 yesterday afternoon. Some delay at *douane.* Cepa here (Hôtel du Rhin) at the same time as us; *et puis Ida.* We dined quickly and unpacked and dressed with marvellous haste, and were at the Théâtre du Vieux Colombier at 8.30 for dress rehearsal of *Une Femme Tuée par la Douceur,* and *L'Amour Médecin,*[1] with Copeau in charge. Crowded with first-night public, and literary public. Many women trying to look young and only succeeding at a distance, with worn-out skins. Many very cheaply dressed. In fact nearly all the literary public had the air of beng *dans la dèche.* Extraordinary muddle at *vestiaire.* A slight feeling of preciosity. But play well and sincerely done. A *naïf* thing, getting fairly strong towards the end.

Sunday, October 26th.

Thursday afternoon Calvo took us to Salle des Fêtes du *Journal* to see a Russian *danseuse nue—séance particulière.* She was not *nue,* but with a "diaphony" that was better. About 20 people, including the most serious, such as Kostilev, the Russian. The offices of *Journal* vast. *Salle* overdecorated and without originality; still, in a recognizable style. Nothing in the slightest degree *troublant* in the dancing. Middle-aged *dame* at piano. A well-known little sculptor explained. . . .

Friday, October 31st.

Yesterday afternoon I went with Cepa to Hessel, 26 Rue La Boétie,

---

[1] *A Woman Killed with Kindness* by Thomas Heywood; *L'Amour Médecin* by Molière.

and bought a small Vuillard for £100. Tea alone. Then with M. to view Rue du Faubourg St.-Honoré. Just dark. Nothing like this in London for luxurious shoppiness. Bought books.

Monday, November 3rd.

Lunch at Martin's.[1] Tea at Cornillier's, where Janvier, Roy Devereux, Esther Swanson. Dined at Henri's, and then with Mme. Edwards to *Le Secret* by Bernstein—Bouffes Parisiens. The rottenest piece by Bernstein, and almost by any one, that I ever saw. I had to go twice to see Simone[2] in her *loge*. (Electric light in quantities, both at top and at bottom of her *psyché*, burning all the time.) Dark eyelids. She said she liked *Le Secret* very much and thought *Le Vieil Homme* idiotic. However, I gave my view. I said, *"Vous êtes magnifique, mais sans vous la pièce ne serait rien du tout."* She swallowed it with ease. She spoke English very well indeed, but with an accent.

Wednesday, November 5th.

Yesterday afternoon, Ravel, Mme. Andrée, the Godebskis, and Calvo came for tea. The Bions dined with us at Ciro's, and then to the revue at La Cigale—which might have been worse. Indigestion yesterday and today. The strangest phenomenon in Paris is the interest excited among sane people such as the Godebskis by the appointment of a new director of the Opéra.

Thursday, November 20th. England.

I meant to begin writing of my play *Don Juan* on Saturday the 15th, but was somewhat indisposed. I began it on Monday 17th. . . . Fred and Stanley Alcock[3] came last Thursday (13). Stan. left on Saturday and Fred on Sunday, in his car. Marguerite and I went to London yesterday for the first Sharpe concert. Lunched at Carlton. Lack of *chic* among

---

[1] Emile Martin was an intimate friend who had introduced Bennett to the life in Paris and had helped him to settle there when he first came.

[2] Mme. Simone had appeared in *Le Secret* at the New Theatre, London, in June of this year.

[3] Early friends of Bennett.

women there. As Nisia Edwards said of Savoy—*vieux chameaux*. I then went to Reform and conversed with Methuen. Last week (motor-show week) was the finest *The Great Adventure* has had. On Saturday we all went over to a special Red Cross matinée of *The G. A.* at Colchester, with Shiel Davy and Athene Seyler in principal parts. It was an admirable performance. I went and saw Athene and Shiel in their retreats.

Friday, November 21st.

Walking last night for exercise along the Station Road (6.30 P.M.), I saw the light of Clacton (not the lights—the light) and of Frinton, over the brows; a reflection in the sky. . . . Idea of a desolate coast (relatively) with the human settlements rather precariously here and there upon it. Darkness everywhere and just those lights on the clouds from below. Sense of the adventure of living on the earth at all; and of the essential similarity of all human existences. Idiocy of loathing or scorning a different kind of existence from your own; e.g. my attitude towards the primness of Frinton and its golf club.

I am putting rather more work into draft of *Don Juan* than usually in my drafts of plays. The realistic idea has gone nearly altogether in this play. In its ignoring of realistic detail in order to get an effect required, it is rather impressionistic. This is the first time I have realized the possibility of a similarity between literature and art in impressionism. I expect that in looking for a parallelism to art in literature I had been looking for the wrong thing, while the right thing was under my nose all the time.

Monday, November 24th.

I finished the draft of the first act of *Don Juan* this morning. It is not a good draft, but it is perhaps a better one than any draft of any previous play of mine.

As I was reading history this afternoon, I thought: "I am 46. On the decline. Why fill my head with knowledge?" An absurd reflection, but it passed several times through my mind.

Friday, November 28th.

Deranged slightly all week with a chill on the colon. B. came yesterday for the day to discuss wills and leases. He told me with perfect seriousness a story of a commercial enterprise in which he was interested —a search for the Ark of the Covenant, Urim and Thummim, plate of the Temple, etc.—based on a cipher discovered by a Finnish scholar in an early copy of the book of Ezekiel at St. Petersburg. Over £3000 already spent on the excavations, stopped by Turkish authorities, who have now given permission again; but the affair is in suspense at present, as the principal contributor of funds (who has already given £20,000 alone) is in a lunatic asylum. The singular irony of this did not seem to strike B.

Thursday, December 4th.

On Tuesday Arthur L. Humphreys[1] came up to lunch, and to inspect my books with a view to a catalogue. He told us how he had walked from London to Land's End, and from London to Edinburgh, at 37 miles a day. We took him to Landermere, Kirby-le-Soken, Walton, and Frinton. He seemed determined to find out about the history of Comarques. Often in France, but incapable of speaking French with any fluency. He said that he thought novels of today immensely superior to those of 20 years ago. He said that at Xmas, numbers of people made up their minds to buy *"Whitaker*[2] and one other book." The other book might be a volume of devotional verse. He said that novels more and more dominated the book market.

Monday, December 8th.

J. C. Squire came on Saturday. Long hair; Jaegerishly dressed. But sound, competent, honest in argument. He was highly in favour of the Webbs etc. and said the *New Statesman* was going on excellently, as to finance. He could not appreciate Tailhade's verse. Left this morning, very Jaegerish.

---

[1] Partner in the firm of Hatchards, booksellers.
[2] *Whitaker's Almanack.*

Monday, December 15th.

Excursion to Ipswich, Saturday. Shops closed at 1 P.M.—at least all good ones except antiquaries. We went into three and bought a number of things. Ravel [1] also. Walpole came in the afternoon—6.40.

I began the actual writing of *Don Juan* on Friday afternoon, and it seemed to go fairly well. I read *Bubu de Montparnasse* lately. A little book; good. *Dans les Rues,* of Rosny *aîné,* which describes the making of an *apache.* This is a less absorbing book, by a greater man than C. L. Philippe. Some of the scenes in it are magnificent. It did not enchant me as did some of *Bubu,* but it held me.

Saturday, December 27th.

Rickards came on Christmas Eve. Doran came on Sunday morning. Hysterical cook of 40-odd left on Tuesday, and we did without. Doran left this morning, to spend week-end with Ernest Hodder Williams. He said that while he was there he didn't have to go to chapel, and Ernest didn't go either. Wednesday, Thursday, and yesterday I wrote 4500 words of a short story, in spite of guests and eating.

Sunday, December 28th.

Sketch, "Buttercup-Night," by Galsworthy, in yesterday's *Nation.* He calls buttercups "those little bright pieces of flower china out of the Great Pottery." Another phrase: "Man playing his little, not unworthy, part in the great game of Perfection." I object to this kind of thing. Much of the sketch is very good.

I am now re-reading *The Way of All Flesh.* It stands it. There is very little wrong with this book, even technically. But the trick of reading a piece of the narrative to the hero himself and then writing down what the hero's comment on it was is a mistake—especially when it is repeated.

Wednesday, December 31st.

I finished *The Way of All Flesh* yesterday. All this book is good. I even suspect it may be better than I think it is.

---

[1] Maurice Ravel, the composer, was then Bennett's guest at Comarques.

I finished the first act of *Don Juan* yesterday. It seems *assez bien*.

According to Miss Nerney's[1] calculations there have been over 2700 performances of my plays during this year. I have published *The Regent, Paris Nights, The Plain Man and His Wife* and *The Great Adventure*. I have written most of *The Price of Love,* the whole of *The Story Teller's Craft*,[2] sundry articles, 2 short stories, and one act of my new play. I did no work for over a month when we moved into Comarques; I took the whole of August for a holiday in the Baltic, and 3 weeks in Belgium, and Paris in October and November.

Added later.

Net earnings received during 1913: Books, £6924 18s. 1d. Plays, £8524 19s. 0d. Total, 15,449 17s. 1d. The gross sum (before paying agents' fees) was £17,166 10s. 1d. In addition, interest on investments, £405 11s. 3d. All this handsomely beats last year's record.

---

[1] Miss W. Nerney, Arnold Bennett's secretary.
[2] Published in America in 1914 as *The Author's Craft.*

1914

Thursday, January 1st.

I read J. H. Rosny's *Les Xipéhuz*. It is like early Wells. Good, but entirely arid, as it has no individual human interest, or scarcely any. Also it is short. Also there is no explanation, or theory given of the "Farms." Thus a question is raised without being settled, and legitimate curiosity unsatisfied. Nevertheless it has interest. Evidently the book has reached some permanency of fame despite its extreme shortness, as mine is the *édition définitive*.

I met Dr. Hare on road this morning and again as I was coming into the house. In the meantime he had been to a labourer's cottage. Mother of 15 kids, youngest 4 months old and fed on Nestlé's. Father earned 15*s.* a week. Two boys helped to support. Eldest boy not son of husband; a bastard of somebody else, accepted as a matter of course. No trouble. Said woman: "I'm washing. It's a lot o' work—washing for ten people." Cottage absolutely clean and tidy. One son down with influenza. Several children still living at home.

Hard snow on ground, bluish tinted (I suppose from sky) with blue shadows. Birds seem to be a little less shy just now.

January 3rd.

The Spences came over to dinner on Thursday night from the Grand Hotel, Frinton. Spence said that Mrs. Maybrick was understood to be guilty,[1] and that she had confessed to wardresses immediately after sentence. It was said that she had arsenic in pocket of her *peignoir* and administered it by means of a handkerchief pressed to Maybrick's mouth when he complained of dry lips or something of that kind. But Spence did not explain how Charles Russell remained always persuaded of her innocence.

Monday, January 5th.

Finished *Marie Donadieu* in the night. On the whole it is not as good as *Bubu,* but it contains fine scenes. But they nearly all talk too much. And they nearly all talk as Jean alone (and the author himself) would really have talked. It is wonderful talking *per se.* Some of the love scenes are perhaps more vivid than any great novelist could have written (e.g. Dostoievsky and Turgenev), and yet the book is not great. It has no large architectonic quality. Some of it is dull, also; but this may happen in almost any book.

I walked all yesterday morning, and worked all the afternoon. I did over 3 mortal hours on *Don Juan* this morning. It exhausted me. I had meant to go on with it this afternoon, but by the time I had done a lot of damnable correspondence about other people's affairs, I had nothing left in me except the desire for exercise.

Referring to Vedrenne's habitual phrase in negotiational bluffings—"I'll throw all my cards on the table"—I was told that Marie Tempest and Graham Browne, at Pall Mall Restaurant, crowded, saw Vedrenne come in and look round, and Marie said, "What's Vedrenne looking for?" whereupon Browne replied, "He must be looking for a table to throw his cards on."

I finished big love scene in Act II this morning.

No work yesterday as I had almost no sleep the night before (and very little the night before that).

Monday, January 12th.

This morning I finished the second act of *Don Juan.*

---

[1] Of poisoning her husband. She was tried in 1889.

More information as to the L.C. holiday in August. A specimen of the co-operative holiday of the middle class, where under the strain of idleness and new conditions most of the manners (mediocre at best) of the middle class go all to pieces at one moment or another. The secret provincialism of the whole crowd (except the younger generation) came out clearly. A set that frequents only itself.

Sunday, January 18th.

Barber's yesterday at Frinton. Read [1] said he had been there and that it was smart and clean, but lacked things. Behind tobacco shop. Long white curtains over window (clean) to hide back yard. Very small room. Very small fire. 3 marble basins with fitments.

No antiseptic arrangements so far as I could see. Room cold. Sturdy small boy who opened door for me, knickers, apron (not clean). "Shall you operate on me?" "No, sir," with a grin. Man doing shaving. No greetings from barber. Dirty apron and coat hanging up on wall. Array of mugs with sponges. I stood with back to fire and looked at *Daily Mirror*. Had not to wait long. Place looked clean but wasn't. Thick dust on gas shades and many cobwebs. Chair too high, a modern chair, which required footstool. I commented on height. Barber said: "It's not high enough for me as it is. I always have to stoop." I suggested footstool. He said, "They do have them in some places." I asked if business was good. "No, very short season." A nice mild man, tall, badly shaven; baggy, worn knees. But decent. No energy. Had to go out in middle to talk to a customer about mending a pipe—"Excuse me, sir." Parted my hair on wrong side and badly. Shoved his sleeve in my eye. Didn't show me the back of my head. Doubtful towels. India-rubber sponge. Price 10*d*. Still, a decent chap. (If I write an article out of this, I might describe Paris barbers, and insist on inferiority of English barbers, with general reference to slackness and inefficiency.)

I finished 3rd act *Don Juan* on Friday night, after fairly huge labours. Read nearly all of Tristan Bernard's *Amants et Voleurs*. The first tale (long), "Sabre et Casque," is admirable. The rest are merely brief *fait-divers*.

---

[1] Bennett's chauffeur.

Also in John Mitchel's *Jail Journal*.[1] This is a good browsing book. Much of the self-analysis or self-description is tedious. It could be cut down and made manageable.

Lastly, Conrad's *Chance* came yesterday. Read 150 pp. This is a discouraging book for a writer, because he damn well knows he can't write as well as this. The episode of the arrival of the news of De Barral's bankruptcy at his house in Hove where his daughter and her superb friend of a governess are living is simply sublime. I know nothing better than this, and precious little as good. I happened to read it in the night.

Saturday, January 24th.

Touching the alleged fact that a name scarely counts with a theatrical manager in choosing a play, Nancy Price offered Pryce's version of *Helen with the High Hand* to Frohman, who offered to do it only on the condition that I would sign it. As I had always declined to do this, of course the thing was off.

I finished Conrad's *Chance* in the middle of the night. It is very fine. The best chapters are "The Governess" and the last one. The tea party chapter and "On the Pavement" chapter are too long. The indirect narrative is successfully managed on the whole, even to fourth-hand narrative, but here and there recounted dialogue and gesture is so minute as to be unconvincing.

In P. G. Hamerton's *Round My House* (p. 160) he says that rise in prices during "last ten years" in France had been so great as to induce some French people to dispense with servants. No date on this book. No clue to its date. But I should put it in the seventies. I suppose this rise-of-price business recurs at intervals, and always makes the same upset and then adjusts itself.

All this week I have taken a long walk in the mornings and worked on *Don Juan* in the afternoons, with some success. I am now on the last scene of the last act.

---

[1] John Mitchel, the Irish Nationalist, was sentenced to 14 years' penal servitude for inciting to rebellion. After some years he escaped from the penal settlement in Tasmania and settled in the United States. His *Jail Journal, or Five Years in British Prisons* appeared in 1854. It has been re-issued many times.

Saturday, January 31st. London.

I finished *Don Juan* on Sunday night, rather to my surprise. Got to Berkeley Hotel at noon on Wednesday. I lunched with Mrs. Lee Matthews. Scott-James came at 5 to beat me down in price of an article for his new paper.[1] Sharpe concert at night. Acute neuralgia. Little sleep. Thursday—Pinker in morning. Bob Davis and wife to lunch. Much pleased with them. Lucas to tea, Atkins and Rickards to dinner—then to Olympia. Not bad. Friday, McKinnel, Wheeler, and Pryce here at 11. Then to Vaudeville Theatre. Welch ill. Rosher and Methuen to lunch at Reform. Henry James joined us afterwards and reminisced excellently. Hy. James said of Reform: "This is for me now a club of ghosts. There were special corners and chairs. It is fuller, too, now than it used to be." He also said that the club was built before clubs were fully understood, and he objected to largeness of atrium or *cortile,* making all rooms round it seem small. He described in full James Payn's[2] daily life: drove down from Maida Vale or somewhere to Smith Elder's, and left there before 1 in order to be at club at 1. Numberless friends. Amusing companion. Played whist, etc., every afternoon and got home (driving) about 7. Never walked. Never wanted other interests. No intellectual curiosity. Large family, but was not interested in it. I asked when he did his work. James said he certainly never worked either afternoon or night. He was continually politely sarcastic about Payn. He now lives on river at Chelsea. He likes pavements, shopfronts, and the convenient taxi. He said, "If I was rich, instead of being in grovelling poverty—" He made as if to go once; then asked if he might stay a little longer, and did so.

Monday, February 9th.

Thursday last we went to London by car and ran into a coal cart at 11.10 A.M. in Lee Bridge Road. Much excitement and crowd. It gave me a headache, which grew capriciously and lasted. Marguerite absolutely calm throughout. Back axle bent and much damage to coachwork. Still, we finished journey in car.

---

[1] R. A. Scott-James started the *New Weekly.*
[2] Editor of the *Cornhill Magazine.*

Afternoon, 5 P.M., *Parsifal* at Covent Garden. Putrid performance. Bodanzky commonplace conductor. Poor orchestra. Appalling scenery, costumes, and scenic effects. Ugly. Kundry, good singer. Rotten female chorus, amazingly ugly and ill-dressed. Also long stretches of dull music. I never saw uglier scenery. I went to sleep in middle of each act. Over after 11. Great deal of music fine; better than I expected. Friday, Pinker to lunch at Berkeley. Vernon came. Details settled for production of *A Good Woman*[1] ("Be sure your sins will find you out") at Palace Theatre on Monday 16th. At night, first night of *A Midsummer Night's Dream* at Savoy. Stylistic quality of much of this play is marvellous. But the two love stories and the love-philtre-ing tedious. Scenery not really good, but exquisite after Covent Garden.

Saturday, February 14th.

I finished the third of the *Velsa* articles for the *Century* on Thursday morning, and finished reading and correcting typescript of *Don Juan* on Thursday afternoon. Also I finished reading Jules Romains's *Mort de Quelqu'un*. This short novel, though often amateurish and indeed sometimes puerile in technique, is a really original work. The collective feeling of groups of men, and the influence of thought on thought, are remarkably done. It could properly be called "psychic."

Yesterday morning we came to London. Lunch at hotel. Then rehearsal of *Helen with the High Hand* at the Vaudeville. Dined at hotel. Then Zangwill's *Melting Pot* at Queen's Theatre. A dreadfully bad piece. We left after the 3rd act. All *vieux jeu;* hollow, reverberating with clumsy echoes of old-style eloquence. No human nature in it, except a bit regarding home life of Jews.

Monday, February 16th.

Schmitt for lunch, ½ hour late. Drank a lot of stout, and thoroughly enjoyed eating and drinking. Upstairs in sitting-room he objected to having a small table by his side for coffee, as it morally prevented him from getting up and walking about at will. We took him (Rickards also,

---

[1] *Rivals for Rosamund.* See p. 100.

who came to lunch) to Wallace Collection. I noted a fine "Music Lesson" of Steer, and a small picture by Léopold Robert. We left Schmitt and his Baedeker in street to find his way to Russell Sq. alone. Then all of us to South Place Institute for concert. Quartet of Ravel, and Quintet of Schmitt.

Wednesday, February 18th.

Rivals for Rosamund received with amiable indifference at Palace Theatre on Monday night. Last night I went to see it myself with J. Atkins. The first half was quite well received; the last half coldly. This was right. It is no real good, and if I had realized this earlier I would not have let it be done. Production and acting goodish.

Characteristic of theatrical methods. My name was misspelt on the painted notice in front of the Vaudeville Theatre, and the title of the short play was given wrongly in the illuminated sign in front of the Palace Theatre.

Dress rehearsal of *H. with High Hand* on Monday night was good. The original end had been restored, with my chief emendation preserved.

Thursday, February 19th.

Returned home yesterday afternoon. I bought *Autobiography of Mark Rutherford* and *Mark Rutherford's Deliverance* in 7d. editions at station. And in the night I had finished reading the latter. Very impressive and original. Fine style; no scheme of construction. As a continuous narrative, extraordinarily amateurish. The man had no notion of fiction. But a work not easily forgotten. Full of wisdom and high things.

Middle-aged couple in our compartment yesterday. Well and quietly dressed. Upper class. Restrained. Extremely good natural and trained manners. The woman (35) especially was charming in her admirable breeding. Evidently wealthy. They talked in such a low tone that, although the articulation was perfectly clear, one did not hear unless one listened. After about an hour the woman, reading *Daily Mail,* said, "What is a tympani solo?" The man made a gesture of non-comprehension. She passed him the paper. He read the passage and made a scarcely perceptible sign of ignorance. "Don't you know?" she asked quietly. He repeated the sign—would not speak (as they were not alone). Her glance seemed to say to him, "Pardon me asking you such an outlandish impossible thing." She took back the *Daily Mail*.

Saturday, February 21st.

Pianoforte recital by F.M. at Frinton Hall last night in aid of Tendring parish funds. Hall centrally heated, but draughty. Uncomfortable chairs. Rush-bottomed chair (cost about 3*s*.) for pianist. Old Broadwood baby grand. Pedal creaked. Rotten tone. Ladies of Frinton and of Tendring parishes in evening dress. Two parsons, who felt they must speechify afterwards. Pianist a man about 40; agreeable, slightly curt smile. Ferocious look when he was playing, often. Beethoven, Rameau, Chopin, Scarlatti, Debussy, Liszt, etc. Piano impossible. Intense, almost tragic sadness of provincial musical affairs, second-rate or tenth-rate under bad conditions. A gentle snobbishness (artistically) among the women. One man (friend of pianist) called out 2 or 3 times after a piece, amid the applause, " 'Core, 'core," very loudly and staccato. And he had his encore. Audience determined to appreciate high-class music, and applauding the noisiest and most showy. Crass inertia and stupidity of sundry women around me, determined to understand and to enjoy nothing.

Saturday, March 14th. On board Velsa.

I finished the last of the 6 articles *From the Log of the* Velsa on Monday March 2nd and was exhausted. Tuesday I packed and arranged, and on Wednesday March 4th we came to London. Dined with Rickards and Pryce at Pall Mall Restaurant and then to see *Helen with High Hand* at Vaudeville. The audience were very pleased by the play.

On Friday we came to Paris. Roughish crossing. On Saturday, March 7th, Théâtre du Vieux Colombier. *Le Testament du Père Leleu* (Martin du Gard), *La Jalousie de Barbouillé,* and *La Navette*.[1] Excellent. Quite a good audience. Met Morrell and Lady Ottoline M. Previously to this we

---

[1] *La Jalousie* was by Alexandre, after Molière. *La Navette* is by Henri Becque. Jacques Copeau was the director of all three.

had been to a *conférence* on "Musical Geography" by Calvo. Dined at Cepa's. Bions called before dinner. Fargue, Vignès, Sert, and Aubry came in afterwards.

Wednesday, March 11th, we came to Hyères. We joined the yacht on Friday morning.

Tuesday, April 21st. Orvieto.

Left the yacht yesterday.[1] *Histoire avec octroi.* The head thereof said our baggage ought to be examined by customs. At last, after much worrying of himself, he told us to go. Fine weather. Rather windy. Dusty. Splendid skyscapes. The Campagna full of purples and bright greens. Turned off high road to Viterbo in order to see Capricola and palace thereof. Lunch at Viterbo after a sharp descent from chilly hills. Old waiter at hotel said he had always been honest. Thus he was a Roman, and did not like to say that Viterbo water was better even than Roman water, but it was, though it was against the interest of the hotel trade in mineral water to say so. I drank it. Curious medieval (S. Pellegrino) quarter at Viterbo.

Then to Montefiascone. Great view of purple and bright greens. Hundreds of sq. miles. Then descent to Lake of Bolsena and Bolsena town and then rise to hills, and sudden view of Orvieto in midst of amphitheatre of hills. Unsurpassed. Like a slow mushroom grown there. Serrated outline of towers. We were met by hotel boy at gate of town. Hotel dei Belli Arti. Dear. Fairish. Slept in a longish room of a palace with large paintings of Judith and Holofernes, etc. Marble floor. Plenty of pre-Renaissance architecture in this town. I walked to bottom end of Corso Cavour last night (clear—after rain) and heard voices and saw groups and lights behind blinds. Everything was alive up the dark courts, lighted by one electric lamp. At 9, groups of well-dressed families began to emerge from courts to see last performance of a Fregoli imitator named Marbis, who was doing *Zaza* all by himself.

---

[1] The *Velsa* had been sent by canal through France to Marseilles, where Arnold Bennett boarded her, and coasted along the Riviera and Italy. His wife went by car. The *Velsa* was lent to the Admiralty during the War and was afterwards sold.

Wednesday, April 22nd. Siena.

Too ill most of yesterday to sit up in the car and be intelligent. Before leaving Orvieto we went into cathedral. A fiendishly noisy office going on between 3 or 4 old priests with awful voices. No audience. Chapels good. Well pleased. Then round town. Went to find very early church, S. Giovanni, *très* primitive. After we had entered it and gone away, it occurred to me that we had not seen it at all, but another quite ordinary church. So much for one's artistic education. *On gobe tout.* Gorgeous and glorious drive over mountains from Orvieto. At first we couldn't see Orvieto Cathedral; then we saw its peaks, and then we couldn't see anything else; it was the one thing that stood out on Orvieto's hill. Lunch at Montepulciano. I couldn't see it, but I walked about a bit, after taking a room at Albergo Marzocco to sleep in. Fine palaces. A great deal of Garibaldi.

Then to Pienza, where the piazza is small but fine. At S. Quirico, Read wouldn't stop, and we had a lovely glimpse of a primitive carved church. Had I known the name of the place I should have stopped the car, but I didn't. As it is, the glimpse remains exquisitely in the memory. This is a good way of seeing things occasionally.

Arrived at Siena at 3.50. Surprised at liveliness and beauty of this town. Drove to Duomo, 7.15. Office going on. Crowds entering, large crowds. Priests at a large desk transacting business with the faithful in front of a large box marked *oblazioni*. Then a monk in a brown robe appeared in a high pulpit and began to preach. We had to leave.

Thursday, April 23rd.

Yesterday spent chiefly in following Baedeker up and down Siena, with good results. The most memorable single thing we saw was a picture by Sano di Pietro (with a woman in it) on the ground floor of the Palazzo Communale. The charm of the cathedral is extreme. Fine Renaissance altars and things in various small churches. Casa di S. Caterina. Very little of it left. A bit of alleged old floor, carefully boarded, with hinges here and there. The place chiefly a series of very ugly chapels. In charge of a young agreeable priest.

On piazza of S. Agostino I essayed a drawing, with bad results. I managed to convey to the *cocher* that I wanted some picturesque scene to draw. He tumbled instantly. He found 3 all good, but only one in the least suitable for me.

Friday, April 24th. Pisa.

San Gimignano and Volterra, both visited yesterday *en route* from Siena to Pisa. In each place we had a man who described himself as *le seule guide de la ville* and who was intelligent. Both places=reputation. Etruscan Museum at Volterra *très bien arrangé*. At lunch there we saw a man whom I took for an English archæologist, but he was an American alabaster merchant. San Gimignano the most complete place we have seen. Roads excellent up to halfway from Volterra to Pisa. Then baddish. Two tire bursts, and a kid with handcart ran into us. Pisa very sad. *Tristesse* of Piazza del Duomo. Leaning Tower just as idiotic as I thought.

Saturday, April 25th. Albenga.

Yesterday, Pisa to Massa, Spezia and Genova. Vile, dusty, busy road to Massa and beyond. Flat. Marmoreal environs of Carrara. Over hills for a few miles into Spezia good. Fine hill road (1700 ft.) to Sestri di Levanti. With snow peaks in very far distance. This was truly sublime. From Sestri to Rapallo, road follows coast. Got Max's [1] address at post office and went to Villino Chiaso for tea. Max in whites, no waistcoat, and a calico sort of jacket. Fine tiled terrace. He was engaged in altering a portrait of George Moore in *Century* in order to tease Moore. Fine tea. Good servant. Picked a lemon off tree for tea. Arrived at Genoa 7.55. Left there this morning at 9.30 and reached Albenga at 1.25. Level crossings rather lucky, but up to Savona progress very slow.

Sunday, April 26th. Menton.

Quite decent roads all the way yesterday. Read ran out of essence near San Remo. Also pump went wrong and tire flat. Sundry delays. It began to rain. Arrived at Menton 6.40 (French time).

---

[1] Max Beerbohm.

Monday, April 27th. Aix-en-Provence.

Pneu troubles up to Cannes and delay there. Left Cannes at 2.30. Slow through the Esterel, but after Fréjus a tremendous pace. We reached here (152 k. from Cannes) at 6.20. General elections; everywhere streets full of outbursts of chairs and tables from cafés. Fête. After I was in bed, silly asinine cheering of crowds swindled by astute politicians. Such fragments of election literature as I saw were just as absurd as in England, but not more so.

Tuesday, April 28th. Carcassonne.

Row with Jewish landlady at Aix yesterday. Lunch at Avignon. Now, all the way yesterday and today, vineyards for hundreds of miles, and men with tanks on their backs syringing them with sulphurous stuff. Sunny, breezy; roads good only in parts. Cathedral good.

Went on in afternoon to Nîmes-Arènes, then on to Montpellier. A great noisy city. Scarcely any sleep. Large theatre. Really very many large cafés round about it. This morn. we came straight through Béziers to Carcassonne, 146 k. in 3¾ hours over very indifferent but straight roads. I had quite a wrong idea of Carcassonne. I thought the town itself (30,000 inhabitants) was a monument. However, the *cité* as restored by Viollet-le-Duc is highly curious. Also church therein. Guide thereat (*né dans la cité*) who said, apropos of *embrassement général* after annual Comédie Française show, that *"le forum de Rome et le Kremlin de Moscou ne sont rrrrien à côté de cela."*

Thursday, April 30th. Toulouse.

Rain last night, the first appreciable for about a month or more. Drove aimlessly about in the afternoon. Lift boy in this hotel, aged 13, works from 6.30 to 11 P.M. or later every day. He has been here a month and looks aged. He is very nicely and smartly dressed, and very small, and he spoils the hotel for "thinking people." The young man aged 17 or 18 who served our *petits déjeuners* this morning excused his delay with *"Je suis seul."* Certainly overworked. Last night in the rain, paper-sellers and tram-conductors in felt sandals that would sop up water like a sponge.

Friday, May 1st. Tulle (Corrèze).

Left Toulouse at 8.50 A.M. Not a *ville sympathique*. Population brusque and rude and *vie dure pour les pauvres*. Rain stopped us from going to S. Sernin yesterday afternoon, but the antique church of St. Étienne was close by, so we went to that. The valley of the Corrèze between Brive and Tulle is lovely. The Corrèze runs rapidly through the length of this town. An important place for only 15,000 inhabitants.

Sunday, May 3rd. Bourges.

250 kil. yesterday. Generally over 1st-class roads. Up to Gueret mountainous. Afterwards for the most part long, straight roads. Arrived at Bourges at 4.45. Very windy. A good deal of praying in churches just now. Many women, but not one man in cathedral. Some young girls doing the stations of the cross while taking an unfeigned interest in me.

Monday, May 4th. Paris.

We reached Fontainebleau at 12.20 yesterday. Have done about 150 k. in 3 hours on the way. Long, straight, pretty good roads. We left F'bleau at 1.30. All right to Villeneuve St.-Georges. Then the *entrée dans Paris était fantastique. Gare à Vincennes,* etc., etc. Arrived at hotel at 3.45 P.M., having motored from Rome without killing even a fowl. Sole incident—a boy and handcart ran into us near Pisa.

Monday, May 11th. London.

Dined at Godebski's last Wednesday, and lunched with Martins. I came to London Thursday. On boat long talk with Pullman agent, once coachman to British Embassy. Atkins dined with me at Reform Club, and Maurice Baring joined us afterwards. Visits to his flat and to Atkins. Friday, lunch with Pinker and son at Arts Club.

Wednesday, May 20th. Comarques.

Two watercolours with Rickards. Too much tennis. Bad nights. I resumed *Universal History*[1] reading yesterday, and also began to write an article for the *New Weekly* and *Harper's Weekly* on *The Barber*. I finished it this morning. This is the first writing work I have done since early in March. All last week I planned the first part of *Clayhanger III*, but I seemed to get little inspirational force for it. I turned to Turgenev, which caused my blood to flow. But the mere reviews of Mrs. Parnell's *Life of Parnell*[2] (publ. yesterday) inspired me much more than Turgenev—gave me the heroic mood. For Clayhanger also is irremediably in love.

Tuesday, May 26th.

Two aquarelles on Sunday.

Yesterday at 5.55 A.M. I began to write the third *Clayhanger* and did 1200 words in the morning.

Thursday, May 28th.

47 yesterday. Very sleepless night. Many annoyances in the morning; chief, a summons to Chelmsford jury for June 11th, the week I have made all arrangements for being in London. Fatigue, and this, put me right off the novel. M. returned home, uncured of her special complaint, but otherwise well. I finished *A House of Gentlefolk*.[3] Somewhat disappointed with the latter half. But it was a book after Mrs. O'Shea's *Life of Parnell*. Some of the latter is *really* interesting, but most of it dull, and all of it marked by a character fundamentally vulgar. But she was a beautiful woman.

Tuesday, June 2nd.

On Sunday before breakfast I wrote a play, *The Alarm,* in one act, for the Actors' Orphanage Garden Party on June 23. Intended to play 5 minutes.

Read Ransome's *Oscar Wilde*. Well-meant stuff. Curious that a man

---

[1] *L'Histoire Générale du IVe Siècle jusqu'à nos Jours.* See pages 82, 84.
[2] Mrs. Parnell was the former Mrs. O'Shea, whose relations with Charles Stewart Parnell, the Irish political leader, had caused a celebrated scandal contributing to his downfall.
[3] By Turgenev, also translated as *A Nest of Nobles.*

with such decent notions on style should have none. After reading Dostoievsky's *Les Précoces* it suddenly occurred to me, a few pages from the end, that it was merely an episode lifted from *Les Frères Karamazov*. The name Karamazov does not occur in the first part of the book, and when it does occur the translators somehow transmogrify it into Chestamazov.

Sunday, June 7th.

Vernon came for lunch Tuesday, and had no progress to report.

The Edgar Selwyns came for lunch and tea Friday. Edgar told us about Al. Woods, once a cheap-theatre manager, thence out of that by cinemas, and now one of the chief N.Y. producers. It was he who said after 1st Act of *Milestones,* "Who is this guy Bennett?"—after second, "No, you couldn't give it to me!" and after 3rd: "He's got me. It'll never *stop* running in N.Y." He says he *smells* a good or a bad play. Showing MS. of an accepted play to Edgar, he said: "Smell that. Smell it. Doesn't it smell good?" Once when listening to an idea for a play, he sniffed all the time—sniff, sniff, sniff—and at the end said, "No, that don't seem to me to smell very good." Once Michael Morton intruded on him; he refused to listen, but Michael made him. Michael said: "My idea is for a little Russian girl who wants to study, and she can't get away unless she takes the prostitute's ticket—the yellow ticket as it is called. That's what they have to do, you know." Said Woods, startled: "It *is?* It *is?* I'll buy your play." Morton said it wasn't finished. "Never mind. I'll buy." And he bought it on the spot. He always thus makes up his mind at once and won't wait. The legend is that he never makes a mistake. But it can't be so.

Walpole came yesterday for the week-end, without collars or toilet things. Great croquet this afternoon.

Yesterday I finished 1st chapter of *These Twain,* 5900 words, and I think it fairly good.

Sunday, June 14th.

Went to London by car last Wednesday morn. Two tire breakdowns. Acute liver attack on previous day, and not recovered.

We dined at Ritz, with Robert Loraine and Mimi Godebski, as guests of Edgar Selwyn and wife. I took them all, and the Retingers, to 500th performance of *Great Adventure*. After that with M. to Granville-Barker's supper and dance at Connaught Rooms. Lillah was my partner, but Asquith came uninvited, and she had to look after him. He took Ainley's place on her left. When I bet Ainley a quid that play would not be running on September 1st, Asquith took the stakes. He was in great spirits. He drank a little, but more mineral water than champagne. We left at 2.15. Met Meyerfeld, translator of *Milestones* into German. Went home at 2.15 A.M.

Thursday morning Pinker came to breakfast. May Wilson Preston and Dr. Carl Otto came for tea. Friday, Ellen Glasgow and Mrs. Westmore Willcox to tea. The former deaf, but pretty, plump, intelligent, and extremely well read.

Friday, June 26th.

Sculpture in garden to be finished tomorrow. Sundry watercolours. Nevertheless I have never in my life worked better than this week, despite liver on Tuesday. I have now written over 20,000 words of *Clayhanger III* and got to the end of the party which opens the book and the quarrel after it. Seems all right. Written with ease on the whole. I was up most mornings at 6.

Monday, July 13th.

I returned from yacht last Monday. Much interested now in question of getting a new yacht. 150-ton schooner, crew of 8, speed 8 knots, draft 7 ft. This is what I want.

I went to London on Friday. Collins came on Saturday morning and read his Grand Babylon Hotel play to me. I joined yacht, with Swinnerton, at Westminster Bridge at 3 P.M. I returned home at 9.35 A.M. today by yacht.

Tuesday, July 21st.

Marguerite went to Paris to be operated on. She returned home cured on

Saturday the 18th. I did no work whatever on my novel all last week, and have not yet resumed.

Thursday, July 30th.

Between the last entry and Wednesday week I did no work at all. Felt queer and couldn't collect ideas. I think it was a chill in the head. But thenceforward I worked well and did an average of over 1000 words a day for ten days. I finished a long chapter yesterday. Last week-end on Broads in yacht; did 2500 words in the two days. I go on board the yacht tonight for an excursion to Cowes, timed to leave tomorrow morning at 6 A.M.

WAR JOURNALS

1914-1918

1914

Thursday, August 6th. Thorpe-le-Soken.

On arriving at Brightlingsea on Monday afternoon, I was told that petrol could not be got in the district, that it was fetching up to 10s. a tin at Clacton, and that Baggaley, the regular hirer of motor cars at B'sea, had gone forth in an attempt to get petrol. At Clacton yesterday the price was 2s. 3d. or 2s. 4d. a gallon. I have 60 gallons in stock.

A great crowd of holiday makers at Clacton in the showers yesterday. No difficulty about getting change for a £10 note in gold and silver. At the fish shop, slight increases of price in poultry and eggs. The man said there was no chance for him to make money (in response to a friendly jibe of M.'s). He said he expected to get no more fish after that day.

Yesterday we heard noise of explosions destroying inconvenient houses at Harwich. The sensations of Harwich people must be poignant. Nevertheless the G.E.R., in yesterday evening's paper, was advertising its Hook of Holland service (with restaurant cars, etc.) exactly as usual, and I believe the boat left last night. We also heard thunder, and the children affirm that they distinctly heard the noise of firing—not explosions. (Report of action in North Sea in evening papers.) I saw one warship in the offing at Clacton, but an ordinary steamer coming to the pier, and a barge sailing northwards.

An officer came yesterday to complain of a fox terrier (? ours) which flew at dispatch-riders on motor bicycles. He said it would be shot if found loose. These dispatch-riders are the most picturesque feature of the war, here. They rush through the village at speeds estimated up to 50 miles an hour. I am willing to concede 40.

I agree that Russia is the real enemy, and not Germany; and that a *rapprochement* between England and Germany is a certainty. But I doubt whether it is wise, in the actual conduct of affairs, to try to see so far ahead. I think that the belligerency of England is a mistake—for England. Yet if I had had to choose, I believe my instinct would have forced me to make war.

Sir Edward Grey's astounding mistake, in his big speech, was the assertion that the making of war would not much increase our suffering. It will enormously increase it. The hope for us is in the honesty and efficiency of our administration. The fear for France springs from the fact that the majority of French politicians are notoriously rascals, out for plunder. The corruption of Russian administration is probably even worse. The seriousness of the average French private will atone for a lot, but it will not—for instance—create boots for him. The hope for France is that the German army, arrogant in its traditions, etc., may be lower than its reputation.

After reading the diplomatic papers leading up to the rupture between England and Germany, this morning, one has to admit that Sir E. Grey did everything he could, once he had stated his position. The war is a mistake on our part, but other things leading to it were a mistake, and, these things approved or condoned, the war must be admitted to be inevitable. Judged by any current standard, Sir E. Grey is a man of high common sense. He has not yet grasped the movement of social evolution, but then very few people have. And you cannot properly or fairly try to govern a country on a plane of common sense *too* high above its own general plane.

Apart from Germany two countries are pre-eminently suffering at the beginning of the war—France and Belgium. Both are quite innocent, Belgium touchingly so. I can imagine the Germans among them if they get the upper hand. The Germans are evidently quite ruthless and brutal and savage in war. This is logical, but a large part of their conduct is due to the arrogant military tradition, which will one day be smashed. If Germany is smashed in this war, the man most imperilled will be the German Emperor. If she is not smashed, the man most imperilled may be the Tsar.

I am told, convincingly, that a firm at Clacton is making an extra £50 a week out of bread, through increased charges for which there is no justification. It appears that the farmers all round have raised the price of butter 3*d*. a lb.

Miss Osborne and a girl friend came round yesterday afternoon to ask for linen or subscriptions for the local branch of the Red Cross Society. Mrs. Byng is ready to lend Thorpe Hall for a hospital. These young ladies have no orders or permission yet from the War Office, but they wish to be in readiness. This instinct to do something on the part of idle young women, or half idle, is satisfactory to behold. All about this district and all about many other country districts are many middle-class young women, and scarcely any young men for them to consort with—I mean even in ordinary times. Now, there will be fewer young men than ever.

On the day after the war the boys[1] wanted a tent. They had one, beyond the pond. It cost one day's labour of a carpenter. This tent is used by everybody except me nearly all the time. The whole household seems to live in it. Today the boys are making wooden swords. Yesterday a village boy gave me a military salute.

Edith Johnston recounts how her father is laying in ammunition against the time when the populace will raid the countryside demanding provisions; he, being a farmer, is to be called on early in the proceedings, and he is determined to give out his stores evenly and not to the strongest. Each morning he summons all his men and explains to them the course of the war, so that they shall not be misled by rumours. Edith thinks that a war is necessary and advisable, as the population is too thick.

Friday, August 7th.

The news of the sinking of the *Amphion,* by striking a mine, and of

---

[1] Nephews, who were staying at Comarques when war was declared.

the weakening of the defence of Liège made a silent breakfast table. Nevertheless, these things are preliminary trifles of infinitesimal importance. My Central News service of war telegrams began at 6 P.M. tonight with an unofficial (Raffles) statement that the Germans before Liège had asked for a day's armistice, having lost 20,000 men. This uncertain news animated me much. The postmaster himself brought the telegram. I asked him if he would like to put it in the post-office window. He said he should. In reply to a question he said he had been having very little sleep lately (P.O. being open continuously night and day), but that he had had a good night last night; he had the telephone by his bed, but no call.

Rumour through M. this morning that Read might have to join forces as ex-Territorial, and that Lockyer as captain of rifle club might also have to go, made me think, startled, "We should have no electricity and should have to use candles." This seemed dreadful at first, but by the afternoon I was reconciled to the idea of no electricity and also to the idea of the garden being neglected.

Lockyer told me that it was suspected that 8 or 9000 Colchester men had already been shipped to Belgium, leaving last Friday, long before war was declared. Certainly the silence of the newspapers as to the Expeditionary Force is superb. He said that miniature rifle clubs had been in existence and full practice for six years now and that the members had been told that the object was to repel a German invasion. He suggested that the captains of clubs should be called together with a view to preparing some definite general organization to offer to the Govt. in case of need (not for an invasion, but for anything) and that I should write to J. Parkes, secretary to Clacton district. This I did. He was quite ready to serve himself, and Cook also is ready to go (as ex-Reserve man); both have families. I asked Read if he thought of offering himself as an ex-Territorial. He said he had no thought of going unless it was compulsory.

Saturday, August 8th.

Miss Nerney told me that while people were reading the copy of the telegram to me, shown in the post-office window yesterday afternoon, one man asked, "Who is Arnold Bennett?" The reply was, "He's the War minister." Then, in correction: "Oh, no, he isn't. He's the actor chap that lives down the road."

Rumour that a miller at W., settled there some years with his family and often suspected of being a German spy, is now proved to be a German officer, and plans of Harwich, etc., have been found at his place; and that he and 2 others are now imprisoned at the hotel.

Today I got postal orders as currency.

The boats were still running to Flushing.

We received the Paris *Journal* for Wednesday. It consisted of one sheet, 2 pages, and gave chiefly the news of Germany's declaration of war on England and a report of the *séance* in the Chamber. M., in her pleasure at a French paper, pinned it to the hall curtains for all to see and read, long after all had read it.

Sunday, August 9th.

Yesterday Johnson, ex-tobacco merchant, called on me in a state of some excitement. Tall, thin, nervous man. He began by saying, "I am a great patriot." He said superiorly: "I know the Germans. They are traitors. I have seen this coming for years. I have £3000 in cash. I am prepared to use it for the country." His scheme was that the Government should give authority to take over the small mills (why 'only small?) of the district, and that he should manage them without profit, so as to prevent the exploitation of small people now going on. He had already got promises of produce of 4000 acres at rather less than market price. The extreme improbability of such a scheme's ever being sanctioned, the absurdity of it, the rights on which it trampled, the excessive difficulty of it—these things seemed not to have occurred to him at all. It was all simple and patriotic to him. He wanted me to guarantee £1000 and to give the support of my name (this was what he came for), and he had got Syme to guarantee £1000. On this he was prepared to start.

To soothe him I said I would write to some one high up as a preliminary, and I wrote to Spender,[1] without, however, concealing my view from Spender. Johnson was soon launched on his camping experiences in Turkey, where he went to buy tobacco. He is a very decent, agreeable, well-intentioned oldish man, speaking fairly correctly except that he adds *r* to the end of too many words. He farms his own land.

Then the Mathewses came. The Rev. M.,[2] a very nice chap indeed, had suddenly discovered that Redmond was a good man; but he learnt from me for the first time at 5 P.M., 8th Augt 1914, that Ulster is not all Protestant. He was staggered to learn that quite 50 per cent of Ulster is Roman Catholic. Although he had to make an announcement about it in the pulpit tomorrow, he had not yet understood the object of the Prince of Wales's Relief Fund. I explained it to him. By the way, I have no desire whatever to contribute to this spectacular affair. I have taken measures to be told of any bad cases in the village (none at present), and I have authorized Pinker to use £100 privately among really necessitous authors. I have the same feeling against funds as I have against committees.

Referring to my permission to postmaster to exhibit my war telegrams at the post office, I read the following on a telegraph form outside the P.O. yesterday: "British Gold Coast Forces Take German Togoland. No resistance by permission of Arnold Bennett Esquire."

Monday, August 10th.

The alleged spy (ex-Austrian officer) is perhaps not a spy. But he has to report himself to the authorities every twelve hours.

The only important rise in price is in butter, 3*d.* a lb. The rise in bread is not the same everywhere.

Daking came to see me yesterday about taking the farm. He is in charge of the National Service League in this district. He asked me if he could hold a committee meeting here. I said he could. He said he had spent £25 himself on the League. He was quite prepared to go on

---

[1] J. A. Spender, editor of the *Westminster Gazette.*
[2] Rev. H. G. S. Mathews, rector of Beaumont with Moze, Essex, the Bennetts' neighbour.

with the preparations for taking the farm, but he said, "I shall look nice if the Germans come and take it from me." At the back of the mind of every one is a demi-semi fear lest the Germans should after all, by some *coup,* contrive an invasion. And that is the only fear. The fear of revolution or serious social uproar after the War does not trouble anybody. Few even think of it.

When one sees young men idling in the lanes on Sunday, one thinks, "Why are they not at the war?" All one's pacific ideas have been rudely disturbed. One is becoming militarist. And the usefulness of certain organizations upon which one looked with disdainful tolerance is now proved by events.

The alleged spy has to report himself only once a day at noon. Nothing incriminating has been found in his house.

The family went to Clacton this morning. They said it was practically emptied of visitors and sundry of the big shops closed until 6 P.M., being out of supplies. Nevertheless, in a four-mile walk round about here this afternoon, I met a quite unusually large number of motors and other vehicles, many of them obviously pleasure and tripper parties.

Mrs. and Miss W. have taken the pictures down in their house and otherwise dismantled it and sent the silver to the bank. But why they have done this neither they nor anybody else seems to know. I suppose it is the mere result of a vague fear.

Wednesday, August 12th.

No definite news yesterday, and probably there will be none today. I am in *full* work, and only a defeat of the Allies will put me off work.

Thursday, August 13th.

Tennis meeting at Mathews's, Beaumont, yesterday. The universal tale of ladies was that they were going to begin Red Cross shirt-making, etc. Our house alone had actually bought its materials and begun. It was said that a band of ladies had collected and gone to —— Hall to scrub, and when they got there found they had not one scrubbing-brush. The idea of certain ladies was to cut out the garments and then send them to cottage women to sew, without payment. Butter only, among provisions, is definitely higher, by 3*d*. a lb. Best sugar between 4*d*. and 4½*d*. I am paying 1*d*. extra per gallon of petrol; that is, the same price as before the reduction a few weeks ago.

I have now had the following hits:

Serial publication of *The Price of Love* suspended in *Daily News,* ostensibly on account of paper famine.

Book publication of ditto indefinitely postponed.

Other autumn books probably ditto.

Vedrenne announced today that autumn tours of *Milestones,* if railways permitted them to go out at all, would be a heavy loss, and would I forgo my fees? I declined. Knoblock, he said, had agreed.

Receipts of *The Great Adventure* at the Kingsway showed a fall of about £500 on the previous week.

No definite news again today, except formal declaration of war last night by England against Austria.

Monday, August 17th.

In the midst of this war I wrote over 7000 words in six days, ending Friday.

No war news till last night, when Japan's ultimatum to Germany reached me by wire after I had gone to bed and to sleep. The dog, hearing the telegraph messenger, woke me.

Yesterday, a request from the *Daily News* to write on the War. Today, ditto from *Everybody's Mag.* Yesterday, inspired somewhat by *D.N.'s* request, I wrote an article on *What the German Conscript Thinks,* this in addition to 2 hours' revision work on novel.

Friday, August 21st.

Davray [1] wrote me the other day from Paris, stating without any hint of scepticism (1) that the menu of the dinner which the Kaiser was to eat in Paris on August 12th had been prepared in advance. And (2) that

---

[1] Henry D. Davray had translated Bennett's novels into French.

in the cellars of the Hôtel du Rhin a garlanded bust of the Emperor had been found ready to expose in the Place Vendôme when the Kaiser should pass through.

Great spectacular depressing fact of the surrender of Brussels to the Germans this morning. But by the afternoon I had got quite used to it and was convinced that it was part of the Allies' preconceived plan and that all was well. But before getting this reassuring conviction I had gone upstairs and written 1200 words in 2 hours.

Sunday, August 23rd.

A tale yesterday that eighty men had been engaged all day in searching for a spy who had not been found (in this neighborhood, that is)!

Sullivan [1] said that he had an enormous belief in the British Expeditionary Force and that he thought it would "cause consternation"! Nevertheless he was sure that the Germans would get to Paris, and he bet me a present worth £5 that they would.

Tuesday, August 25th.

Yesterday's rumours. Mathews (who came with wife and daughter to play tennis) said that a friend of his had a friend who with others had been sent out to Belgium, a fortnight before the declaration of war, with British guns for the Liège forts and to instruct the Belgians in the use of the said guns. This friend's friend had not returned. The theory held by the friend was that the Germans were taken by surprise by the range of the Liège guns. This reminds me that, though we had constant news that the Liège forts were holding out, we have only had indirect news that they have fallen. Clemenceau is right in demanding full news of defeats.

Psychological consequence of fall of Namur: We were all discussing last night what we in this house ought to do if Germans came. The general result was: nothing.

---

[1] The late Herbert Sullivan. He collaborated with Newman Flower in publishing the life of the composer, Sir Arthur Sullivan.

Thursday, August 27th.

Talk with old farmer down Golden Lane this morning. Said he was 78 ("but I'm done for") and had farmed there for 50 years. He said he had often been to Brussels as cattle dealer. What surprised him there was that people kept pigs in cellars under their houses. He said he didn't know my opinion, but he thought Germany was short of money and couldn't last. Then he said, "Now tell me, Mr. Bennett, is it true they're a-killing women and children?" He said the harvest was very good, and that at Laudermere Farm they had got 20 sacks of wheat to the acre. Many farms, he said, got only 3, 4, or 5. One of his larger fields was being used for cavalry (or perhaps field-artillery) manœuvres. I asked him whether he charged the Government anything for the field. He said: "No. They've got enough to pay for." Lastly he suggested to me "a matter of business." "I know you're a business man, Mr. Bennett; I can see it in yer face." To wit, that I should have my mare covered by a piebald pony that he knew. He said I could work her up to the day she foaled and begin again a week afterwards.

Saturday, August 29th.

It is now reported that Dr. H. (who nevertheless knows colonial and frontier quasi-military and military life), as well as Mr. Johnston, can do nothing but read the papers, and think, think, think, and mourn because English youths will not enlist. It was given forth that while at Tendring and Weeley and other villages the response to the call was excellent, the response in Thorpe was miserable—indeed, it was said, only one man. No doubt every village is saying the same. In any case the alleged state of affairs would be explicable by the fact there is a camp at Tendring and another at Weeley and youths are thereby fired.

However, on inquiry from other sources I found that Thorpe was doing excellently. Lockyer, a grim and very serious patriot and the chief pillar of the Rifle Club, said that 5 men had gone from his club alone. Cook, second gardener, who belongs already to the National Reserve, put down his name again, and was told that for the present he was not wanted. Few young men, eligible for recruiting and able to go, remain.

Miss Nerney said the same. It was she who told me that Mrs. Wood (parson's[1] wife) had said to a young man who offered certain sorts of help: "You can only help in one way. You can enlist." As parson's wife and familiar with the village, she knew or ought to have known that the young man had a widowed mother depending on him. Mrs. Wood is a very decent woman, and that she should have said such a thing shows how far the feeling of the middle classes will carry them.

Yesterday morning I wrote an article telling some incontrovertible truths about this recruiting question. Mrs. Sharpe "agreed with every word of it" but did not think it ought to be published. Marguerite did not like it at all. Both were afraid of it. I should not be at all surprised if the *Daily News* is not also afraid of it. In that case I shall probably send it to the *New Statesman*.

Monday, August 31st.

Rickards and I met H. in the street. Jaunty but gloomy. He said there was only one thing "to save this country"—vastly increased recruiting. When I said that soldiers could be had quite easily if we would pay fairly for them, he at once said: "Bounty? Yes, the U.S.A. paid a bounty of £20." The usual charitable idea, not a proper salary. He said it was the middle classes that shirked, not the lower and not the upper. It did not seem to occur to him that the whole organization of the army was such as to keep the middle classes out of it—save as privates.

Our young women and M. paid another visit to another camp yesterday. Officers wire appointments here, etc. They call here in motors to make appointments. Good news yesterday, as to moving of German troops from western frontier. The bill came for the British stand, between 5000 and 6000 losses, but the news that they were thoroughly reinforced was good. The girls came home with a positive statement from the camp that 160,000 Russians were being landed in Britain, to be taken to France. The Colonel had brought the news from Colchester.

The statement was so positive that at first I almost believed it. But after about an hour I grew quite sceptical. Only the Archangel route

---

[1] Rev. A. R. Wood, vicar of Thorpe-le-Soken.

could have been used. Think of the number of ships and the amount of convoying necessary. In the end I dismissed it and yet could not help hoping. . . . Rumours in village as to it also. Debarkation said variously to take place at Harwich and in Scotland, etc. Numbers went up to 400,000. The most curious embroidery on this rumour was from Mrs. A.W., who told Mrs. W. that the Russians were coming via us to France, where they would turn treacherous to France and join Germans in taking Paris. "We could not trust the Russians." This rumour I think took the cake. Yet Mrs. Sharpe asked me seriously whether there was any fear of such a thing.

Wednesday, September 2nd.

Yesterday I received an official invitation to go to London to meet Masterman [1] as to the war.

The agent for Mrs. Cowley came and rounded up six men for recruits on Monday night. Cook, second gardener, left this morning. Lockyer says that practically all available men in village have gone or belong to some reserve or other.

Thursday, September 3rd.

London absolutely as usual in summer, except the "call to arms" on the taxis. Atkins lunched with me at Reform. Atkins believed in Russian troops story, but had not much inside news. Belloc said it was a question whether Germans would break through Allies' line yesterday or today. Spender told me a lot of useful stuff for articles. He also said that Kitch. had 150,000 recruits before he would admit 100,000, and that he now actually had over 200,000 while still advertising for them. Recruiting organization had broken down, and the recruiting campaign was off.

Conference at Wellington House of "eminent authors," Hall Caine, Zangwill, Parker, among them. Masterman in chair. Zangwill talked a great deal too much. The sense was talked by Wells and Chesterton. Rather disappointed in Gilbert Murray, but I liked the look of little

---

[1] Rt. Hon. C. F. G. Masterman, Chancellor of the Duchy of Lancaster.

R. H. Benson.[1] Masterman directed pretty well, and Claud Schuster and the Foreign Office representative were not bad. Thomas Hardy was all right. Barrie introduced himself to me; Scotch accent, sardonic canniness. Afterwards I went with Wells to his flat; all alone there. A young Vowles came in with his own recruiting story, which I arranged to turn into an article. I was much pleased with the serious, confident, and kind demeanour of every one. But Spender told me that the military clubs were full of old officers in a panic. I had such a fearful headache after the conference that I had to dine alone at the club. I bought *The Riddle of the Sands*—very annoying style.

Saturday, September 5th.

Joseph Retinger came yesterday for the night. He had taken 3 weeks from the Russian-Polish frontier to London—six days in prison at Vienna and six days in prison at Paris. He said that there were no uniforms for 800,000 French reservists, and that for three days no reply had been given to a patriotic offer of 200 combined tailors to set to work on the uniforms, materials being plentiful. He also said that Messinez (ex-Ministre de Guerre) was a *cas pathologique,* often fainted at Cabinet meetings, etc. He said that such men as Berthelot (now practically in charge of French foreign politics) were very sanguine as to the result of the War. He had plans for Poland but did not strike me as having lost any of his impracticalness, nor did he inspire any confidence. He was fairly wrong in his estimate of U.S.A. opinion.

Monday, September 14th.

Nothing much happens. I wrote *Liberty* last week for the *Saturday Evening Post,* and *Daily News* article last Sunday but one and yesterday. Pinker came up on Friday for week-end. He confirmed a tale of Miss Nerney's (from France) that the lack of support to British army in early stages was due to a general forgetting a dispatch in his pocket for two days and that this general was shot.

---

[1] Monsignor Benson died this same year. He was the author of several works on Catholic subjects, and the brother of two other distinguished writers, A. C. and E. F. Benson.

The theatrical business varies with the war news, I think. Week ending Friday 4th it was more than £100 less than previous week. I am expecting that for last week, with German army in retreat most of the time, it will be up again considerably.

No certainty yet as to the alleged Russian army in France. Military officers up to yesterday have always believed the tale, and indeed positively asserted it, here. But yesterday Miss Hatchett found a colonel who said it was false and who could explain how the rumour first arose.

Sunday, September 20th.

Yachts, dinghies, and other small boats were moved inland from Brightlingsea creek last week, as part of a plan for defending Brightlingsea and the Colne in case of a German invasion. The notion seemed to be that the G.'s might use them as pontoons. I said to old Capt. Brand that it was only done because a number of people had a desire to do something, and this strange proceeding could not do any harm. He said the same thought had occurred to him. We met a lot of these boats in military carts. Sullivan told me there were about 200 of them.

No news last week.

Constant flow of one or two military officers in and through this house, on account of Mimi[1] and Miss Hatchett. The latest move—a night excursion in car to see searchlights playing on the sea off Frinton.

Tuesday, September 22nd.

News of sinking of *Aboukir, Hogue,* and *Cressy* (12,000 tons each), by submarine or submarines, startled me in the middle of my work this afternoon. I thought: Suppose all our fleet sank in this way? But then I thought: We have twice as many submarines as Germany, and the trick ought to work both ways. Nothing in the war yet has affected me like this news, of which no details to hand. Thursday I contemplated an article about terms of peace to be imposed on Germany.

Monday, September 28th.

Cook came to see me last Sunday but one. He was happy in camp at

---

[1] Mimi Godebski.

Dovercourt. He said that inoculation was being practised against enteric and that it was useless. I contradicted him firmly, but probably without effect. He said that tattooing was a better preventive of enteric. He is extensively tattooed. I think he was tattooed in India. His chief argument in favour of the excellence of tattooing as a preventive was that "they put gold in it" where he was tattooed.

I met Dr. H. yesterday morning. He had been having a pow-wow with an old friend not seen for 20 years, Col. Robertson, in command of new battalion at Colchester—a great maker of soldiers, keen, etc., etc. He had come back with the usual fine crop of rumours that flourish in camps and in naval ports. Serious misunderstandings between French and English commanders. French short of ammunition. Serious leakage at the Admiralty in the very highest quarters. Our 3 cruisers were given away, etc., etc. A French general shot by court-martial, etc. I disposed at once of the last tale, and sniffed at all the others, and I especially protested against the implication, every time the word "German" was used, that the Germans were superhuman. His wife in the afternoon said that I had quite changed him. But I bet he is the same as ever today. I learnt from Mrs. H. that there is a serious undercurrent of fear of a German raid in the village.

Friday, October 9th.

Last week I learnt that, owing to the glut of English authors' "distinguished 'copy'" in U.S.A. offered practically for nothing either in order to get it published quickly, or because American copyright had been sacrificed to instant publication in England, there was no longer any market for such copy in U.S.A., American editors, with characteristic foolishness, setting down as valueless that which they could get cheap. I was told that they now adopted a patronizing smile towards all English war-"copy" other than news. Thus our literary patriotism has cost us authors money and done no good. Personally, a contract for 10 articles for £1000 was practically arranged for me and then called off. This was for American use of *Daily News* article; so it was a clear net loss.

Today I acted on notice to reduce lights, on account of Zeppelins.

Monday, October 12th.

Lunch at Mrs. Hausberg's. I met a really intelligent officer—the first —Captain Montagu Browne, brigade-major or something at Colchester. He, of course, did not believe in the possibility of an invasion. But others did, and were ready to bet on it. With him a Colonel D., retired for many years, but now at work again administratively. Amiable and decent, superficially smart, but politically a fool. Said (quite nicely) that since the Boer War there had been nobody interested in British Empire. "Party" was the chief concern, and how longest to remain in power. When I asked, "Who *has* been looking after the British Empire, then?" he made no answer. Afterwards he took me aside and said how interesting it was to meet me, and praised my books, and even showed knowledge of them. He had a Rolls-Royce car, which he looks after entirely himself, except washing it. Said, even then he couldn't afford it.

German bomb dropped on roof of Notre Dame yesterday.

Sunday, October 25th.

No news except newspaper news, and no time to write it down even if there was any. I spend 1½ days a week on war articles. Village lamps not used for a time. Now they have been blacked halfway down the sides. A useless precaution. Our house is now heavily curtained everywhere except on top floor, where curtains are most needed. I only do what I can there, servants being incurable. I saw a regiment moving on Friday. Wretchedly badly made, cheap-looking uniforms. A red coat here and there. Marguerite had a letter from Auguste this morning from Marseilles to say that his regiment was starting in the direction of Belfort on the 20th.

Charles Wyndham and F. Harrison both opened their theatres every afternoon last week and gave only two performances in the evenings. Most other theatres begin their evening performances earlier. From tomorrow *The Great Adventure* begins at 7 P.M. and finishes at 9.45.

Wednesday, October 28th.

F. W. Wile (*Chicago Tribune*) came to interview me yesterday, and

I gave him a scheme for a court of Belgian inquiry to be held at The Hague under ægis of U.S.A. during the war—not to affect the course of the war or to attempt to stop the war.

He told me that T. P. O'Connor told him that the authorities made recruiting in Ireland as difficult as they possibly could. Also that Kitchener, as usual, said the war would last 3 years.

Wounded announced to arrive in a day or two at our hospital, Thorpe Hall.

Wile said that Northcliffe presided every night at the nightly editorial council of *Daily Mail*.

Also that *Chicago Tribune's* first correspondents at the war were collared by German staff and spoilt and became pro-German, and were deeply impressed because they had never seen a big army before. *Tribune* continued pro-German, as 25 per cent of its readers at least were Germans. Took Wile's first impartial article with fear, but it had a great success. *Tribune* had rather forgotten its 75 per cent. Attitude changed.

Friday, October 30th.

On Wednesday I finished the second part of *These Twain*.

This afternoon I wrote my contribution to *King Albert's Book*—Hall Caine's scheme.[1]

Wednesday, November 4th.

Came to London yesterday morning. The Atkinses arrived on Saturday and left on Monday. An impression of off-season half-emptiness throughout West End. Girls driving motor cars. If one thinks about recruiting one soon gets obsessed by number of young men about the streets. Lunch with Pinker at Arts Club. *Price of Love* had sold 6700 in England and 3500 colonial. Season good, at shops; but libraries "obstructive," as Pinker said.

---

[1] *King Albert's Book* was published as "A Tribute to the Belgian King and People from Representative Men and Women throughout the World," and was sold for the benefit of the *Daily Telegraph* Belgian Fund. Arnold Bennett's contribution was *The Return*, an account of his first visit to Belgium and an anticipation of the feelings of expatriated Belgians on their return after the War.

He had seen Conrad that morning, just returned from Austrian Poland. C. had no opinion of Russian army and had come to England to influence public opinion to get good terms for Austria! As if he could. Pinker had also seen Henry James, who often goes to see Page, American Ambassador, in afternoons. They have long quiet talks together. First time H.J. opened his heart to Page, he stopped and said, "But I oughtn't to talk like this to you, a neutral." Said Page, "My dear man, if you knew how it does me good to hear it!" Hy. James is strongly pro-English and comes to weeping-point sometimes.

Then tea at A.B.C. shop opposite Charing Cross. Down into smoking-room. A few gloomy and rather nice men. One couple of men deliberately attacking dish of hot tea-cakes. Terrible. Familiar smell of hot tea. A.B.C. shops are still, for me, one of the most characteristic things in London. *Milestones* on buses again. Same servants at hotels and clubs.

After tea to N.L.C., but I saw nobody I knew. Then, through latest dusk, to Reform, where Rickards and I dined. London not so dark as I expected, owing to lamps in centre of roads throwing down a volume of light in the shape of a lamp-shade (they are blackened at top). After dinner, Ponting's Antarctic cinema,[1] followed by poor war pictures. Provincial-seeming audience. Woman behind me continually exclaimed under her breath, with a sharp, low intake of breath, "Oh," "Oh."

Two nice old Johnnies at Reform Club, phlegmy-voiced, one fat, one thin, quoting Latin to each other over their reading. One said he had a music professor from Liège coming to stay with him—seemed rather naïvely proud of it. Many old men at Reform. Their humanness, almost boyishness, comes out. Lying placards on evening papers. *P.M.G.:* "Great German retreat," on strength of a phrase in Belgian *communiqué* affecting one small part of battle line only.

Thursday, November 5th.

Morning. Print Room, Brit. Museum, to see watercolours by Cotman, Bonington, and Girtin. Several Cotmans were inspiring. The finest thing

---

[1] Herbert G. Ponting accompanied the Scott South Pole Expedition, in charge of the photographic department, 1901–13, and was in 1914 lecturing in London on the Scott Expedition and its findings.

seen was a small sketch by Bonington. These in new gallery of B.M. Very bad direct light. New galleries very ugly and crude.

Then to see Humphreys at Hatchards, where I bought a Baskerville Congreve in 3 vols. There Lucas telephoned me. He came here for tea. Said he had written his *Swollen-Headed William* [1] in 3 hours and that 42,000 had been sold up to yesterday. He is doing a revue for Hippodrome; a cheap production, Harry Tate the only expensive item. He told me about the war visit of Barrie and Mason to U.S.A. It was decided without consulting Spring-Rice (Ambass. at Washington), and Masterman forgot even to tell him of the visit until visitors were within 36 hours of New York. Spring-Rice didn't want anything said by English visitors just then—and rightly. He had the steamer met, and he stopped all talking by Barrie and Mason. Mason returned home at once, and Barrie remained in concealment with Frohman for three weeks.

Then to see Vedrenne (and Berman) at Royalty. Returns of *Milestones* revival bad. Vedrenne said if he couldn't take £400 a week he should close the theatre.

Sunday, November 8th.

The Great Adventure finished its London run last night (673 performances).

I came home on Thursday.

Yesterday sale and show at Frinton, organized by Marguerite for Belgian refugees. Total gross receipts, £82 6s. 7d. and about £3 more to come. Expenses under £5, I think. Opened by Marguerite, who during her speech kept jabbing a pair of scissors into green cloth of table. Hall full of exhibits, plants, flowers, jam, vegetables, and sundries; and of visitors.

I walked out to sea. Lovely afternoon. I went home for tea and wrote most of a war article and returned at 8 P.M. for auction of things left. This auction, worked with difficulty by a good auctioneer, fetched over £8. Young housewives hesitated to buy astounding bargains in fruit, etc. The affair as a whole was a very striking success.

---

[1] E. V. Lucas's *Swollen-Headed William* was published with drawings by G. Morrow.

Tuesday, November 10th.

Alcock came yesterday. He told us a lot about transport work. He said Newhaven port had a huge sealed envelope of orders to be executed on receipt of code telegrams. When the first telegram came, the orders proved to be dated 1911. This was rather good. The orders, as I heard them, seemed excellent.

Telegram that cruiser *Emden* destroyed.[1]

Friday, November 13th.

Last Saturday Miss Nerney began her services at the hospital (Thorpe Hall). She was to work from 7.30 to 3.30 and from 7.30 to 6.30, alternate days. This was adhered to for two days, but afterwards she was kept till 8 each night. She says there is no rest all day. Nevertheless there must be women in the village who could do this work in part. Every other week she has free. As the arrangement of 7.30 to 8.30 every day brought her work for me to a standstill, I gave notice that it would have to be altered.

More wounded came at the beginning of this week, 14 English. There were already over 20 Belgians.

Knowledge of soldiers: a grenadier at Thorpe Hall, wounded, told Alcock on Wednesday that the Germans had a gun with a range of 22 miles!

Monday, November 16th.

Yesterday I received a letter from Maj.-Gen. Heath (commanding South Midland Div.), asking if I would be military representative on Thorpe Division Emergency Committee (for preparations against invasion). I answered I would, but that as I was regularly criticizing the War Office in the press, and might continue to do so, perhaps he would not care to have me. This morning he wired me to meet him at 1.45 at Crown Hotel here. As I was going there two cars full of him and his

---

[1] This German cruiser had done much damage in the East and had kept nearly the whole of Admiral Jerram's fleet in search of her, when she was finally run down by H.M.S. *Sydney* at Cocos Island.

staff passed me. I can't distinguish ranks by uniforms, but most of these men had red round their hats, and I knew that that meant importance. Ryder (landlord) took my card into the room where the officers were. A middle-aged officer came out: "Are you General Heath?" I asked. "Oh, no," he said, rather alarmed.

General Heath then came out, and took me into the room. A man about 55, tallish and thin, with a good grey moustache. He had just begun to smoke a briar. He said at once that my journalism needn't affect the situation at all. He asked me whether I was in favour of civilians sniping at soldiers—"murdering" them. I said emphatically I was not, and that I thought the idea absurd. (Evidently he had read Wells's letter to *The Times* advocating this, and had heard it discussed.) He said he was glad to hear my view, which was his own. Speaking with slight feeling, he said that if he caught any civilian "over there" doing it, he should deal with him. I suppose he meant after the Britons had reached German territory. He then said, laughing, that Sullivan (who was in the room, and on his staff as interpreter!) believed in sniping by civilians. He said one of my duties would be to get intelligence. He introduced me to his representative, Captain Chesney, and thanked me very much, and I said: "Not at all. Not at all. Only too glad," and I departed, after ten minutes.

Later, Bertie Sullivan came here. He said he was doing the same sort of thing at Brightlingsea. He told me of astonishing "coincidences" at B'sea. How on the same day the customs officer's telephone wouldn't work, signalling was thought to be seen from the second martello tower (belonging to a suspicious family) on Beacon Hill, and a man had seen bubbles (indicative of a submarine) in B'sea Reach, and two other coincidences which I forget. Next day the Blackwater was "swept" by the new apparatus for a submarine, also the Colne, but naught found; and in fact there was nothing in the whole thing.

He told me that the Wallet was being closed by a boom. The War Office theory was that if an invasion was attempted it would be within the next fortnight. He said there was absolutely no co-ordination of effort against invasion, and in particular no co-ordination between Navy and Army. Yet almost in same breath he gave me two instances of the Admiralty's informing War Office of certain facts. He said B'sea had between 8 and 9 per cent of its population in the forces. As sergeant of special constables his difficulty was the utter stupidity of people. Men kept writing week after week that B'sea water works ought to be guarded etc. and at last demanded a military guard for it. In the end I think they got it, but I am not sure. Sullivan agreed with me that the chance of an invasion was nil. Also he couldn't see the use of more new armies beyond what we have in training, as we wouldn't arm them etc., etc. He said Kitchener didn't believe in invasion.

Friday, November 20th.

It is said that 40 troop trains went from the South, Cromer-way, to supply troops against a feared invasion last Monday. All I know is that the traffic was considerably upset by troop trains, and newspapers were 3 hours late.

An Emergency Committee meeting for Thorpe Petty Sessional Division called at Colchester for tomorrow, but I received a letter this morning from Capt. Chesney, S.M. Division, to say that it had been found that such divisions were too big and that they would be split up, and would I act as military representative on the Tendring (Thorpe) Police Division. Now I don't know if I am to attend the Colchester meeting tomorrow.

On Wednesday afternoon I went to Burslem to see Mater, reported to be past hope. I saw her at 8 P.M. and remained alone with her for about half an hour. She looked very small, especially her head in the hollow of the pillows. The outlines of her face very sharp; hectic cheeks; breathed with her mouth open, and much rumour of breath in her body; her nose was more hooked, had in fact become hooked. Scanty hair. She had a very weak, self-pitying voice, but with sudden outbursts of strong voice, imperative, and flinging out of arms. She still had a great deal of strength. She forgot most times in the middle of a sentence, and it took her a long time to recall.

She was very glad to see me and held my hand all the time under bedclothes. She spoke of the most trifling things as if tremendously important—as e.g. decisions as if they were momentous and dictated by profound sagacity. She was seldom fully conscious, and often dozed and woke up with a start. "What do you say?" rather loud. She had no pain, but often muttered in anguish: "What am I to do? What am I to do?" Amid tossed bedclothes you could see numbers on corners of blankets. On medicine table siphon, saucer, spoon, large soap-dish, brass flower-bowl (empty). The gas (very bad burner) screened by a contraption of Family Bible, some wooden thing, and a newspaper. It wasn't level. She had it altered. She said it annoyed her terribly. Gas stove burning. Temperature barely 60°. Damp chill, penetrating my legs. The clock had a very light, delicate striking sound. Trams and buses did not disturb her, though sometimes they made talking difficult.

Round-topped panels of wardrobe. She wanted to be satisfied that her purse was on a particular tray of the wardrobe. The Mater has arterial sclerosis and patchy congestion of the lungs. Her condition was very distressing (though less so than the Pater's), and it seemed strange that this should necessarily be the end of a life, that a life couldn't always end more easily. I went in again at 11.45 P.M. She was asleep, breathing noisily. Nurse, in black, installed for night. The Mater had a frequent very bright smile, but it would go in an instant. She asked for her false teeth, and she wanted her ears syringed again, so that she could hear better. This morning she was easier, after a good night, but certainly weaker. Mouth closed and eyes shut tight today. Lifting of chin right up to get head in line with body for breathing. A bad sign.

Monday, November 23rd.

Sisters Campion dined here Saturday. They explained that there were only 60 soldiers at Frinton and that they had a tremendous lot done for them in the way of entertainment and comforts. They said, however, that after quitting the social club at night—cocoa etc.—the men could go to their canteen and get drunk, and did so. These sisters run a Badminton Club, a choral society, the Women's Liberal Association branch, and other things, yet play a round of golf every day. Wesleyans. Father a great Wesleyan. Orphans, with a trustee; live in a little house

with one servant, are very active, and seem to have a jolly fine time.
Almost laid up with a liver attack this week-end.

Tuesday, November 24th.

The Mater died, unconscious, yesterday at noon. The telegram awaited
us when we came back from tea at Mrs. Tollinton's at Tendring yesterday. Cold upstairs room, with bedroom grate—a bedroom used as a
secondary drawing-room. Three great windows. I got near the morsel of
fire. Mrs. Tollinton *mère* a widow with cap. The wife's sister in black,
with a nervous habit of shrugging her shoulders as if in amiable protest
or agreement with a protest or a humorous comment.

Friday, November 27th.

M. and I went down to Burslem for the Mater's funeral on Tuesday
afternoon.

The Mater died about 1 P.M. on Monday.

I learnt from Jennings that the "last journey" had to be "the longest,"
i.e. corpse must always go longest way to cemetery. I asked why. He
sniggered, "So as to prolong the agony, I suppose." Real reason nowadays
and for long past must be ostentation. We naturally altered this.

Walk downtown. Some bricks dry before others. Prominent yellow
painted stone-facings of Macintyre's. Abolition of most crossings in Waterloo Road, to disgust of residents. I saw new Coliseum Theatre. New
window in Mr. Povey's side-room at top of Church St. Church St. was
cleaner and better kept.

Funeral. Too soon. Orange light through blinds in front of room.
Coffin in centre on 2 chairs. Covered with flowers. Bad reading, and stum-
bling of parson. Clichés and halting prayer. Small thin book out of which
parson read. In dim light, cheap new carving on oak of coffin seemed
like fine oak carving. Sham brass handles on coffin. Horrible lettering.
Had to wait after service for hearse to arrive. Men hung their hats on
spikes of hearse before coming in. No trouble in carrying coffin. I kept
Uncle J.L.'s arm most of the time, as he is nearly blind. He told me he
still managed 700 accounts. Long walk from cemetery gates to region

of chapel. By the way, the lodge at gates is rented as an ordinary house to a schoolmaster. John Ford's vault next to Longson, with records of his young wives ("The flower fadeth," etc.). This could be exaggerated into a fine story. No sign of any other coffins, of course, in Longson vault.

Curious jacket and apron of first gravedigger. Second stood apart. Both with hats off. Parson put on a skull-cap. On return, carriages trotted down slope from cemetery, but walked as we got to houses near Cobridge station. "Nest Egg Factory" en route. 2 cottages turned into works.

Saturday, November 28th.

I met Colonel Tabor (of Cyclists) in the road yesterday. He said that the War Office was apparently taking quite seriously the danger of a raid. He said that many officers were now having a few days' leave and that one had breakfasted in the trenches and dined in his club in London.

The Colchester road is being mined just east of the point where the Tendring road branches off. Four or six soldiers digging holes on either side of the road (4 in all), about 4 feet cube. The bridge next to the railway station is also being mined. Twelve engineers in the village, and more to come. B. told us that an officer on Submarine E9, which sank the *Hela,* had told him that E9 only rose to surface by chance, because some one wanted to excrete, and W.C. can only be used when at surface.

Commander refused at first; told man to wait ½ hour. Man couldn't. Boat therefore rose. *Hela* was seen and torpedoed. Such was the tale. It seemed to me odd that defecation on board a submarine could only take place when she was at surface.

Tuesday, December 1st.

On Saturday ended the run of the first revival of *Milestones.* For nearly three years I had had a performance, and frequently two, every night without intermission in the West End of London.

Two officers of the North Devon Hussars came for tea on Sunday, Money-Coutts and Solomon. Both very intelligent. The first writes. The second paints; I showed him all my pictures. They told us of a subaltern of engineers who had charge of a squad of sappers at work mining in the village and that he was billeted in a cottage here and very lonely. I went with them to find him; Michaelis, Australian, and obviously a Jew. Very intelligent and with a sense of humour. He came to dinner on Sunday, and today he installed himself here entirely. He is of the 2nd Field Company (Territorials). Aged only 18. A boy. Yet he is in command here.

Friday, December 4th.

Patriotic concert last night in village schoolroom. Full. All the toffs of the village were there. Rev. Mathews and family dined with us before it. Most of the programme was given by soldiers, except one pro. It was far more amusing than one could have expected. Corporal Snell, with a really superb bass voice, sang two very patriotic, sentimental songs, sound in sentiment but extremely bad in expression. They would have been excruciating in an ordinary voice but he was thrilling in them. Our Lieutenant Michaelis was there, after mining the roads, together with a number of his men. The great joke which appealed to parsons and every one was of a fat lady sitting on a man's hat in a bus. "Madam, do you know what you're sitting on?" "I ought to. I've been sitting on it for 54 years."

This morning, with an endorsement by G.B.S. himself, I received a suggestion from Mark Judge [1] that I should edit Shaw's manifesto for volume publication.

Gales blowing for days.

Sunday, December 6th.

Major Danielsen asked me on Tuesday to write to the press about behaviour of civilians in case of a raid. I did so, and sent the letter to, *inter alia, The Times,* where it made a great effect. Major-General Heath, G.O.C. South Midland Division, wrote me on Friday, saying that he agreed with every word of the letter, but that I ought not to have written it in my capacity of military representative or to have mentioned him as

---

[1] The Chairman of the Committee on War Damage. He published *The War and the Neutral Powers—International Law* in 1914.

my authority. This is very characteristic of the official fear of responsibility. The military are really *very* anxious for their views to prevail, but they don't want anybody to know!

Meeting yesterday of Emergency Committee at Colchester. Representative of police there—an awful, beefy, decent piece of stupidity. I paid for maps for parish councils. Badges for special constables simply cannot be got.

Returning to Emergency Committee, we haven't yet been able to get out of headquarters what roads they will want if there is a raid nor to settle with police what the signal is to be.

I am now fairly *in* the last part of the third *Clayhanger*.

Wednesday, December 9th.

Sub-committee meeting yesterday with H. Sullivan here as to signalling order to evacuate. I found he knew more about handling populace than any one I had yet met. He said, "I ought to have been chairman of the committee." He was right.

Today I communicate with banks as to what they will do.

Saturday, December 12th.

I heard of some documented account of work in trenches, so awful that it could not be printed. Maj.-General Heath, however, said he should send it to some people. Colonel Phipps, who had just left a man who had just arrived from the front, said that in some places trenches of English and Germans were only 5 and 7 yards apart. Heath told me he had got into a row with 3rd Army about my letter to *The Times*. But it was now all "purged." To make conversation, or perhaps because he thought it was the proper friendly thing to do, he began talking about books—*The Crock of Gold*, etc. He had no use *at all* for Wells. I caught 5.41 home. Very wet.

Tuesday, December 15th.

London yesterday. Visit to L. G. Brock, secy. of National Relief Fund, at 3 Queen Anne's Gate. Formerly house of Sir E. Grey.

I then went to inspect establishment of Women's Emergency Corps at Old Bedford College, Baker St. Miss Ashwell in charge. Vast effect of femininity. A general exhilarating effect. The young women badged as messengers, standing in two lines in outer entrance hall, earnest, eager, braced, made a specially characteristic feminine effect. One stopped me at once as I entered and asked me if she could do anything for me and then if I was A.B. I returned by 5.30 train.

Wednesday, December 16th.

Concert in aid of National Fund by Frinton Choral Society last night at Frinton Exhibition Hall. Very bad music, especially the ballads—all appallingly dull. A madrigal by Beale, fine, badly sung. Also in a pot-pourri of national airs, the air *The Minstrel Boy* seemed a masterpiece. It is. Orchestral suite rotten. Two apparently professional female singers sang with some skill the most putrid things; their gestures and facial movements comic, but of course they are too close to the audience in these small halls. The ordeal is too much. Audience asked for a lot of encores, especially of the worst things, that were freely given. The only fun in these affairs is comic remarks to your friends and the examination of all these ingenuous English faces that are nevertheless so difficult to decipher. I imagine all the people in their homes, in natural poses. A few tolerably dressed women in the audience. But for the most part a fright-fully inartistic audience, showing their lack of taste in everything except their reserved demeanour.

Saturday, December 19th.

Major Danielsen and Lieut. Goodhart called on me this afternoon. Danielsen told me that their intelligence department was extraordinarily good and that they had news of the visit of German ships this week at 5 o'clock on the evening before they arrived. I did not, however, under-stand why sufficient big English ships could not arrive in time to deal with them.

From Thursday in last week to last Thursday I did nothing on my novel. I was fairly free to go on with it on Wednesday, but I had neuralgia. I wrote 2500 words of it yesterday.

Monday, December 21st.

Gen. Heath, Col. Ryley and a sub called to see me yesterday morning. Heath, still greatly preoccupied with the question of civilian behaviour in an invasion, showed me a proclamation which he was having printed about sniping etc. He also showed me a draft proclamation to coastal population about bombardment. It was clumsy. I offered, with proper diffidence, to re-draft it. He consented. The others seemed slightly staggered. I posted him the new draft last night.

Two naval officers, Lieut. Hogg and Assistant Paymaster Simmons, on motor bikes for tea. Hogg told me tale of a soldier (cavalry) wounded in a charge, who lay on field with the spear of a lance sticking in him. Another English soldier came along and was asked to remove spear. Just as he started to do so he was shot through the brain. Then a group of Germans came along and began to loot. Without troubling as to the spear, they took the wrist-watch off the cavalryman's wrist, but just then a shell burst among them, killing or disabling all of them, but leaving the cavalryman untouched. He was ultimately saved.

Tuesday, December 22nd.

Major Danielsen came over again to see me yesterday afternoon, with a letter from G.O.C. saying that my amended form of his proclamation about bombardment was much better than his. They have accepted our suggestions for dispensing with the police as a means of transmitting the emergency order. This must have been a great step for Heath to take. Danielsen gave me the secret word with which any emergency order will begin.

Today I heard firing at sea which seemed to be like a battle and not like firing-practice. The first time I have had this impression since the war began, though we have heard firing scores of times.

This is the most gruesome item I have seen in any newspaper. It is from an account of life in Brussels in *Daily Telegraph,* December 15th:

"Since the fatal attacks on Ypres and the Yser a new recreation has been created for the Bruxellois, namely the trains of the dead. These pass through the suburb of Laeken, and go by way of Louvain and Liège to Germany, to be burnt in the blast furnaces. The dead are stripped, tied together like bunches of asparagus, and stacked upright on their feet, sometimes bound together with cords, but for the most part with iron wire. Two to three thousand pass with each train, sometimes in closed meat-trucks, sometimes in open trucks, just as it happens. The mighty organization will not suffer a truck to go back empty; a dead man has no further interest for them."

Referring to the firing, Brig.-General Hoare called on me yesterday afternoon, and, after doing business, asked me if I had heard the rumour that Yarmouth had been bombarded. He had heard the rumour and (characteristically) had started out to trace it and curse the originator. He traced it to the stationmaster at Thorpe, who said he had had it from a Clacton journalist who passed through in the train. Apparently it was quite untrue.

I forgot to say earlier that Maj.-Gen. Heath told me he thought of having a proclamation printed in German for the benefit of invading Germans, warning them that if they did certain things certain punishments would without fail ultimately follow. Rather good.

Wednesday, December 30th.

Great storm on Monday night. We lost 5 trees. A large elm blew across the road, broke telegraph wires, and broke through the vicarage fence, and blocked the road all night. While I was out at 10.30 P.M. inspecting I heard another tree crashing and fled. Old oak fell into the pond.

Thursday, December 31st.

Mr. F., maltster, with £200,000 worth of buildings and stock at Mistley, called with the secretary of his company as to order for destruction of the whole thing in case of emergency. He, of course, wanted a proper guarantee of compensation. His best argument, however, was that a fire would block both the railway and the highroad to Harwich. Speaking of military measures, he told me he had been to the Home Office and that there had actually been drawn up an order to prevent certain things' being imported in this part of the world, lest advantage might accrue to invading enemy. The order was never promulgated.

1915

Thursday, January 7th.

Dr. H. called this afternoon in a great state of excitement: "I've called about a most unpleasant thing. But I thought I ought to tell you," etc. His news was that the village was seething with the news that R. was a pro-German, and taking advantage of his position as chauffeur to the military representative to transmit secret information as to English plans through his sweetheart, a German girl, to the German authorities. H. believed it, or half believed it.

Friday, January 8th.

I wrote to the police inspector last night and he called to see me today. He said he was constantly having complaints about signalling etc., all absurd. I told him that R. was engaged to an English girl and that the whole thing was idiotic. He said he had received a letter about it (signed) and had to make a few inquiries, but expected, of course, no result. A very decent sort.

Tuesday, January 12th.

Captain Bath and Lieut. Way of Ammunition Column of W. Somersets billeted here yesterday. 40 horses in Daking's yard. Bath told me a tale of a party of German officers who spent some time in his town, Glastonbury—I think last year—with a fleet of cars in which they went out every night. They had a field and pretended to be perfecting a process for getting petrol from peat. They showed some petrol stated to be so obtained. Then they departed suddenly and mysteriously. I asked: Why all this? He said it was to reconnoitre the country. I asked why they should reconnoitre the country at night when they were free to do it in the daytime, but he had no answer. Anyhow, he was fully persuaded that it was a great case of "intelligence."

Danielsen came to see me yesterday as to the case of the postmaster at X., an alleged spy. The contents of a military telegram of no importance had been divulged. I knew that this had happened to civil telegrams up there in the past. I sent for the postmaster here and questioned him, but fruitlessly. Speaking yesterday of the difficulty of dealing with spies, Maj. Danielsen said: "It's this damned vote-catching government. They're out to get the vote of the alien." He is a quite honest man and seemed to believe this. That the spy business was the exclusive affair of the War Office and that he was arraigning the beloved K. of K.[1] did not seem to occur to him.

Saturday, January 16th.

London, to see work of Queen's Fund. I took Mary and Richard to London, and Tertia[2] met us at L'pool St. Train late. I have never known the 10.07 not late. Lunch at Mrs. McKenna's.[3] Largish house in Smith Sq., designed by Lutyens. Very bare and lacking in furniture. But there was some good furniture. Present: Masterman, full of good humour; Brock, secretary of National Relief Fund; and Mary MacArthur,[4] stoutish matron, with a marked Scotch accent. I met her on doorstep and introduced myself. I liked her. Mrs. MacArthur had prepared a timed programme of our pilgrimage, with times in it for leaving, like 2.48. We kept to it fairly well.

Sunday, January 24th.

In pursuance of rumour that 30,000 Germans were to land at once,

---

[1] Kitchener of Khartum.
[2] Tertia was Arnold Bennett's sister, and Richard and Mary were his nephew and niece.
[3] Rt. Hon. Reginald McKenna was Chancellor of the Exchequer in 1915.
[4] Mary MacArthur was also secretary of the Women's Trade Union League and of the National Federation of Women Workers.

S—— of Tendring made all his household sleep in clothes on ground floor.

Monday, February 1st.

Meeting of T.E. committee at Colchester on Saturday.

Richmond came on Saturday for week-end to give me all particulars of slacking by members of the Amalg. Soc. of Engineers in war contracts. His firm is making shells, mines, and submarine engines. He said there was not a great deal of money in it, and that the contracts supervision dept. of War Office was saving enormous sums.

Richmond told me that a submarine had attacked Barrow. This must have been the same vessel that sank several steamers in the Irish Sea on Saturday. But nothing as to the attack has appeared in the papers.

Went down to see trenches made by Michaelis's men today.

Thursday, February 4th.

A wealthy maltster called to tell me all he knew about spies and suspects at Mistley. He said there was nothing of the sort, and all he could speak of was one or two people afflicted with "cussedness"—people who *would* argue that the English were no good and that the Germans must win, etc. He saw this cussedness in various forms all over the country. I agreed. But he said that it was all due to the abolition of flogging. He brought ingenious old arguments in support of flogging. The chief was that if you fined or imprisoned a man you punished his wife and children; whereas if you flogged him you punished *him*, and the thing was over at once. He got quite excited on this subject and could scarcely leave. A quiet, nervous man—public school etc.

Saturday, February 6th.

Yesterday Brig.-Gen. Hoare (called the Brig) came to inspect ammunition column's horses. He asked W. full details of every horse. W. only knew about 20. He invented the rest. He says you must never say "I don't know" in the Army. Hoare asked him if horses were getting chaff. He said they were (it was true). When asked how, he was floored and ultimately said he bought the chaff himself. A lie! "I must speak to you about that later." Later Hoare took him on one side and said: "It's very kind of you to pay for that chaff out of your own pocket. Don't do it in future. The proper thing to do is to exchange spare horse-rations with farmers for chaff."

Saturday, March 6th.

I finished *These Twain* yesterday. Doran came for week-end.

Monday, February 22nd.

Friday, Saturday, and Sunday I corrected *These Twain* and cut it from 128,000 to 100,000 words.

Saturday, March 6th.

Marguerite went to London on Monday, and I (in the car, and taking Michaelis) went Tuesday. Michaelis had to go to Braintree for an "explosives course," and *un nommé* Rogers came here to take his place. Miss Weeley as usual came to stay in the house during our absence.

Committee meeting of Allies Wounded as usual on Tuesday afternoon. Before that, lunch with Eve at R. Thames Yacht Club. Good club, with good bedrooms to be had. Met there an infernal bore, red-faced, middle-aged man, owner of a fair-sized and smart cutter at Brightlingsea. He said a vast number of silly things. "When I trust a person, and that person breaks his faith—especially if he belongs to the working classes—then I'm death on him. Now the son of my steward—my steward that I had for 25 years and who venerated me; he kissed my hand when I went to see him when he was ill in bed etc.—now the son of that steward," etc., etc.

Dinner with Atkinses as guests, at Treviglio's. Then to Coliseum, but there wasn't a seat. Then to Alhambra, which was almost empty. A ghastly show. Wet night. Wednesday, National Gallery. Rickards. He and M. lunched at Appenrodt's. I lunched alone. Afternoon, tea at Cedric's. Betty and M. went to theatre together. I dined alone at Reform, and listened to some amazingly dull talk by 3 old jossers at table next to mine. Cedric came to see me there. Thursday, I had Masterman, L. G. Brock, and Lanchester to lunch, and the last explained admirably his scheme for finding work for prof. classes by making surveys of towns. Afterwards when Masterman and I were alone, I expressed to him my notion of the way he had been treated, and he seemed rather touched. He told me that Kitchener was no great shakes. Obstinate, not open to new ideas; no great brain power. But he had the quality of acknowledging that he was wrong, after an interval. Tea at Rickards's. M. and I dined at C. P. Trevelyan's.[1] F. W. Hirst, editor of *Economist;* Noel Buxton, with a new and beautiful wife. Norman Angell[2] later. In the end I should like Trevelyan. My *D. News* article was really appreciated. Norman Angell was markedly affected by the war. When I said that worrying was useless, he became even graver and said, "It's very serious, very serious." He is a good man.

Nothing much Friday morning, except drilling and physical exercising of troops in Hyde Park. Very varied. Echoing of commands over Kensington Water and so on. Drove home in the afternoon.

Saturday, March 13th.

Went to London Tuesday morning. Pinker called at the hotel after lunch. Harmsworths[3] starting a new weekly (he didn't know what—afterwards disclosed as the *Sunday Pictorial*) and they wanted some star contributions—1500 words. They came to him for advice and help. Their idea was Corelli and Haggard! He suggested me at £100 and said I was the greatest and most expensive star. They at once accepted. I wrote the article on Wednesday and it was advertised on Thursday. Pinker offered H. G. Wells, but when approached, Wells said he had already written on the subject suggested, and moreover he was very busy with his novel. In the end the *Sunday Pictorial's* star trio was me, Horatio Bottomley, and Austin Harrison!

---

[1] Charles Philips Trevelyan resigned from the Government in protest at the policies that involved England in the War. He was the eldest son of Sir George Trevelyan, the biographer of Garibaldi.

[2] The present editor of *Foreign Affairs* was knighted in 1931. His most widely read book is *The Great Illusion.*

[3] The family name of Lords Northcliffe and Rothermere.

Lunch every day at hotel. Wednesday night, Bach's *Passion* at St. James's Church. Much material in this assemblage. Performance mediocre, with vast cuts. We dined at A.B.C. restaurant for 1s. 9d. the two, because I had written a £100 article that day. Thursday, Pauline came to lunch. Night: *The Man Who Stayed at Home* at Royalty. Very mediocre. Very well acted. Returned home yesterday.

Sunday, March 21st.

We went to London on Tuesday. Auction sale of pictures etc. on behalf of Wounded Allies' Relief Committee at Hotel Victoria in the afternoon. Spent over £12. Evening, M. went to Kennerleys.[1] Sydney Harrison came to talk at Reform Club after dinner. Very polite and amiable, but a perfect infant in literature. Wednesday, the Morrells to lunch. Evening, *The Man Who Stayed at Home,* with Emily at Royalty. Thursday, Hirst and Lowndes lunched with me at Reform. Afterwards, I had a long talk with Clutton-Brock—a first-class man. Dinner at Websters'. Tremendous Englishness of their house. Came home Friday afternoon. I wrote half an article at Reform Club Library. Knoblock came on Saturday for week-end. On Saturday a new cook arrived, drunk.

Tuesday, March 23rd.

We brought Knoblock to town yesterday morning in the car. Previously I had got rid of temporary cook, a drunkard. Lunch at Reform, where I met G. W. S. Russell and Clutton-Brock. I stayed in all afternoon reading Hueffer's *When Blood Is Their Argument,* which is not good. Dined in grill-room. Then to *première* of Barrie's *Rosy Rapture.* Met Vedrenne, Algar Thorold,[2] Spencer, and Charlton, editor of *Sunday Pictorial,* who said he was, and really seemed to be, very pleased with my article last week. He said that circulation of their second number was a million and a half. *Lever de rideau, The New Word,* quite good in a small way.

---

[1] W. W. Kennerley (brother of Mitchell Kennerley of New York) was born in Burslem and was an intimate of the Bennetts from childhood. He married Bennett's sister Tertia, and is the "W.W.K." to whom *The Old Wives' Tale* is dedicated.

[2] He was then on the editorial staff of *The Truth,* and the author of a few biographies. In 1917 he joined the Foreign Office and served in Italy on a Mission of Propaganda.

Rosy Rapture good here and there, but on the whole very tedious, and mostly conventional. Tons of flowers for Gaby Deslys at the end. On entering I was greeted by cries of my name in the pit. I think this never before happened to me. Much difficulty in getting car at the end of the show. Wet night.

Wednesday, March 24th.

Mair [1] and Sullivan came to lunch. As usual, Mair was full of authentic information on things. Meeting of W.A.R.C., 4–5. Then I went to see Sharp and Squire [2] at *New Statesman* office. Rumours as to its imminent death untrue. They asked me to qualify as a director. I said I would.

Webster dined with me at the Reform.

Thursday, March 25th.

Lunch at Knoblock's. A Marquis de Rosalis, Italian, speaking French and English fairly well, and emitting platitudes on the situation throughout.

Mrs. Lowndes gave dinner at Sesame Club. Mrs. Reg. McKenna, Lockwood (an American Rhodes scholar), us, and Sir George Riddell, who came very late. He said the Press Bureau had sent out a notice to newspapers, asking them to stop being optimistic. On the top of this came the interview (Havas Agency) with Sir J. French, predicting a short war.

Friday, March 26th.

E. V. Lucas and wife to lunch. We went to picture show, "London Group" at Goupil. Cubists idiotic. Some nice things, but all imitative. Dinner at Morrells': Lowes Dickinson, Bertrand Russell, Whitehouse.[3] All these very much upset by the war, convinced that the war and government both wrong etc. Afterwards, an immense reunion of art students,

---

[1] G. H. Mair, formerly on the editorial staff of the *Manchester Guardian,* and later of the *Daily Chronicle,* had resigned from the latter position to work for the Foreign Office. He was appointed to the League of Nations Secretariat in 1919.

[2] Clifford Sharp, editor of the *New Statesman* since its foundation in 1913. J. C. Squire, the present editor of *The London Mercury,* was then a leading contributor.

[3] Lady Ottoline Morrell's house was at this time the centre of a group that included D. H. Lawrence as well as Bertrand Russell and which looked upon the War as a moral crime.

painters, and queer people. Girls in fancy male costume, queer dancing, etc. A Japanese dancer. We left at 12.15. Pianola. Fine pictures. Glorious drawings by Picasso. Excellent impression of host and hostess.

Saturday, March 27th.

Lunch with Clutton-Brock at Reform. Natl. Portrait Society in morning and Natl. Gallery in the afternoon. Dinner with G. H. Mair at Carlton. He is in the secret service, and told us a lot of really interesting things about the war—wireless, submarines, press campaigns in Europe, British spies, etc., etc. He was quite as optimistic as I am.

Sunday, March 28th.

Rickards dined with me at Reform. Then music—Mina Parkes—at his place. F.L. came in, fat, intellectual, and inartistic, and began explaining how Brahms ought to be sung, and rather mucked up the show. I played accompaniments. This morning, R. and Miss Parkes and I were at Westminster Cathedral at 9.45 for the blessing of palms by Cardinal Archbp., and High mass, with an old St. Matthew Passion sung. All this cathedral scene ought to be described in detail. We met Webster. Then to St. Paul's Cathedral, which seemed very English and narrow. I had not been inside St. Paul's for about 20 years. It seemed small, very Italian, and splendid.

Wednesday, March 31st.

I dined with Knoblock at the Garrick and then to Nat. Sporting Club. Digger Stanley *v.* Berry Barnards. Eagerness of seconds. Four seconds for the swell boxers. I met James Pryde and Arthur Morrison, the latter small and shrewd.

Yesterday Swinnerton, with a new brown beard, lunched with me at Reform.

At 6.45 I was at St. Paul's Cathedral to meet Webster for Bach *St. Matthew Passion*. The scene from the stall was superb, with the aged white-haired figure of the conductor (surpliced) at the west end of the choir. Choir boys seated on benches in corners to help in singing.

Thursday, April 1st.

I returned home yesterday afternoon. Lunched with Pinker at the Arts Club and discussed project of me going to the front.

Superb weather.

Good Friday, April 2nd.

Having cleared up all my correspondence and found room for all accumulations of new books, I decided yesterday to get ideas into order and begin my new novel, *The Lion's Share*, today. I was rather disturbed by the prospect of going to the front with G. H. Mair.

Saturday, April 10th.

I finished the first instalment of *The Lion's Share*, 12,500 words, today, having begun it on Good Friday and written an article as well.

The novel is light and of intent not deeply imagined, but it seems to me to be fairly good and interesting.

Thursday, April 15th.

The Ammunition Col. of the Somerset Battery (Capt. Bath and Lieut. Way, officers) left here this morning to go into huts with the Battery at Great Bentley. Last night we went to Marguerite's Soldiers' Club, but very little was going on there, except a gramophone actuated by a young woman who sat between two soldiers. It seemed that many of the soldiers had asked for passes to go out to supper. There must have been many farewells. The woman in charge of the refreshments had the same monotonous faint smile that she always has. Her husband is at the front.

We went and came in the car and met officers with a lamp on their rounds. I walked round by the sea wall, and as I came home old Carter told me that there was a deserter from the Battery and that 8 or 10 cyclists were out after him. He was a young man who hated being in the Army. Still, being a Territorial, he chose it early.

Saturday, April 17th.

Frank Swinnerton came last night. He and I dined together while

Marguerite and Edith Johnston went to dine with Hope at the Grand Hotel, Clacton. Swinnerton told me that all the publishers were in an appalling funk at the beginning of the war, and that H—— sacked half his men and reduced the other half to half salaries. The ghastly vileness of this proceeding ought to be dwelt on. It must have been very common. He said publishers were doing well, and that his firm, Chatto & Windus, were calmly proceeding with their autumn list. Collins's edition of Keats was selling jolly well.

Report in *Chronicle* yesterday that a Zeppelin had dropped bombs on Clacton, on its way to Harwich, in the middle of previous night. Untrue. Miss Nerney, however, coming home from some kick-up at 12.45 A.M., said that she and her friends heard the airship and that it was very loud indeed. They could not see it. I was asleep.

Monday, April 19th.

Owing to alleged existence of a German spy in British officer's clothing and in a car, in this district, order that no officer shall be out at night in a car unless on duty and with the password of the day. Personally, I don't see what good this will do. Highly inconvenient for officers. One officer coming through Chelmsford got stopped on his way to this district. He did not know of order and had no password. He telephoned for help. A dispatch cyclist was sent from Great Bentley to give him the password. This cyclist, although on General Hoare's orders, was not allowed to go through Colchester, and in the end the officer had to get home by train.

Rickards and Pinker came on Saturday. Yesterday, R., P., Swinnerton, and I went for a walk to Laudermere and had drinks at the pub. Pinker told me he had arranged to sell my "front" articles (if I go) to the *New York Times* for £100 each, for America. He also told me that Hy. James had intimately conversed with two men sent on missions by Wilson through Germany. One, unofficial (the "King of Texas," great friend of Wilson's),[1] to ascertain state of Germany (? and Austria); the other, official, to try to arrange something as to complex social relations (Ger-

---

[1] Colonel Edward M. House.

mans with American wives etc.). These two men only met at the end of their work, and in London. They agreed in their observations.

1. German Government had no hope whatever of a victory.

2. German Government was in a "state of *terror*" as to the British Navy, feeling themselves like men in a room from which the air was being slowly withdrawn.

3. Food question likely to be very troublesome before harvest.

4. No first-class leader in Germany.

Wednesday, April 28th.

I finished the 3rd instalment of *The Lion's Share* on Sunday, wrote an article on Monday, and went to London yesterday for Wounded Allies' Committee meeting, at which I was in the chair.

After lunch I had a talk with Spender, who told me that Italy had "signed on" definitely in the Quadruple Alliance. He gave the war another 18 months. I asked him if he kept a diary. He said no. He said that at the beginning of his intimate friendship with Rosebery, Rosebery asked him if he kept a diary. "I'm glad," said Rosebery when he had the answer; "now I can be free with you."

Saturday, May 8th.

Lusitania sunk at 2.30 near Cork Harbour. It was on the posters at 5.45. At first I did not believe it. It made almost no impression on me. Then I went back to buy a paper.

Pinker told me some good new small things about the conduct of the war. He gets most of his information through Henry James.

Wednesday, May 12th.

We came to London yesterday, bringing Pauline Smith.[1]

Shopping all afternoon with Marguerite. Two dresses bought at Selfridge's by Marguerite. Crowds of women in Oxford Street and Regent Street just as usual, and shops just as usual.

The *chic* of the women in Piccadilly collecting for Russian wounded

---

[1] Bennett had written a preface for her novel, *The Little Karoo*.

was quite remarkable, and the total improvement of Englishwomen in this respect in recent years is astounding.

Festival of British music at Queen's Hall last night, alone.

I met Ernest Newman, who was very canny and very himself.

Thursday, May 13th.

Lunch yesterday with Wells and Gardiner at Automobile Club. Wells said he knew that French (Sir J.) believed the war would be over in June. Afterwards with H.G. to Royal Academy. I had no use for Sargents, Orpens, or Clausens. A fairish crowd there. Then to tea with him at Carlyle Club. First time I had been in this club. Furnished in a horrible manner. The tea, however, was good.

Then to meeting of executive committee of Wounded Allies at Sardinia House. It lasted from 5 to 7.35, and Lord Swaythling kept relighting *one* cigar the whole time.

Dined with M. at hotel. Then to reception at Charles Trevelyan's to meet the managing committee of the Union of Democratic Control. But the only member that I found there was Arthur Ponsonby; a pale, light, large-foreheaded man. Seemed surprised when I said that Germans would be beaten and that Government would stand. All these chaps have twisted ideas.

Monday, May 17th.

Saturday, I re-wrote the London-to-Paris chapter of *The Lion's Share*. I added an amusing incident, but did not treat it very marvellously.

I saw coming up Whitehall the Cadet Corps, with many shrill bands, a long snake curving through the Mall into the gardens of Buckingham Palace, where they were to be received by the King. Nearly all were in uniform, and all had rifles. They marched excellently, putting all their brain into marching and marking time. Command from time to time to change shoulders with rifle. Also *left*—right, *left*—right. Also lowering of big drum by white-leather-aproned drummer, sometimes with aid of a companion, to his side after end of a *morceau*.

May and Emily came to dinner. Then Coliseum, which was excessively dull. But we had a good box for 10s. 6d., and the sight of the immense crammed house was very good. Everything in this place is so damned ugly. Genée danced old-fashionedly well, amid rotten scenery. Great difficulty in getting taxis nowadays at night. On three evenings (1) we took motor bus, (2) we took four-wheeler, (3) we took motor bus.

Yesterday I wrote my *Daily News* article, *The Pogrom*, at the Reform Club, lunched there, and slept there afterwards. Very agreeable.

Tuesday, May 18th.

Sir George Riddell sent a man and a car to conduct me to St. Dunstan's, Regent's Park, where Arthur Pearson has established a home for blinded soldiers. Very large place; belongs to an American financier named Kahn. 15-acre garden etc.

Pearson very natty, and a constant and rapid talker. Practically *quite* blind. He may have vague sensations of dark and light. His wife came. He kissed her hand when she left. I liked her. Two blind officers, a secretary of Blind Institute, Pearson's secretary, the matron, a wounded soldier, and the Bishop of London for lunch. The last is certainly clever—for the *mot* particularly. He is, perhaps excusably, deeply impressed by the fact that he is Bishop of London, but he turns it off always into a joke. Thus: "When I get into a car it always breaks down. People say the Bishop of London is a Jonah," etc. "A strange thing for the Bishop of London." Small, thin, sharp face, with small trembling eyes. Ordinary Tory ideas. He told us that every general had told him to impress upon the country that the Army was very short of ammunition, and one general told him he was only allowed 2 rounds a day! He spoke agreeably, with simple wellworn forms of jokes, to the men after lunch about his experiences at the front.

Wednesday, May 19th.

Wells, Archer, and Sep [1] lunched with me at the Reform. Archer, Wells, and I arranged a scheme for an organized protest against yellow pressism concerning aliens etc.

---

[1] Arnold Bennett's youngest brother.

Friday, May 21st.

Yesterday I lunched and dined at the McKennas' and learnt a lot about the crisis. Runciman fine. McKenna and Asquith and others extremely hurt and pained by the crisis. Kitchener not very good. Crisis made by Repington's article in *The Times*. Churchill with French at same time as Repington. Rep's article "arranged." Excellent War Office defence against charge of lack of shells; namely that French, knowing circumstances, demanded a certain quantity, and that this quantity was not only supplied but doubled. Fault therefore with leaders at front. French not now liked by Army, who want Robertson. Battle of Aubervilliers of Saturday, 8th, bloodiest of war. Not a defeat, because men could not be shifted, but we lost 28,000 men. Operation undertaken against advice of other generals.

In evening, after dinner, Hobhouse, Postmaster-General, came in to learn from McKenna his fate, who, however, couldn't tell him. As I had been attacking Hobhouse fiercely in *Daily News*, McKenna saw him alone in the drawing-room. I just caught a glimpse of him.

Saturday, May 29th.

London yesterday for the day. New English Art Club. Very interesting water-colours of Steer etc.

Lunch with Mair at Garrick Club. Mair said that *Princess Irene* blew up with 300 mines on board. He said that whereas Fisher went to bed at 10 and rose at 5, Churchill stayed up later and would come to Admiralty after dinner and alter disposition of ships while Fisher was asleep. Churchill sent in a telegram to be approved by Fisher; Fisher declined to approve it. On the intermediary's suggesting that instead of sending a blank refusal he should draft a new telegram, he did so.

Mair said that Simon was going to be much more strict with the censorship and that it was intended to prosecute *The Times*. He also said that Fisher, on being appointed, ordered 300 craft of various sorts. One firm alone made 24 light cruisers. There are special craft for going up the Danube and special monitors for running over mine fields to attack Cuxhaven.

Thursday, June 3rd.

Dance last night in aid of blinded soldiers and sailors. About 40 people paid, and something over 30 came. Receipts about £11. Curious method of sitting out. Couples went to sit out in the motor cars waiting in the stable yard. Coldish night. The earnest air of young couples, especially the girls, and the short-statured girls sitting about in my study, my bedroom, and M.'s rooms, also on the top stairs, was just as comic to me as ever it was. It is the small girls who seem to take the dalliance so seriously. I danced with six women—a record.

Monday, June 7th.

Now that Zeppelin fatalities are no longer fully reported in the papers, it may be noted (from Miss Nerney's brother, who is in an anti-aircraft train and knows) that eighty houses were destroyed at Sittingbourne the other day and not one life lost.

Official telegram today that 5 killed and 40 injured in raid on east coast last night.

Sunday, June 13th.

The *Strand Magazine* objected to my novel *The Lion's Share* on the ground that it contained suffragette scenes. They held a meeting of directors and solemnly decided that the *Strand* could not print a suffragette serial. However, I think that I have reassured them.

Wednesday, June 16th.

Still waiting for a telegram permitting me to go to the French front.

I was told positively on Monday that Dardanelles were forced. Last night Asquith said that there was no truth whatever in the rumour. This rumour has been very strong.

Sunday, June 20th.

London on Friday. I paid three visits to Godfrey, Mair's secretary, to get my passport for France and police pass, and in the end the police pass was wrongly filled up. The passport had been marked Havre instead of

Boulogne, although no passengers are allowed to land at Havre. Godfrey's calm under these provocations was remarkable.

I leave for London and France tonight.

[Arnold Bennett went to the western front, June 21st, 1915, and was there until July 13th, 1915.—EDITOR.]

Monday, June 21st.

Victoria Station 7.45. Given a form to fill up. Couldn't get a big bag through without registering. People coming off train. Shabby, respectable girls etc. Hot summer's morning. Soldiers, officers. Staff officers on train.

A general: crossed sword and baton with star: "What I should really like to know is how they relieve those trenches at night."

Fine voyage.

My police pass saved me a great deal of trouble of waiting at Folkestone, more at Boulogne. Channel covered with shipping. Boom for several miles outside Folkestone, buoyed at about every 100 yards.

Impression at Boulogne of men of military age not engaged, similar to that at Folkestone.

Arrival of bevy of nurses, white starched muslin blue- and red-edged in car at "Stationary Hospital." Arrival of Army Postal Van, with legends about Y.M.C.A. and Kaiser written with a finger in the white dust on the sides.

Étaples. Hospitals and camp. As English as England. Hay in some places made and laid in cocks. Arrived Abbéville 4.15, having taken 3 hours to do 80 or 90 kil. The whole line, station and scene, makes an impression like perpetual Sunday, except for soldiers and camps.

Amiens. Very old man in a new long blue blouse and swagger check trousers showing beneath, acting as porter and shoving a truck along. Probably had retired and been brought back again.

Paris. I had at first a rather false impression about streets; in big streets over half the shops were closed. Then I recollected that the hour was after 7. A peculiar feeling, certainly, all over Paris. No auto buses, but trams. Few taxis. I saw the horse bus, Madeleine-Bastille, with a woman in charge, bareheaded, and with a great black bag over her abdomen. About 40; on easy terms with the passengers.

Mair and I went to Godebski's after dinner. Godebski would not believe 33 submarines sunk. Very harsh on Italy. Paris even darker than London. Same impression in Paris as in London of young men not in uniform. Plenty of young men in streets.

Wednesday, June 23rd. Paris.

I learnt yesterday that it was impossible to leave yesterday for the front. Gide, Godebski, and Mair came to lunch. Gide intellectually more than ever like an orchid.

General Sketch of Impression of Paris.

View from hotel. Destruction of gardens and architecture; St.-Clotilde. Station. Trees. Young man and woman playing silly ball game in dust. Shops. No buses. Concierges sitting out at night on pavements. Very close and hot, and as it were expectant. Number of young men for various reasons left. Lack of chicory and salt. Sound of guns at St.-Mair-Georges. Variety of uniforms. Bad puttees. Women's heavy mourning.

Thursday, June 24th. Paris.

Dinner last night at Mme. Edwards's. An astounding flat. Ph. Berthelot, Gide, Mair, the Godebskis, and Legrix (young novelist). Berthelot was as mysterious as ever. When I flattered him about *Le Livre Jaune*, he told me that he had to leave documents out. One an absolute prophecy of the course of the outbreak of war, from a Pole, received a month in advance. It was too true for any one to believe that it wasn't a fake. The other a quite authentic statement of the war plans of the Germans, as to aeroplanes, shells, trenches, strategy etc. This was received a year before the war. It couldn't be published because the French War Office had taken no action on the strength of it, though they knew it was authentic. It was tremendous accusation of the French War Office. Only a summary was given in *Le Livre Jaune*.

June 24th. Meaux.

House by roadside, roof damaged, contents taken away by G.'s. Why? What they couldn't take they destroyed.

Trenches. Character of country: rolling upwards. Farms. Wheat, oats, *poppies.* Heavily wooded in places. High horizon of tree-lined roads. Tombs here and there.

Thence to Chambry. Many tombs in wheat and hidden by wheat. Barbed wire on four stout posts (a bird on post), white wooden cross. Always a small white flag. Not always a name. On every side in these fields the gleam of cross or flag, as far as you can see. Scores and scores. Dark green-purple of distant wooded hills against high green of fields.

Cemetery used for firing from. Holes in wall.

Wheat absolutely growing out of a German.

The battlefield is between Barcy and Chambry. Barcy is high; Chambry is low, like Meaux. Round through battlefield German Army was going southeast, and chiefly east.

General impression: How little is left. How cultivation and civilization have covered the disaster over!

June 25th. Paris.

Mair and I dined at Meaux. Lord Esher came in, wearing a fancy military costume—perhaps that of constable of Windsor Castle. A star was depending from his neck. As soon as he saw my eye on it he tucked it inside his double-breasted khaki coat.

We are to go to Rheims on Saturday.

June 26th. Rheims.

Château Pommary.

Trenches at 80 metres apart. German first-line trenches like a road. Champagne proprietor who didn't want me to drink water.

Low, short sound of firing. A little smoke and dust.

Crowded roads. 80,000 men entrenched in front of us. Desolation. Days when 3000 *obus* fell. Shrapnel last week—no good except to break windows.

June 28th. Château-Thierry.

Arrived here last night at 7.20. We took drinks at headquarters of a commandant of whom I didn't catch the name. This drink (lemon and water and sugar) restored me more than any drink I ever had. We did a great deal of rough walking yesterday—estimated 20 miles. I put it at 12.

June 28th. Merval.

German prisoners collecting muck in a courtyard under a guard. When told of possible exchange of prisoners they said, "No."

Ambulance de premier ligne. Tent operating-hospital. Ether smell. This is the first hospital after the *poste de secours* near trenches (30 yards). Some cases operated on here in an hour after wound.

In one case at Tirlemont an ambulance (field hospital) with 200 *blessés* departed in 60 minutes.

June 30th. Paris.

Ravel came to lunch. He is a *second* in autos. He wanted to be in aviation, but his friends would not help him on account of danger.

July 8th. Near Ablain.

Young prisoner, 21, just caught. Trousers and coat pierced by bullet. Consumptive, enfeebled. Called up in Dec. 1914. Examined by officer, then went off with a soldier. Had work in paper factory. Infinitely pathetic. Scared little consumptive. Why military ambition?

Ablain, seen from here, is merely rafters.

Passage of wounded.

After car came to Road 2 Souchez, Germans began to fire on Road 78, high explosives. Searching road at 50 yards' distance or 100 up and down each shot. Almost every 2 minutes, and 1 minute sometimes. Tremendous waste of ammunition. The thing burst before sound of sizzling had finished reaching your ears.

Nearest shot 100 yards.

TROOPS GOING THROUGH SERVIN, 5.45 P.M., JULY 8, 1915
From a sketch in the War Journal

ABLAIN ST. NAZAIRE, JULY 5, 1915
From a sketch in the War Journal

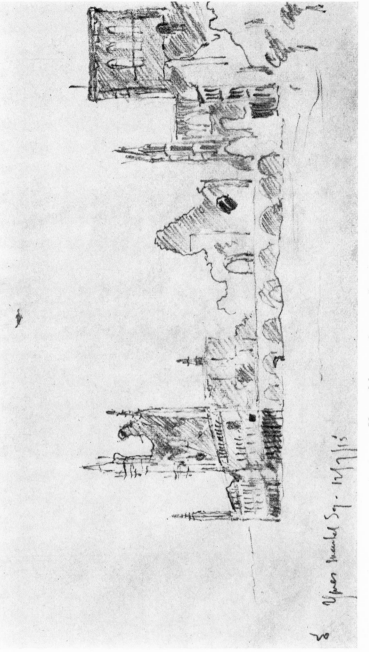

YPRES MARKET SQUARE, JULY 12, 1915

From a sketch in the War Journal

ARRAS TOWN HALL, JULY 7, 1915
From a sketch in the War Journal

Friday, July 9th. Doullens.

405 and 407th Reg. passed through in auto buses, chiefly Berliet. Many roofed in, others with canvas tops, and window holes either empty or mica-ed. Young and jolly.

1200 lb. meat in wire safe per day.

26,000 meals a week.

July 12th. Ypres.

Market place full of people, up to April 22. Acacia trees still flourishing. St. Martin's stands, but irreparable. Only walls left, and tower skeleton. Organ stands. Apse blown out. Vast heaps of bricks in meeting of transept and nave etc. All yellowed by picric acid.

Big guns. Wireless report of shot reaches Germans before sound of explosion.

Boches shelling towns by sections.

Behind cathedral 50-ft. hole by 17-inch gun into graveyard; bones all over hole.

Grande Place—except for one white building (convent) all the rest jagged needles of walls.

Sat in a shell-hole to do sketch in front of convent. Aeroplanes overhead.

High wind. English guns booming. Fitments in houses creaking and rattling and cracking.

Houses full of disordered belongings.

On ramparts, dug-outs, birds lustily enjoying odour of gas from shell. *We never saw a Boche aeroplane.*

Friday, July 16th. England.

I returned home from the front yesterday, after 2 nights in London at the Savoy. By the evening I had dealt with all arrears.

The *Strand* people are obstinate in their objection to *The Lion's Share*. On the other hand, the *Metropolitan* (New York) are delighted with the work, and openly say so.

Considerable movement of troops round about here. Towns apparently being fortified etc. General coming down from London to confabulate with Brig.-Gen. Hoare on the spot. A current belief that the War Office expects a raid from the German fleet. I don't think the War Office does. If it does, why does it let the Somersets go a whole year without firing a single shot of any kind in practice?

Thursday, July 22nd.

Mysteriously and intestinally ill for a week. Unable to work. Convalescent this morning only. Miss Weeley told me yesterday at dinner that all the bees had died in this district, and that the reason was they had not been "told" about the war.

It appears that bees should always be "told" about deaths in the family and other important happenings; otherwise they will die. She met a woman in the road with a lot of honey and asked her how it was that she almost alone had succeeded with her bees. The woman said: "Ah! But as soon as the war broke out I went and told my bees all about it." Miss Weeley believed in this superstition. Edith Johnston said that her parents had lost 7 hives out of 9.

Monday, August 9th.

After my return home I was ill with colitis until the end of July and in bed for 9 days. I did not resume my visits to London until August 6th, when I had a long talk with Spender and Masterman, who agreed that not only was the Russian administration corrupt, but the War Office was thoroughly Germanized until after the beginning of the war. Even Witte was pro-German until Turkey came in. Spender said Russia had 7 million men trained but not armed yet.

Renewed activity up this coast about preparations for invasion. Generals came down from town, and I had communications with Lieut.-General Sir A. R. Martin, K.C.B.

Saturday, August 14th.

London. Masterman lunched with me at Reform.

W.A.R. Committee. George Whale [1] joined it. Tea with Pinker after it.

Then long talk with Dr. Brend afterwards. He had brought over wounded from Ostend in October and was very impressive about official incompetence. A positive man; rather agreeable.

I dined with Clifford Sharp at Romano's. He told me that Brooks had told him Brooks was in Northcliffe's room when N. himself dictated the *Daily Mail* article about Kitchener, and that it was very much stronger then than in print. It seems Northcliffe, having no sons, is very keen on his nephews. He has already lost two in the war, if not three, and he regards them as having been murdered by Lord K. When remonstrated with about his attitude to Lord K., he burst out, "But he's murdered my nephews!"

Saturday, August 21st.

It now appears from my official correspondence with headquarters that in case of invasion the military people have not yet got their transport into order; they admit that it will not be in order for 2 months, and they are still "going to" indent. They want to indent from this coastal division, where transport is already inadequate and any evacuation would be very sudden. I am trying to stop them.

Also, without any corresponding change in the arrangements for evacuation, the direction of the evacuation has been taken out of the hands of the committees which organized it and put into the hands of the police, who know nothing about the arrangements.

Pinker told me that British Army now held 160 miles of French front; that new horizontally effective bombs were now perfect. War Office had said that no bombs could be effective at 50 yards away on the level. Inventors said it could. Bomb made and tried. An officer was to let it off electrically at 70 yards. War Office protested that he could not be in danger. He was killed—hit in the breast by a bit of projectile.

Also great muddle in landing at Suvla, Dardanelles. Troops 24 hours late. Otherwise they might have got right across peninsula. Fearful row.

---

[1] Solicitor, ex-mayor of Woolwich, and one of the founders of the Omar Khayyam and Pepys Clubs.

2 Generals sent home. I talked somewhat with a Russian in N.L.C. (in French). He had great blame for his countrymen's administrators—*"ces voleurs."*

Thursday, August 26th.

An oldish woman was carrying a pail of water past the nearest cottage of the row of cottages on the left of the Harwich road; at Thorpe Green.

"It don't get no nearer," said another woman within the cottage.

She was referring to the well in the field, two or three hundred yards away, which supplies these cottages with water.

"No, and it don't get no lighter," said the water-carrier.

"It's too far," they agreed.

So it is. There is a water-main runs down the road or very close to it; and yet these cottagers have to carry water a ridiculous distance in pails. It is astonishing that they don't contrive a water-cart on wheels, easy to push. To get enough water for a bath would take a woman several hours by the present system.

The chaplain to this brigade told me yesterday at tea in the garden that he was very friendly with Y.Z., the composer, and that Y.Z. would ultimately rank with Wagner. He was arranging for the performance of one of Y.Z.'s works with due solemnity when somebody told him that this composer's alleged wife was not his real wife, who still lived. The chaplain had to retire from direction of arrangements, but he was not acutely disturbed. He said to Y.Z., "Don't you think you could make a clean breast of it and explain things fully to people?" And Y.Z. did so to the organizers. He explained how he could not work when living with his real wife, whereas now, with No. 2, he had composed so-and-so and so-and-so. Further, No. 2's money was necessary to his material existence. Whereupon somebody in the room offered to give an income to Y.Z. so that he could quit No. 2! The thing had not been settled when the chaplain last heard. I asked if Y.Z. was a communicant. He said: "No, he doesn't quite know where he is. He's trying to find himself. I tell him to take his time."

Yesterday I finished sixth and last article on the front.

Saturday, August 28th.

The other day, when I reminded an officer concerned with emergency arrangements here that a secret word had been given without which no order to evacuate was to be considered genuine, he replied that he had never heard of such a word, but would look into it. This is a good example of official negligence. Had I not brought up the matter, the whole emergency scheme might have been vitiated if an invasion had suddenly taken place.

To Harwich yesterday. I took a map in the car. I asked sentry at entrance to search the car. He declined. Nothing said as to maps. No printed notice as to maps. On leaving, I was stopped and sent back with a soldier to headquarters. Maps were not allowed. The A.P.M. himself had seen me looking at the map. The attitude of the A.P.M. and another official, who both interviewed me, was grotesque, and I have written formally to wake them up.

Wednesday, September 1st.

After over a week's delay I received my first article on the British front back from the censor at G.H.Q. With the exception of about three words the whole of the censoring struck me as entirely futile. I keep the censored copy as a curiosity.

Thursday, September 9th.

Yesterday I finished a supplementary article (hospital) on the front. I am now quit of all this, except that I may write a preface for the book form. I can now turn to the last half of *The Lion's Share*. Besides this I have my next (London) novel in my mind, and my war play, which will advance every time I think about it for an hour.

I read a year or two of De Goncourt's journal recently. Very good. In fact it had the finest effect on me when I was exceedingly annoyed.

Saturday, September 11th.

Tea with Pinker at A.B.C. He told me about a new and marvellous brand of British mines that would float into German harbours, but wouldn't float out again.

During the day, from Davray, Waller, and Rickards, I got information as to Zeppelin raid on Wednesday night.[1] Davray on roof of the Waldorf. He said Zeppelin was fairly low over roof. Searchlights on it. Star-lights. Fairy-like. Shots at it. Then it rose and went northwards. Spectacle agreed to be superb. Noise of bombs agreed to be absolutely intimidating. And noise of our guns merely noise of popguns. One bomb in garden of Queen's Sq. had smashed windows and indented walls and smashed window frames on three sides. Two hospitals here. A lot of the glazing had already been repaired. Much damage at Wood Street, Cheapside. I didn't see it. Two motor buses demolished with passengers. Rickards, who went out at 11.15 (visitation at 10.50—he was in bed and went to cellar), said it was very strange to see motor buses going along just as usual, and a man selling fruit just as usual at a corner. People spoke to each other in the streets. Waller said streets near bomb in City were two inches deep in glass etc. I didn't see damage in Theobald's Road. It appears there had been a raid over New Cross on Tuesday night. Queen's Square was rather like the front—Arras, for example.

Mrs. T. to lunch. Her father, a bishop, has just lost his wife. A grand-nephew was told to write condolences to him. The boy, aged 11, wrote first: "Dear Grandad: I am very sorry Grannie is dead, but we must make the best of these things." Told that this wouldn't do, he tried again: "I am very sorry Grannie is dead. But you may be sure she is far happier where she is." This also being condemned, he wrote a conventional letter about Grannie having always been kind to them all, etc.

Wednesday, September 15th.

Zeppelin excitements nightly. It was said in the village that a Zeppelin hung over the village church for an hour on Monday night, but I did not believe this. A station porter, however, told me that they could see a Zeppelin on Sunday night, as it passed. He said that another Zeppelin or

---

[1] On the evening of September 8 a number of Zeppelins raided London and the suburbs. Considerable damage was done, 20 killed and 86 injured.

some Zeppelins had been signalled for that night (Monday). It was dark when I talked to him on the dark platform. (They had had instructions as to lights by telegraph.) The only lights were the reds of the signals, high up. I asked him as to Marguerite's train. He said that the train had "asked" for the line and would arrive soon. This mysteriousness of unseen things known to be coming—such as Zeppelins and trains—was rather impressive. Then suddenly a red light changes to green in the air. Two engines attached to each other rumble through the station. Then M.'s train. And after a long delay Marguerite's silhouette very darkly far down the platform.

Monday, September 27th.

Capt. B. called late last night. He said he had heard that the *Mauretania* had been sunk with 6000 soldiers on board, but did not believe it. He liked telling it. He said that a friend of his, commander of a T.P.D., had told him that 21 German transports had recently been within a comparatively short distance of the English coast. "They got away again 'by a miracle,' " said the commander. "I can't give you particulars, but it was a miracle." The commander told him that in the affair he had been responsible for sinking 10 German submarines and that 11 were sunk altogether. All had double crews. I said to Captain B., "Did the commander tell you this with his own lips?" He replied: "He did. He is a friend of mine." B. said he believed the transports were empty.

B. also related how a man who had gone to the Dardanelles had promised to send a bit of blue ribbon in an envelope as soon as they were forced. No word. Just the blue ribbon. Thus no trouble with censor. Well, the ribbon arrived on Friday, and the man who had received it (in police force) had himself told B. yesterday of the incident.

Saturday, October 2nd.

London yesterday. Tailor's. Then to McKenna's for lunch. Reggie came in late and left early. There were also Marguerite, John Burns, and a young doctor whose name I missed. McKenna was very strong against conscription. He said it would lose the war. He said the army was already too large for our resources, that the demands of the Allies were always growing, and that the financial strain was very great. John Burns was in great form and less vain than usual; in fact, scarcely at all vain. He gave most amusing and convincing pictures of artisan family life, etc. He said that when he had been buying a book too many he would leave it at the club and then take it home last thing at night, after his wife was in bed, and hide it.

Then to National Liberal Club to meet Percy Alden, M.P., who interviewed me for a syndicate of papers. He said there were only two things he could do really well, sail a small yacht and control a meeting. Driving with him to Liverpool St. Station afterwards, I heard of his speechifying tour round the world. He said that in Japan he saw a factory where between 2000 and 3000 girls were employed. Girls gathered from country districts with dreams of town life, flower festivals, etc. These girls worked in two 12-hour shifts, night and day, Sundays included. They slept in huge dormitories. The sight of them, dirty, dishevelled, crowded, asleep in the dormitories—and the Japanese by predilection such a clean and neat people—was awful. It was absolutely forbidden to leave the factory at all. They were bound for three years (sort of apprenticeship), and they earned $2\frac{1}{2}d$. a day, of which $2d$. was deducted for food. Food chiefly consisted of soup with fish-tails and heads therein, bodies of fish being reserved for managers etc. When he talked to a big Japanese statesman about industrial conditions, statesman (I forget his name) said that there was no need for trades unions in Japan as all Japanese loved each other so much that abuses would be impossible. Alden said things had slightly improved.

Home by restaurant train.

Monday, October 4th.

Mrs. Green today said that she had been talking to a young sub at Queen Alexandra's Hospital, Millbank, wounded in Dardanelles. He told her that one day they had to put up wire entanglements and there were no posts. A number of stiff corpses of Turks were lying about. They upended them and stuck them into the ground like posts, and fastened the wire to their heads. Mrs. Green said to us, "What will the youths of 19 be like afterwards, who have been through this kind of thing and got used to it?"

I should say that in most respects, and to all appearance, they will be like others who have not been through it.

Started 6th instalment of *The Lion's Share* today.

Saturday, October 9th.

Left home at 10 A.M. and drove over slippery roads in a Scotch mist to Little Easton. I walked with Wells in the park at dusk. Stag rutting season. All the bucks were roaring like lions, and we were somewhat intimidated. Two of them made a show of fighting, but funked it. Before this, original ball games in the arranged barn, in front of which a farmyard and cesspool had been turned into a very sightly sunk garden with bathing tank in the middle.

Immense park, belonging to Lady Warwick, and practically wasted for useful purposes. And there must be hundreds such.

"It ought to be taxed out," said H.G.

Tuesday, October 12th.

I returned from Wells's yesterday morning and wrote my article in the afternoon. I had a great time there. There were about 18 people to hockey on Sunday afternoon. Newman Flower, of Cassell's, came on Sunday for the night, and Clarkson, chairman of National Steam Car, and others, came for supper on Sunday night. It is Wells's tremendous energy that makes the place so entertaining. If there is no real talking, then he must instantly play at some game. I played at Badminton, hockey, his own patball, etc. He has turned a barn and a farmyard into something very nice, and a great "escape" from the house. He works in his bedroom at a very small table and has a primus stove to make tea there. He sometimes gets up and works in the night. The house is partly steam-heated and is fairly comfortable and very bright, but some of it is badly planned and arranged. It is like a large cottage made comfortable by people rich but capricious. H.G. drives a car very indifferent bad, but he enjoys driving.

Saturday, October 16th.

London yesterday. Show of French drawings about war at Leicester Galleries. I bought a Hermann Paul for 8 guineas. The Forains were very fine indeed. 50 guineas each.

Monday, October 18th.

Capt. K. and Capt. B., stationed here, recounted the Zeppelin attack on their camp in Epping Forest. It was apparently brought on by a light in the officers' mess. It seems that the Zeppelin hung over the camp. It dropped several (4 or 5) explosive bombs right in the camp, a few feet (under 20) away from where K. actually was. None of these bombs exploded. They buried themselves 10 feet in the earth. They were excavated without accident. K. said the soldiers used pick and shovel in digging them out, with perfect indifference to the danger. The Zeppelin also dropped a number of incendiary bombs which the soldiers put out as they fell. It seems to me that the fact that incendiary bombs were dropped shows that the Zepp did not know that it was over a tented camp. The object of setting fire to tents is not clear at all, as the men could easily get away and the damage would be inconsiderable. The explosive bombs weighed one hundredweight each, and the incendiary bombs about 15 lbs. each. K. said he could not assert that he actually saw the Zeppelin. He said the men saw whole fleets of Zeppelins. Apropos, Rickards related last night that Webster came across a crowd in the centre of which was a man pointing to the sky and raging excitedly: "There she is! She's hit! She's hit!" Webster said, "You think that's a Zepp, but it's the moon." The crowd dissolved.

Tuesday, October 26th.

Mr. and Mrs. H. G. Wells came for tea yesterday and left after lunch today. He told me he regarded E. Carson as the really sinister and dangerous figure in politics today. Immediately after it was established that he would not compromise on Home Rule the Austrian note was sent to Serbia. Germany thought she was safe so far as concerned England.

Last week Gardiner kicked against my article showing the financial danger of recruiting. But he printed it in the end, unfortunately cutting out the very part in which I saved myself by blessing the present recruiting campaign and expressing the hope that only at the end of the 6 weeks' trial would recruiting be stopped.

Friday, November 5th.

Chrysanthemum show here yesterday for the Red Cross. Only our own plants. About 60-odd people. A singer who came from London for her expenses, £1 1s. 0d. Of course far more women than men, but still a few men (and officers). It was a success, £23 net. But it is a strange, though ingenious, way of getting money. The people could afford more by paying directly, like income tax; but they prefer to pay more indirectly; that is, to indulge themselves in amusement while "helping the cause." There is something to be said for it.

On Wednesday night my new bookshelves in Miss Nerney's room were inaugurated.

Monday, November 8th.

Lieut. E. came to dinner last night. He had had eight months at front at Armentières and Ypres. Only about 2 officers left out of his original lot. He said they spent 12 days in trenches and 6 out, but frequently 14 or 16 in and 4 or 2 out. They had to walk about 10 miles to and from trenches with 90 pounds on their backs; on arriving in trenches they were so tired that they didn't care whether they were under fire or not. But the return journey was worse, as they had had no exercise for nearly a fortnight, being in trenches. In rest huts, no beds. They had to sleep on wooden floors, so that they hated these rest-huts and preferred the dugouts. He had been out over six months (I think) before he got leave at all. He then could not go to sleep in bed until about 4 A.M. and was strongly tempted to lie on floor, but refrained. Also, being in a room put him off sleep. He said food was fairly good. But Tommies used to put the bully beef on parapet of trenches. The supply of it, of course, could not be stopped. Everybody liked "Maconochie" rations, veg. and meat, which could be taken hot or cold. A certain amount of looting. He took a clock valued by a Harrod's furniture expert out there at 80 guineas. But he left it. He also had a camera. His company commander made him send his camera home so that he could report no cameras. But this C.C. fell ill, and his substitute never asked about cameras; so E. sent for his again. He has a lot of photos. He was particularly calm, simple, measured, and *posé* in his demeanour; he gave very good descriptions, and exaggerated nothing.

Friday, November 12th.

On Wednesday at tea Mrs. M. described the luxury and liveliness of life in the European colony of Shanghai but afterwards admitted that its scourges were typhoid and abscess on the liver. Most of her best friends she had lost through typhoid (males, that is). Later she gave me her views on men and women. She was bringing up her little sons with the idea that they must be nice and helpful and protective to all women. They thoroughly understand that at the earliest moment they must buy a motor car for their mother. She is afraid of scandals, being a young and attractive widow, but gives cocktails to her assembled friends every Sunday morning in a place like Frinton! She said there were three things any man could give to any woman without fear of being misunderstood —flowers, chocolate, music. She was great on what women could expect from men. Doubtless owing to her widowhood. She lamented that labour was so dear in England. "It was because the working classes lived too well." I expect she has all the usual colonial social political ideas. In the end she displayed a pleasant conception of life—limited to her own class, of course. The general impression of her ideal was very agreeable.

Wednesday, November 17th.

Yesterday morning, barber's. Reform. Directors' meeting, at noon, of *New Statesman,* Shaw, Webb, Simon (large employer at Manchester), and Clifford Sharp. Shaw said we ought to attack Asquith. Said we ought to make Haldane P.M. Shaw had no conception of public opinion at all. Afterwards, in the street, he told me he had talked like that as a "hygienic operation" and that it was necessary to exaggerate in such hygiene; he wanted to stir Sharp up. He said he went to Torquay sometimes for a holiday and worked harder than ever. The fundamental decency and kindliness of Shaw were evident throughout.

Sunday, November 28th.

London on Thursday. Drummond Fraser, managing director of Manchester & Liverpool District Bank, told me positively that America had quite failed to take advantage of chance of becoming the world's financial centre and that after the war everything would revert to England as before.

Saturday, December 4th.

London, Thursday. Slept at R.T.Y.C.[1] Very good. I finished *The Lion's Share* on Wednesday night and slept very ill and was really too fatigued for London, but I took a tonic, which did me good. Max Beerbohm lunched with me at Reform, and I urged him to start on some cartoons.

Tuesday, December 7th.

Came to Manchester by Midland 4.30. On arrival at Central Station a young officer who had slept and in between had made much litter in the train was met by his family, one by one. First father. "Hello, Dad," etc. Dad was a tall, thin, grey man; they kissed. Then little sister running along; then big sister, more reserved, but very welcoming, with a touch of sisterly superiority. All this was a very agreeable sight on the worn wooden platform, strangely out of date, of the Central Station.

Thursday, December 30th.

I wrote 272,200 words this year, not counting journals. I had the best book and serial year I have ever had (though I didn't issue a single new novel), and by far the worst theatrical year since before *The Honeymoon,* I think.

I finished re-reading *Esther Waters* last night, after a bad bilious attack. It still vigorously lives.

---

[1] The Royal Thames Yacht Club.

1916

Saturday, January 1st. Comarques.

Masterman had lunch with me, and R. Ross[1] joined us. Masterman said that in the still existing crisis, McKenna and Runciman had both actually resigned, as they could not get a guarantee that the army should not be allowed to exceed a given total, they being convinced that we could not financially carry on unless a strict limit was set. Asquith then implored etc., wrote letters etc., and the subject was reopened.

Wednesday, January 5th.

After an immense day's work on Monday I came to London with M. yesterday. The Italian *maître d'hôtel* of the restaurant spoke with amazement and respect of the British. "They spend as much as ever. We are doing more business than in peacetime. They do not look at their bills. They do not inquire about prices. They pay. They have money. They can afford to wait and make Germany wait. They never give in. They always win. They are prodigious!"

At night my second visit to *Romance* with Doris Keane in it. She played even better than before. She has a most powerful personality. Yet afterwards in her loge, embracing and stroking Marguerite, whom she had never seen before, she told us that she thought she had played rottenly. After 9 performances the previous week she had got gastritis and

---

[1] Robert Ross, journalist and art critic, was the executor of Oscar Wilde's literary estate.

had taken practically nothing but hot water for 4 days. She is a very attractive woman.

Saturday, January 15th.

I went to London Wednesday and returned Friday and was ill nearly all the time with dyspepsia. Edward Garnett lunched with me on Wednesday. He said he had an important matter to discuss. It was a project for a weekly penny political paper to tell the truth about politics. He wanted me to give up everything and edit it, also to start it and organize it. He had the title and a plan of contents, including chiefly a series of "Fables for Liberals." He had written the first fable himself. When I asked him what he would do, he said he only meant to contribute, himself. He was quite sincere and had not begun to suspect that the scheme originated in his idea for a fable about Liberals who had lost their trousers.

From the Reform I went to the *Statesman* to discuss with Sharp the notion of some plainer writing about political facts. I had previously seen McKenna's brother, who told me that Reginald was still quite determined to leave the Cabinet if it tried to outrun the constable. He indicated that the financial situation was exceedingly grave.

At night I dined with Atkins, who told us he had met an old friend that day, an American journalist named Marshall whom he had known in the Cuban War and who had been shot in the spine in a very interesting way, so much so that it ought to have been impossible for him to live, and two medical books had been written about him. He walks with a stick or sticks. This man was coming to Europe journalistically, and Bernstorff had him in at the Waldorf-Astoria and said to him, "You can have £50,000, not dollars, before you leave this hotel, if you will go to Europe in German interests." Marshall refused. Bernstorff then went further and told him he could have the biggest journalistic scoop that any journalist ever had; namely, he should be taken from Belgium to Berlin in a Zeppelin and there have an interview with the Kaiser and be brought back. Marshall refused. Atkins said he knew Marshall very well and vouched for his honesty. The Zeppelin excursion was afterwards accepted by another American journalist, whose name I forget, but he died in the Zeppelin on the way. Atkins also told us that Lord Cromer had told him that an English officer out in Russia on military contracts business found himself absolutely unable to do the business without baksheesh to officials, which he refused to give. He then managed to see the Tsar, who affected great surprise and went over the heads of the officials—but how long the Tsar's arrangement "worked" Atkins couldn't say.

Tuesday, January 18th.

Came to London yesterday with M. Lunched at Reform and saw Spender and his new contributor, whose *noms-de-plume* are Action Front and Boyd Cable. He writes descriptive stuff very well. I should say a good soldier, very earnest and obstinate and lacking in humour. He said that the Flanders campaign had done good to the Indian soldiers because it had shown them what western fighting was and how little chance a mutiny could have.

This was *en route* to Assault-at-Arms at National Sporting Club in aid of W.A.R.C. The place not full. Very few ladies, though a ladies' night. Two British and one Russian nurse. The former jealous of latter, who had to stand on platform while her postcards were being sold for £5 and £10 the set. Bookmakers and similar people bought, and allowed to be sold again, a Shetland pony, dogs, a stamp collection. A music-hall star, in an evening dress with a red tie and worn-out boots, was auctioneer part of the time.

Saturday, January 22nd.

Too ill in London to write any notes. I even forget what I did. We dined at the Carlton with Dorziat [1] and Knoblock. She is a little worn physically. Very intelligent and amusing and natural. Then to an absolutely dreadful Scotch play at Royalty, *Bauldy*. As bad as *Bunty* and longer. We saw Eadie, Vedrenne, Vernon, Eaton, and others. Wednesday I lunched with Doran and Messmore Kendal and Wells at Savoy. H.G.

---

[1] Gabrielle Dorziat, the French actress, appeared several times in England and also played in English.

held forth on the future of N. and S. America. Eaton came to tea at Berkeley and explained his triumphant progress. At night (M. having returned to Thorpe in order to go to the Colchester Hippodrome) J. R. Richmond dined with me at the Yacht Club, and we went to *Il Trovatore* at Shaftesbury. Very old-fashioned, with a few good things. Horribly conventional plot and acting. I walked to hotel in thick rain. Thursday, Doris Keane came to lunch. I learnt a lot about her and got some general ideas as to how to write a play to suit her. She said she was very fond of women—and also of men too.

On Friday after a third sleepless night I lunched with Methuen at the Reform. He told me *These Twain* had sold 13,350 in the first week. Some rotten reviews. Apart from other things, the book is too jolly true for some people. They say it lacks the ideal, and mean that it refuses to be untruthful. Several of the best critics have noted this with satisfaction and laudation.

Monday, January 31st.

I only found out last night that Swinnerton was really interested in music. Vernon came up on Saturday. Very military. Yesterday morning I drove him and M. and Swinnerton to Frinton. In the afternoon Corfield persuaded me to go out for a ride with the officers and Vernon. First time across a horse since end of 1902. We went to Frinton. Very fatiguing for me. I did some work before dinner. In the evening piano and discovery of Swinnerton's interest in music.

Friday, February 4th.

I went to 47 Bedford Sq. yesterday morning to see Roscoe, secretary of Teachers' Registration Council. A downright Midlander, with traces of accent. He gave me information for articles on education. The whole feel of 47 is now changed—for the better. Clearer and brighter everywhere.

Lunch at the Reform. I saw Methuen, who said that the Publishers' Association had unanimously decided to issue novels at net prices and at prices varying according to length—from 4s. 6d. net to 7s. 6d. net. I don't think it will work, at 7s. 6d. net anyhow.

Two committee meetings at W.A.R.C. Lady Paget came over half an hour late. She is a master-woman, and well accustomed to command. Every one says she is an unrivalled "beggar." She enunciated her principles of begging, ruthlessly. They were excellent. She is now starting out to collect a million for blind soldiers. If she gets £5000 from our Caledonian Market Show I shall be far more than satisfied.

Monday, February 7th.

On Saturday night great excitement about two men who, challenged by sentry of the ammunition park near the station at 7.15 P.M., had run away. Ammunition of all the district is kept there, including 300,000 rounds of rifle, etc., etc. The marauders vanished, though pursued. Clacton was called up by telephone and kept up most of the night. Officers were called from dinner. The missing men were supposed to correspond with 2 escaped Germans interned from Dorset. The one best seen had a rope and walked noiselessly—hence rubber shoes! Why? Etc., etc. No capture yesterday either. The funniest thing is that one of the guard, or perhaps it was the sentry himself, says that the marauder must be a German, because when he challenged, the fellow distinctly called out "Von."

Way and a Dr. G. of R.A.M.C. came for the day yesterday. The latter bald, thin, big nose, self-assured, goodish talker, but too interested in his own doings. He had not been to Dardanelles, but recounted tales of champagne luncheons, together with rude lack of hospitality to visiting officers, of the administrative staff (seventy-odd) stationed permanently in a ship at either Mudros or Imbros. They had very bad reputation. Soldiers could not get fresh potatoes, though vast stores of potatoes were rotting not far off, because lighters were plied by staff for their sporting excursions. And so on.

Thursday, February 10th.

Came to London yesterday. First good, clear frost of the winter. Very sharp. Lunch at the Reform. Pinker came. Methuen joined us about alleged coming "revolution" in price of novels. It seems that of the council of the Publishers' Assoc., who had suggested it, only four published novels at all, and none published novels on any scale. Characteristic. We told him that the scheme of different prices would never work and coached him as to what he should say at the grand meeting on Monday.

Then to W.A.R.C. offices. Difficulty with Lord X. as to my having put name of Queen Alex. on posters for concert. I flatly disagreed with him, whereupon he said I was logically right, and I drafted a letter for him to write to the Queen.

Friday, February 11th.

E. McKenna gave me an idea for a novel. I pointed out the defects of it, and he was going to think it over further. I met Atkins coming out of the Travellers' Club. He said *These Twain* had kept him from his proper amount of sleep and that every episode in it was true of every husband and every wife. Then 3¾ hours of Wounded Allies' Relief Committee. Rush to Treviglio's at 6.50, where M. and Webster dined with me. Thence to Stanford's new opera, *The Critic*. Thoroughly rotten. The only fun is in the clowning, and this to the accompaniment of music without a spark of humour. One or two primitive musical jokes. Scarcely an original air in the thing, but when he borrows an air from an old song, how fine it sounds!

Monday, February 21st.

Haymarket concert in aid of W.A.R.C. at night. This went off without a hitch, and I was very glad when it was over. I had no particular trouble, but I will never organize another. The theatrical element, Ainley and Nelson Keys,[1] had a much greater success than the musical element. The latter was naturally jealous, but could not help peeping and hugely enjoying the former. One is more struck than ever by the forced cordiality of all greetings and all praise in this *monde*. Miss Ada Crossley, the oldest singer there, has very great charm, and she got the first encore. After Ainley, people began to go, and after Nelson Keys a lot went.

---

[1] Nelson Keys became known to the American public through the very popular first *Charlot's Revue*.

These two had each more than one encore and occupied a great deal of time, so that the concert was not over till 10.25.

Sunday, February 27th.

Went to London on Wednesday afternoon last without this volume. Snow. Dined at Lord Swaythling's. About 12 diners. I sat between Viscountess Camperdown and Lady Asquith. Bad music. Lord Chancellor [1] came late, and informally, straight from House of Lords. He came up to talk to me—said he had often seen me at the Reform. He gave me the best praise of *The O.W. Tale* I ever had *viva voce*. He said he knew Asquith liked my late appreciation of Asquith. I said I didn't always praise ministers, referring to my slanging of himself as head of Press Bureau. He seemed to catch this and smiled. He is a captivating man.

Walker came at noon to discuss Shaw's idiotic proposal for a coalition of intelligentsia. W.A.R.C. meetings all afternoon till 7, after a lunch with Masterman about an article I was to write for him in U.S.A.

At home we learnt that small German raids expected. All local garrisons doubled. Two batteries in the village, etc. Great excitement. I had heard nothing of this in London.

Tuesday, February 29th.

As regards the great invasion scare. The two batteries "stood by" yesterday morning from 4 A.M. till sunrise and today from 5.30 A.M. till sunrise, all ready to move off—except that bits weren't in harness. The assistance which came in a hurry from Colchester here consists of convalescent wounded gunners from the front, appointed only to light duty and to extreme emergency duty. In the fatigue of yesterday's field day (which was utterly useless) the wounds of two of the gunners were reopened. It is considered that the early morning standing by is connected with high water and that some attempt at a landing is feared. Only the Ammunition Column remains in Thorpe. The two batteries have taken with them 100 rounds per gun. The rest is stored in our outbuildings.

---

[1] Lord Buckmaster.

Saturday, March 4th.

Went to London Wednesday. Lunch and sleep at Marriotts'. Then national "economy" meeting at Guildhall, where I sat next but one to Barrie. McKenna spoke well but too slowly. Kitchener read badly a speech which had been prepared for him. Balfour was pleasing.

Then a meeting of the new Art and Industries Association, at Art Workers' Guild. Some of the Labour people were funny. The representative of gold and silver workers drank too much. A successful working bookbinder slanged trades unions. Turner of Shop Assistants was good. A working man got up at the end, and having evidently screwed himself up to the point, said angrily that nobody had asked him to speak, a plain workman, and that most awful bosh had been talked and that nobody there understood working men.

Saturday, March 11th.

Birthday dinner at Mrs. McKenna's. Short dinner, but 3 man-servants. Birrell, very boyish, with much grey hair and short of a front tooth; decided, gay, wary. Edwin Montagu [1] and wife, both very Jewish. Diana Manners in a low-necked short frock, with no shoes and stockings. Nothing seemed to be known about future of war, and McKenna didn't seem to believe in a smashing of Germany; but Montagu did. Montagu rather diffident and quiet. It was stated that nobody *could* be worse at the War Office than Kitchener. He wasn't even a brute.

Friday, March 17th.

To Grafton Gallery, where the most mixed show (Allied Artists' Assocn.) you ever saw. Good modern things and cubism, and the rottenest amateurishness of the worst old-fashioned kind. For instance, a cat sitting on a polished floor, and necklace thereon, with the title "Reflections." No Strand picture dealer would have dared to put it in his window. The place was ready for a reception to Pachmann. I don't know how we managed to be let in. All the snobs began to arrive. We

---

[1] Second son of Lord Swaythling and financial secretary to the Treasury.

left then. Tea at Hatchett's. Then to Westminster Cathedral for even-song. Beautiful darkening empty building, very sad, and a sing-song by six priests and their leader. I dined at the Reform, alone, and alone to the Alhambra. Very empty. *Les grues* allowed to sit in back row of dress-circle. London very wet and dark and many *grues* mysteriously looming out at you in Coventry Street. Impossible to see their faces at all.

I slept at R.T.Y.C. Thursday morning, long séance at barber's. Then to W. Nicholson's. He was in a black leather jacket, covered with paint. He gave me the portrait of Wish Wynne that was used in the production of *The Great Adventure*. He showed me some most ingenious still lifes and Eric Kennington's biggish war picture—very striking.

Monday, March 20th.

The Ammunition Column received the order to depart on Friday night at 10.30—to leave on Saturday. The actual departure, which we witnessed between 5.30 and 6.30 P.M. on Saturday, was a striking proof of the vast inferiority of horse and mule traction to motor traction.

One mule wagon had to be unloaded twice, as the mules wouldn't or couldn't draw it. General mix-up and dinting of gate-posts. Part of confusion may be the fact that the O.C. had lost both his subalterns and had to do everything himself. However, he had an excellent sergeant-major. On one wagon was perched his servant, holding his dog under one arm and a parcel of a large photo under the other. The departure had the air of a circus departure badly managed. Then, of course, on arrival at Weeley (2 miles) they had to take everything to pieces again.

Meantime new units were coming in, and it was getting dusk, and an officers' mess was being fixed up roughly at Culver House. The melancholy of evening over it all, but it was a warm evening. Few drops of rain. Then in darkening village you saw groups of men with piles of kit-bags lying in front of them, waiting to get, or trying to get, into Workmen's Club, where a lot of them billeted.

Lovely night. Bright moon. Trot of a horse occasionally till late.

Wednesday, March 22nd.

According to the Swedish betting, this is the day, at least, on which the German fleet ought to come out.

I received a letter from General Martin, chief military representative for Essex Emergency Committee in case of invasion, this morning, asking me to give him a few more copies of the Tendring Division Instructions, drawn up by me, to be used as a guide for other divisions. This shows that instructions have not yet been issued in some divisions. I thought ours were very late, seeing that the W.O. instructions were revised over six months ago. Also it seems strange that the W.O. should depend on the chance of the instructions in one division being competently drawn up, for the example of other divisions. You would have thought that the Central Emergency Committee would have drawn up a model set of instructions. However, the incident shows that literary merit is appreciated, even in military circles.

Friday, March 24th.

On Wednesday night a Welsh vet officer came here to sleep. 60. Very provincial and polite and talkative. All about Lloyd George [1] and Wales and Stanley Weyman. Just like middle-class provincials in Potteries, except for accent. Speaking of billeting in Manningtree, he said that billetees had to cook for soldiers, while not finding the food. *"Now, many of them didn't like it,"* he said with sympathy and conviction, as middle class speaking of and understanding middle class. It was absolute Five Towns. No member of upper middle class would have said it like that. A member of upper middle class might have laughed, or said it indulgently, or said it comprehendingly, but not with the same unconscious sympathy.

Saturday, April 1st.

Today I began on construction of *Carlotta* play for Doris Keane.

Last night about 8.45 we heard a rattling of windows. denoting distant explosions. We at once thought of Zeppelins.

---

[1] Became Secretary of State for War in 1916.

This morning the post was 80 minutes late, and at 11.45 the newspapers due at 9 A.M. had not come. No sound of a train yet heard. Rumour of a raid with 18 Zeppelins. Magnificent spring morning.

Friday, April 7th.

The end of winter was very sudden last week. On Tuesday last week was the worst blizzard for 50 years (in which our car got smashed up against a tree that had fallen across the Colchester road); snow, slush, etc. And on Saturday the sun was very hot and the roads full of flying dust. Just like summer, even to the E. and the N.E. wind.

I really "got on to" first scene of *Carlotta* play on Wednesday.

Friday, April 14th.

London yesterday. Interview (with Mrs. Scott) with Selfridge [1] in his office. He is very proud of his Information Bureau. He wanted the Christian name of the superintendent of Islington Cattle Market. He got it from his Information Bureau in about 3 minutes. There was a small closed roll-top desk in his room. It is his son's, aged 16. Boy now home for holidays from Winchester. He was upstairs learning accountancy. He takes a boxing lesson every day at 12.30. His father showed us photos of him at his desk in various attitudes, including the attitude of dictating to a girl clerk. I continue to like Selfridge.

Wednesday, April 19th.

Dr. Slimon reports to me that at the meeting of chairmen of Emergency Committees and military representatives at Chelmsford on Friday, which I could not attend, under the chairmanship of General Paget, Paget insisted on the strong probability of an invasion between Harwich and Maldon in July or August.

The naval opinion at Harwich, I hear, is that the Harwich flotilla could not deal with the covering ships of an invading force and that, so far as the Navy was concerned, the force would land and the convoy

---

[1] H. Gordon Selfridge, the American-born owner of one of London's great department stores.

be taken in the rear. It is also said that the German submarines are trying to mine the course of the proposed expedition and that we are sweeping their mines and mining *contra*.

Pauline Smith came on Saturday, having lost her luggage on the way. Voice perhaps feebler than ever. She is highly intelligent.

Wednesday, April 26th.

In addition to marking the opening of the water-colour season, yesterday had some importance in the war. About midnight (previous) an orderly came on a motor bike and looked in the front garden. I challenged from the window. He had an order for Lieut. Myers to report at once at the Orderly Office. Myers was up all night. Then in the morning's papers was the news of the capture of Sir Roger Casement in an attempt at gun-running in Ireland. Then Myers came in with the news (which he had overheard on the telephone) that a German fleet had been within five miles of Lowestoft between 4 and 5 A.M., and also that Zeppelins had been over. Then General Y. and 2 of his staff called to see me. This was in the middle of breakfast. Y. wanted information about the emergency scheme for the civil population. He said he had nearly ordered the evacuation of Frinton, Walton, and Clacton, in the night. I gave him some documents and also wrote him later in the day. One of the dangers in this district is that some one like Y. may try to order an evacuation, either when it isn't necessary or in a manner contrary to the military authorities' own instructions. It was characteristic of the Army that *I* gave him his first copy of the instructions ordered and approved by the Army!

Then came telegram with official news of a short naval action off Lowestoft. Then came telegram that Betty Sharpe had had a daughter. Then came the daily French telegram. Then came telegrams of riots and seizure of the post office at Dublin. Then came telegram as to Zeppelins. To continue the tale, this morning I had a letter from A. G. Gardiner practically putting an end to my connection with the *Daily News*.

By the way, the cyclist who called up Myers, going immediately afterwards to Frinton without any lights (as ordered), ran into a car and broke both his legs and fractured his skull. He is supposed to be recovering.

Friday, April 28th.

London yesterday. Very warm.

At the barber's, while I was being pedicured in the inner room, a young voice came in and asked whether it could cash a cheque for £1. Yes. Well, pay the cabman and have the luggage brought inside, and send down to ——'s and ask for the box of cigarettes that was ordered by Mr. A. The voice, rather high, kept on all the time. Its hands were being manicured. Then it was called to the telephone. A Mr. Barlow. It sprang with enthusiasm to the telephone. It trembled while it greeted "dear old boy." It explained that it was going down to Windsor by the 1.15 to play golf and would return that day but didn't know whether it was expected to play after lunch or after tea. It would "love," "love," "love" to do something with Barlow in the evening. Time passed. It was 12.45, and anxiety for the train began. A friend came in, evidently to join the Windsor excursion. Certain shopping had to be done on the way to Paddington, but evidently this was given up. A taxi was ordered, and it was ordered to be turned in the direction of Piccadilly, and luggage was to be put in. Then one cigarette was to be taken out of the cigarette box and the box put in a certain bag. At last the voice left. What change remained out of the sovereign, or how the voice would get to Windsor, I don't know. By the way, to save time, the cheque was filled up by a member of the staff so that the voice should only have to sign it.

Went to see Lady Paget at 35 Belgrave Square. House in holland covers except one room, in which she saw me. Open door answered by chauffeur, who raised his hat and came into the house to do it. Decent woman; not much humour, but commanding. We got on excellently. She slanged the idleness of society helpers and believed most in American women for charity. She is one.

I came home by 6.38 and had three beef sandwiches at one end of the journey and some cold bread and butter pudding at the other. I walked into Red Cross concert at Vicarage Hall and was instantly called on to sing a comic song, which I did.

Tuesday, May 2nd.

The MS. of *Helen with the High Hand* sold for £27 at the Red Cross sale at Christie's on Friday. This was the last day of the sale. Bookseller Beaumont bought it. Galsworthy's MS. of *The Freelands* sold for £26.

Friday, May 5th.

London yesterday. Mair mysteriously telegraphed me to go to an "important" luncheon at the Garrick to meet a Swedish author. During morning he telephoned that it would be at the Savoy. The author was Brunius. Also present George Alexander, H. B. Irving, W. L. Courtney, another Swede living in England, named Valentin, I think, and Mair's colleague, Carnegie. I had to sit next to Brunius. He seemed a very nice, sound, provincial chap, with pretty bad English. But what the luncheon was for, and why such a strange gathering, I haven't the least idea. It was a Government luncheon, in a private room at the Savoy. Brunius specializes in Shakespeare, and he had come over for the celebrations. Alexander is very well preserved and behaved with great restraint (especially for an actor or any sort of *artiste*); quiet voice. Tells a story lengthily and without a spark of originality, but with effect. I had to leave at 2.50 for meetings.

Invasion alarm getting more acute on this coast.

Monday, May 8th.

Reading Marcel Dupont's *La Campagne* last night and night before. There is no genius in it. 40th edition. But it gives a plain notion of what war is, and some things are moving. Curious sensation lying in bed reading this, nightingale singing violently across the road, and horses and motors passing at intervals, and the thought that exactly similar scenes might be occurring here at any time, and that *this* house might be a ruined château and that *our* furniture might be defiled by German officers. At any rate according to the theory of the War Office. A period of extreme vigilance now on. It is a pity here that at new moon high water is at midnight. If high water was at 6 A.M. at new moon the periods of vigilance would be fewer if there were any at all. One night out of three our lieutenants have to spend at the telephone in the orderly room—8 P.M. to 8. A.M. The defensive works are being increased all along the coast.

Friday, May 12th.

London yesterday. Lunch with the brothers Buxton.[1] The elder told me the younger (my opponent as to pacificism in the *Daily News*) had ruined his sight in reading up land facts for Lloyd George's Land Valuation. He cannot read at all and can write very little. He looks much younger in every way than the bearded M.P. I like both of them very much. The younger thought the Reform Club "uneconomic"—especially the hall—evidently he has very little æsthetic sense.

On the way to Sardinia House a man overtook and accosted me. It was Coveney, once articled clerk at Le Brasseur & Oakley's. I had not seen him for 23 years at least. I knew him at once, and he me. It is true that he had written to me about a year ago asking if I was the A.B. he knew. He told me that Sparks, whom I put into *A Man from the North* as Albert Jenkins, was now a middle-aged man and apparently very able.

Mrs. Selfridge and Olga Nethersole at the W.A.R.C. sub-committee. Olga fat and oldish, with lightish hair, puffy face. She spoke well and sensibly. Mrs. Scott said she had a beautiful house and evidently plenty of money—I don't know where from.

Saturday, May 20th.

I slept at Reform Club. "Kemp! chamberlain!" Kemp is an ageing little man; very precise. "Did you know Mr. Henry James, sir?" Well, this was his room (next to mine) for fifteen years. Of course he had it beautifully furnished. In the morning Kemp came in and brought tea

---

[1] Noel and Charles Roden Buxton. They were both sent on a mission to secure Bulgaria's adherence to the Allied cause in 1914–1915, and they collaborated in a work on the Balkan situation.

and arranged everything in the small room (it really *was* small), and then walked to door, turned round at door, and said formally, "Your room is quite ready, sir," as if you didn't know. He is very careful lest he should give you anything to do, or too much to do. He doesn't say, "If you'll ring, sir, I'll do so and so." He says, "If you'll *just touch* the bell sir," etc., etc.

Friday, May 26th.

Some weeks ago Davray, official press agent of French Government, asked me to write an article on conscription in England. He laid down the lines, which he had taken from previous articles of mine in the *Daily News.* I wrote the article exactly on these lines and he was most enthusiastic about it. It was for *Le Temps,* which the Government now controls. The French censor turned it down entirely, and Davray in a letter to me this week gives the censor's actual words. He says the figures were not official (which they were) and might give rise to polemics; moreover, that conscription was now accomplished and there was no more to be said. But he had kept the article since before the final conscription bill was brought into Parliament. The censor's reason for refusing the article was, of course, purely political. This article gave the arguments on both sides; it stated that conscription—certain to come—would not greatly increase the army—and spoke of the necessity of trade, munitions, etc. The censor didn't like that.

The article would have cleared up misunderstandings into which the French public have fallen. The censor didn't like that, either.

Another curious example of rumour: that passports to soldiers on leave were now endorsed with the words that if the war ended before the leave ended the soldier must report at such and such a place, etc. This rumour, on reflection, is transparently idiotic for lots of reasons; yet many people believed it. I half believed it. Pinker believed yesterday that peace negotiations were on the way.

Monday, May 29th.

Talking with Captain ——, brigade major, last night, apparently an intelligent man, I mentioned the corruption of the Russian administration. He said, "Well, we aren't much better ourselves." I then learnt that he believed that Essen was not attacked by our aeroplanes because Asquith holds shares in Krupps! And yet one is expected to discuss politics seriously with such intelligences.

Thursday, June 1st.

Lieut. Myers told me yesterday that the gas officer came down yesterday to inspect gas-helmet efficiency of troops down here. Asked what would be the effect of gas on horses, he said he didn't know. And he an alleged expert. He afterwards found out from a man in the A.S.C. who had been at the front what the effect was. Myers pointed out that the whole A.S.C. here had only 25 helmets. The gas officer said that that would be all right and that as soon as an alarm was given the necessary helmets would be forwarded! I seem to see it!

Sergeant Humberstone had his son down here yesterday. Humberstone has been all his life in the Army—Coldstreams etc.—and is called "Dad" by all the other non-com. officers.

His son received a commission on the field for gallantry. When he came home, considerably knocked about, and met his father, his father saluted him, whereupon the son threw his arms round his father's neck and kissed him. During his visit here, father has introduced him with restrained pride to Myers and others. Humberstone is a very nice old man.

Monday, June 5th.

A brigade staff captain, speaking of invasion last night, said the Germans were expected to try for it in August and not before. He said they were waiting for a chance all last year. 3 Army corps had been practised in landings for a very long time. The finest troops. But lately, one corps, or part of it, had been taken for Verdun. Asked how he knew all these things, he said, "Intelligence." He spoke of a marvellous intelligence man named ——, now at Harwich, with whom he had talked, and who had recently penetrated the German lines, disguised as a woman, etc. He said the German plan was to land 40,000 men in one mile of coast. Lighters, containing 1000 men each, to be towed over by destroyers. Gas shells. Monitors with 15-in. guns to destroy our coast positions first. He said we had done an enormous lot within the last few months, but that six months ago there was nothing and the original British plan had been to let the Germans penetrate 20 miles or so before tackling them. Now the plan was to stop them from landing, and he thought we should do it. He said they would probably try two places at once—here, and near Newcastle-on-Tyne. Nothing he said altered my view that they couldn't reach the coast at all. I told him this, and he said he was glad, but that all precautions had to be taken.

The Captain said the district was full of spies, which I thought exaggerated. He said tennis lawns were inspected as gun positions prepared, but they had never yet, in digging up a lawn, found any trace of preparation. I should imagine not. The buried gun and the prepared emplacement stories show the inability of staffs to distinguish between rumours probable and rumours grotesque.

Thursday, June 8th.

Came to London Tuesday morning for the Wounded Allies' "War Fair" at the Caledonian Market. Heavy shower. Great success. I sold books at M.'s stall. After 5.30, crowds of young women came to look at books and some to buy. One well-dressed man had never heard of Balzac. Demand for Kipling, Chesterton, Conrad, and me. Difficulty of selling autographs. Enthusiasm for Jepson's *Pollyooly*. Met Pett Ridge, and he looked just like an actor. Various estimates of profits of 2 days, but you can see that the men keep estimates lower than their hopes. Thus Mr. Henry—£8,000 to £15,000. Selfridge estimated attendance first day at from 25 to 30,000. I agree. Yet one man in charge of a gate said that through that gate alone he estimated that 30,000 people had passed. And so on. There were not enough goods, nor stalls. The place looked nearly empty when I arrived, and remained so. It was too big. I did a very good trade in books, but I brought down prices at the end considerably, and autographed favourites were going for 3s. and even 2s. 6d. Habit of women of squealing out in ecstasy over name of a book and then refusing even to consider the purchase of it. Perhaps they were so startled to find that they recognized a title.

News of Kitchener's drowning came at noon on first day. His sister Mrs. Parker was at M.'s stall, but she had left before it came. The rumour in the afternoon that Kitchener was saved roused cheers, again and again. . . . The Fair did not agree very well with my advertised descriptions of it, but it went excellently despite weather, and refreshments were fairly well managed. Bank took £800 of silver alone in car to bank on first night, and 4 or 5 men were counting hard all day.

Monday, June 12th.

Brig.-Gen. Y. dined here last night. He has been a soldier all over the Empire. He said: "I wonder whether they'll give votes to soldiers after the war. . . . The men who do the bulk of the work of the Empire never get a vote because they're always away. Kitchener, Curzon, Milner, never could exercise their votes before they were lords," etc. This was quietly said, but meant. It certainly gave a point of view. It showed a feeling. Of course Y. is in favour of all fit men of military age joining, and thinks tribunals ridiculous. But he is very quiet over it. Equally of course, he sees only the military argument. He has no imagination, no prophetic view, no wish for a better England, except militarily. But he must have done a certain amount of work in his time.

Friday, June 16th.

London yesterday. Spender told us some funny stories of his personal relations with the Kaiser. He said that in a talk about theology, the K. insisted that Boyd Carpenter was our greatest theologian.

In the railway carriages of the G.E.R., after 22½ months of war, they have at last got notices warning about spies and overheard conversations.

Tuesday, June 27th.

C. G., poet and friend of Larbaud, came to see us on Sunday morning. He ought to have arrived on Saturday, but had difficulties with police. He said that a prominent lady of Lyons (his native town) had urged that it was essential that the Croix Rouge should keep its character *mondain*. That in the *midi* most ladies went in for a little mild *croix rouge par pur snobbisme,* and then only in the mornings; afternoons for amusements. He said that the arrangements for wounded were still bad and had been appalling. He gave dreadful first-hand descriptions of wounded journey-ings. He said all French officers were in the first place dandies and in the second place afraid of the *jalon supérieur,* etc. Jealous, and careless of their men's lives; and that thousands (tens of) men's lives had been use-lessly lost simply because C.O.'s did not like to risk the reproach of inactivity. His indictment was terrific and almost wholesale. In brief—men splendid, officers rotten, system bad and corrupt. At the same time he said that the defence of Verdun was one of the very finest things of the war—sublime, etc., etc. But he apparently saw no contradiction be-tween these two attitudes or points of view of his. Much truth, or some truth in all he said, but no perspective, no realization of the good side.

Thursday, July 6th.

Not very optimistic about the big push,[1] which began last Saturday. Was told that minister's secretary had seen a telegram, and told him, to the effect that troops had once more overrun the points at which they had been ordered to stop. I didn't hear at what point or points this occurred.

Friday, July 14th.

London yesterday. Selfridge was extraordinarily eloquent and sane on the matter of the relations between employer and employed. But he was very jealous on politics. He said whenever politics came near their store they trembled. Asked by me what he considered the sphere of politics, he said politics was to govern. Apparently the immense difficulty of defining politics had not occurred to him. He has no trades unions to deal with. He said he gave a lecture at Leeds University and that the atmosphere was clearly hostile to employers. There can be little doubt that the condition of affairs in his store is just about ideal.

---

[1] The great British offensive along the Somme front.

Monday, July 17th.

I finished the *Carlotta* play yesterday morning.

On Thursday last I had a dictaphone installed here.

Saturday, July 22nd.

London, Thursday. Lunched with Pinker at the Arts Club. Club pretty empty. But before this, I walked through the City to Pinker's via Gracechurch St., Monument, etc. Places I had scarcely seen before. Very interesting and material for next novel. Tremendous impression of wealth and of common sense.

I sent *Carlotta* play to Doris Keane last night.

Friday, August 11th.

A fortnight ago last Wednesday we began my first holiday since the war. Slept at St. Pancras Hotel, which is rather like a church inside, with the longest corridor I ever saw.

Next day: Glasgow via Midland because it alone has kept restaurant carriages on its trains—I mean the three Scottish routes. St. Enoch Hotel. Fine suite for 25s. Richmond took us to the Alhambra, at the instigation of Marguerite. I was unwell through sleeplessness next day, so instead of visiting shell works we motored to Loch Lomond and so on. Very successful. Weir dined with us, also Richmond. Next day, Marguerite did shell works in morning. We lunched at W. Weir's, and in the afternoon went with Richmond to his new house at Blanefield, Kirkoswald, Ayrshire.

We stayed at Blanefield from the Saturday evening till Thursday morning. I soon got an effect of the county of Ayrshire, with its own character and industries. It is proud of its agriculture, especially potatoes. Ayr is a granite town, rich, with a good bookshop—out-of-the-way water-colours therein. Turnberry golf course, with big hotel, said by some to be the finest golf links in the world, is about 4 miles off Blanefield, on coast. Diversion from domesticity is to dress up and go there for dinner. I played a few holes (averaging 12) with parson of Kirkoswald.

Parsons have evidently more prestige in Scotland than in England. This one, though a mediocrity, had a lot, and "carried" it well. Absolutely old-fashioned in his ideas, I was told, but he has travelled. His greatest fault was the small joke. Beautiful church by brothers Adam, but when I said it was beautiful he seemed quite surprised, though of course agreeing.

Burns lived in Kirkoswald for 6 months "to complete his education"; so it has fame, and the churchyard draws people—I forget why.[1] Parson's house full of agreeable old things. Many books, but not a good collection.

We also went to Culzean Castle (Marquis of Ailsa). Superbly situated, right on the edge of the sea. Large. Built by Adam. Magnificent, and splendid rooms. But several generations of owners had done nothing to furnish it worthily, and the modern side stairs were terrible in every way. The main stair and the oval well are lovely. I did one or two water-colours at Blanefield, mostly very bad.

Thursday to Airemore, in Strathspey, right in the Highlands. A panorama of Cairngorm mountains in front of hotel. Very fine.

We left for Edinburgh on Monday and were much pleased with Edinburgh. An old driver, a shade drunk, drove us over all the town, and was most informing and useful. Great contrast between the fineness of Edinburgh and the dowdiness of Edinburgh and the dirtiness of its shops and cafés. Its site has really been *très bien compris,* and its natural advantages, scenically, are terrific.

On Wednesday we went to York, and had a very taciturn driver. I got some ideas for my next novel. At Edinburgh and York we stayed at railway hotels. In railway hotels as regards food the thing to do is to stick to the grill and the sideboard, which railway companies understand, for lunch and dinner.

Thursday, August 17th.

Yesterday I cycled to Frinton to see the shooting of the R.F.A. The target was the Frinton lifeboat, about 300 yards out. The guns were at

---

[1] Douglas Graham (Tam O'Shanter) and John Davidson (Souter Johnnie) are buried there.

Coldharbour, north of Frinton, range of about 2500 yards. L. seems to know nothing about artillery (yet he was in H.A.C.), and he was made observation officer so as to save him from having to shoot. He could not observe. He had no notion of observing, beyond marking a plus or a minus. The R.G.A. subs explained things to us, and were useful, at any rate to me. Half the shooting being over, a policeman was clearing people off the beach because of the danger. Last night at dinner I had the account of the shooting itself from one who had had to do some of it. He said the observation officer was supposed always to be a first-class gunner, as everything depended on him, but that an observation officer was not really necessary in this case (direct fire etc.). The generals were kidded accordingly. There were three generals. One of them knew nothing or little about gunnery. He made a great noise, and wanted a great noise made—explosions, and to see shells dropping in the sea. He told the gunners to fire quickly, and to remember that this was not manœuvres but war (which happily it was not). He constantly deranged Gen. Y.X., but Gen. Y.X., being a thorough expert, and not to be ruffled, went ahead and gave quiet orders to the gunners, ignoring Gen. Z.'s notions. Z. wanted rapid firing. Y.X. said, "What is the use of your firing the next shot until you know exactly what was wrong with the last and why?" Y.X. was evidently the bright spot in the proceedings.

What strikes me is the inability of all these generals to control themselves. They behave like kids with autocratic power. People like French merely dashed round, stayed 2 minutes and said, "Excellent, excellent." The whole body of subs is against the plan of defence, and calls it silly.

Speaking with Mason as to this, I said that it seemed improbable that the staff should be all wrong and the subs and captains right (though I agreed with the latter), and Mason said it was not improbable because the subs had had experience and the others hadn't. I think I have forgotten to mention that the observing officer was not informed that the lifeboat was not the target and that the target was an imaginary point beyond it.

Tuesday, August 22nd.

Invasion alarm Saturday night. Warnings to local units in the morning that there was Zepp activity. Second warning, instituting P.O.V. (Period of Vigilance) in the afternoon. At 11.30, after men in bed, orders came to R.G.A. (heavy guns) to take up positions at Frinton. In 45 minutes they had departed. This was good. Their guns were in position at 2.30 A.M. Nothing doing. They still regard the whole scheme of defence here as grotesque. At 3 P.M. Sunday P.O.V. was called off. In the meantime German fleet had definitely retired and we had lost 2 light cruisers.

Sunday, August 27th.

London last Thursday. At 4 P.M. S. S. McClure came by appointment and had a talk. He was very laudatory about England. Frankly considered himself one of the world's greatest experts on public opinion. Said law was respected in England and not in America. Said he had seen a customs official very roughly manhandled on quay at New York before an admiring audience of sailors etc. who thoroughly appreciated it.

Our own anti-aircraft shrapnel fell at Laudermere quay on Thursday night. Getting closer. At first it was thought to be a bomb, but it wasn't.

Saturday, September 2nd.

London Thursday. In the afternoon we saw the films of the Somme offensive. Very instructive and salutary. Dined with Mr. and Mrs. Gilbert Miller, who took us to see *Daddy-Long-Legs* at the Duke of York's, which Miller is at present controlling for America. An absolutely putrid play, with a new actress, Renée Kelly.

Sunday, September 10th.

London Thursday to Saturday. Dorziat lunched with us at Berkeley on Thursday. 2 committee meetings of W.A.R.C. As there was nothing for publicity committee to do we adjourned for a month. The general view among the W.A.R.C. was that the French authorities no longer wanted English hospitals. Wounded were now being treated chiefly just behind the front.

In view of recent round-ups, and my youthful appearance, I am now carrying about my birth certificate and registration card.

Thursday, September 28th.

Corfe Castle. I came down here on Tuesday to join John Wright in half a week of water-colouring. The New Forest was in its best form. All the scenery of the Isle of Purbeck very fine. Corfe Castle is spectacular. It was very wet yesterday. I did a water-colour through the rainy window in the morning, and part of an interior in the afternoon. Wright knows every one in village. He told me how at the beginning of the war there were women here also who carefully explained to their inferiors how they were to behave when the Germans came.

Friday, September 29th.

The butcher's daughter practises the piano close to the hotel very well and brilliantly. Her Chopin is understood to be remarkable. Today it is raining all day, very heavily. Nevertheless, this morning, under an outhouse shed at Wright's, I did one of my best water-colours. Unfortunately I heated the sketching frame to dry it, and it stuck to the varnish and is now torn.

Weather is in fact horrible. Landlord full of theories about Zepps and moon, because once in the Navy. I don't know how it follows, but it does. Last evening I did a water-colour in blacksmith's garden. He related to us how a "picture" hawker had tried to sell him a pair of pictures. "Look here," said blacksmith, "if you can show me a place to hang 'em in my parlour, I'll buy 'em." Hawker entered and looked. "Nay, guv'nor, you've done me. There's no room." And there wasn't, for portraits of Kitchener, French, etc., etc.

Saturday, October 7th.

I went to London on Thursday. Lunched at Lady Paget's. She was late—her doctor being late—and she sent word down to Mrs. Lewis

Harcourt and me that we were to begin. The business was the appeal
I had written for the American Women's Hospital. I liked Mrs. Harcourt. Youngish. Quiet. Self-possessed. She said that they asked her not
to take a maid when she went to the continent, but she met on the
journey an American woman with two maids. Lady Paget came down
when our lunch was nearly over.

She told us private information about the way Zepps are caught.
Two aeroplanes go up with a long wire between them. When they
have got this wire against the Zepp they electrify it and it sets fire to
the Zepp. Also they entangle the Zepp in the wire and thus drag the
Zepp along. She seemed to believe all this. Some people will swallow
anything.

Yesterday, lunch at McKenna's. Runciman (looking ill again). Lord
Fisher, Duchess of Rutland, and Mr., Mrs., and Miss Davison. Davison
is a partner in Pierpont Morgan and is arranging loans. Before lunch
Mrs. —— took me aside and explained that I had to be polite to
Davison, as if people weren't polite to him he wouldn't let us have
any money. She was quite serious. The whole family had been to the
front as far as Rheims. I liked the look of Davison.

I sat between Fisher and the girl. In two minutes he had referred
to "bloody experts." Touching Falkland battle and Cradock's defeat,
he said that a tortoise had been sent to catch a hare, and then two
tortoises. He ordered the two fastest ships there were to go off at once.
People protested. An admiral came up from Portsmouth and said that
really they ought to be overhauled before leaving. "Not at all," said
Fisher, "they must leave tonight." And he said to me: "They only
arrived ten minutes too soon. The only real victory we've had at sea
yet. It doesn't want an expert to see that a tortoise can't catch a hare,
and that a hare has never yet been wounded by a tortoise and won't be."
Then the phrase about bloody experts. He was evidently still feeling his
shunt from the Admiralty. He said: "I was the only one who objected
to the Dardanelles expedition. Kitchener was in favour of it. He's dead.
Won't say anything about him. He got the Order of the Garter. I got
the order of the boot."

He said that in October 1914, having *carte blanche* from Lloyd George, he ordered 612 new vessels for the Navy. He didn't think the German line would be broken in the west, and was in favour of an invasion of Pomerania, only 82 miles from Berlin. He said that this possibility was the only thing that had ever made Frederick the Great afraid. He seemed to have developed this scheme. He told some excellent stories with strong language. They say he is like a boy. He absolutely is. He said: "I'm told I shall live till I'm 110. So I've plenty of time yet." He gave me his favourite quotation:

> Not heaven itself upon the past has power,
> What has been has been, and I have had my hour.

They also say that he smacks more of the forecastle than of the bridge. There is something in this, too.

Monday, October 9th.

Clegg brought a Capt. B. (of his Battery) to lunch. Had been out at Ypres ten months and then wounded in the head, in front of right ear. He carries a good scar. He talked well, and said he should like to write if he could. I told him he could.

He said the newspaper correspondents' descriptions of men eager to go up over the parapet made him laugh. They never were eager. He related how he had seen a whole company of men extremely pale with apprehension and shaking so that they could scarcely load their rifles. Then he said that men who nevertheless *did* go over in that state were really brave. He told us how his battery saw hundreds, thousands, of grey figures coming along only 1000 yards off, and every man thought he would be a prisoner in ten minutes, when suddenly thousands of Canadians appeared from nowhere, and the Boches fled. The cheering was delirious. He told this very dramatically, but without any effort to be effective. He said he really wanted to be back with the battery. For a long time the fellows wrote to him regularly once a fortnight, and every letter ended with "When are you coming back?" He said they had had glorious times now and then, glorious. He said that to sit on a factory chimney and see the Boches going over was better than big-game shooting. He said the Boches had any amount of pluck and grit. And Clegg said that even in hospital they would stand things that an Englishman probably wouldn't. Both Clegg and B. facetiously contrasted the rough, anyhow, bumping treatment the wounded get on their way from the firing line (when they really *are* ill) with the hushed, tender, worshipping treatment they get on arriving in London when many of them are doing pretty well.

Wednesday, October 25th.

On Friday I went to Nottingham under charge of Captain Lloyd, R.N., to inspect a national projectile factory. Article written on this for munitions ministry propaganda.

On Sunday in a dreadful east wind we went to Peldon to see the Zepp. It was worth seeing. Was told, *inter alia,* that Air Department had refused offer of 100 engines a week eight months ago. They said they had placed sufficient orders, and would not believe that some of the firms who had accepted orders would never be able to deliver. Now they want more engines. They also need larger planes to go to Essen. They have refused and still do refuse the only size of plane that will satisfactorily bomb Essen, on the plea that it is "aerodynamically" wrong.

Thursday, October 26th.

Came to London. Lunched with Clutton-Brock and Judge Evans. The latter a collector. Then old Rawlinson came to the same table, also a collector. Their talk was rather refreshing and reassuring. It showed how painters materially live.

Worked on my novel (after a sleep) all afternoon till 5 P.M. I dined alone and went alone to Aldwych in the dark in a creeping taxi to see *Il Seraglio.* In time for second act. Long, tedious waits. A few too-well-dressed women in boxes, attended by their courts. Lovely tunes in opera. But otherwise nearly as ridiculous as musical comedy.

I got some cigarettes yesterday with a card of astronomical information about Mars. Some boys may grow up with cigarette cards their sole education.

Friday, November 3rd.

I came to London on Wednesday and took possession of apartment C at the R. Thames Y.C. which I have rented. Rather like celibate life in Paris again. I dined at the Club and read Macready's diary; extraordinary sensation of having resumed a closed chapter of existence.

Thursday, dined with M. at Elysée Restaurant. Dancing by two nice professional girls at intervals. Young nut who came in at 9.31 and asked whether it was just before or just after drink-closing time. He crossed legs and leaned on stick before beginning to ask waiter.

Caledonian Market this morning. I got there too soon and saw trucks and hand-carts and carts being wheeled up by all sorts of people— many foreigners. Type of pale puffed skin, or pinched and full red lips. I went back to tailor's to try on, and went to market again at noon, when it was in full swing. I bought an eastern bowl.

Thursday, November 9th.

At night I went to Lord Mayor's banquet with Regge of Frinton. I asked usher if I *had* to be received. He said I could please myself; so I wasn't, and joined Pett Ridge and another acquaintance whose name I couldn't recall behind a barrier at the entrance. Fisher got loudest cheers. Funny to see Asquith followed by his wife and daughter. Reception, in library, took at least an hour. Names called from usher to usher, and ushers walked continually up and down the length of the library with guests. In great hall, about 1500 guests. Beef carvers at foot of big sculptures, with rags and knives in sheaths, stood on high platforms carving barons of beef. At the end, a policeman lifted one old carver down. Procession inwards of nobs. Maids of Honour with pink bouquets for Lady Mayoress. Trumpeters. Inauguration march by solicitor, X.Y., awful tosh. Soup tepid. Fish cold. Pheasant good. Cold meat good. No veg. Sweets excellent. Fruit good. Wines good. Box of

2 cigars and 2 cigarettes to each male guest, but no smoking in hall. Awful dowdiness of women, including nobs. After dinner, Maids of Honour appeared in a row in balcony in front of Lord Mayor, and arranged their pink streamers to hang over balcony. Reporters had seats near nobs. Took about 5-minute turns, and handed a watch to each other. Trumpeting before L.M.'s chaplain's grace (short and inaudible) before and after meal. Trumpeting (2 pairs of trumpets, one echoing the other, very good; trumpeters covered with gold braid and with black velvet jockey caps) before each toast. Comic toastmaster who had a huge rosette and scarf, and looked up to skies in announcing toasts. . . . Loving cup never reached us. . . . General effect, old stonework, carving, sculptures, 2 galleries (top: musicians), to left of L.M. wooden beams, gilded roof. Dependent flags. Stone inscriptions round roof. Old flags at one side. City costumes, gilded. Black velvet and lace costumes. Levée costumes. Military ditto. Foreign ditto. Vast epaulettes of Ministers. Lord Mayor leaning back with false ease in his great gilded chair. Many City officials behind him. Look of tradition, city-ness, grooviness, in ugly and yet often decent faces of men.

Councillors had to wear their mazarine (?) costumes (trimmed with fitch fur) at reception, but some took them off for dinner (£12 each). Electric chandeliers. Flowers on tables. Rows of heads. . . . Blackened windows. Policemen at every door. Draught on my head. Ben Davies sang *God Save the King* very well. The name of Venizelos aroused easily the most cheering. Herbert Samuel spoke without conviction. Balfour was resentful, defensive, and then over-confident (as to ability to prevent future Channel raiders from getting back). He said "the service which I for the moment represent." French Ambassador quite inaudible after first few sentences. Lord French perky and sure—kept looking down at MS. Asquith was the best. Diction uneven but phrasing absolutely perfect throughout. He was grim but not boastful.

After Asquith, I left.

Tuesday, November 14th.

I came home from town on Friday afternoon, with Swinnerton and

Marguerite. Swinnerton was walking out on Sunday evening (dark) in the village looking for me, and not finding me, he asked a little boy whether he had seen a gentleman, Mr. Bennett, with 4 dogs. The boy mumbled a negative. Swinnerton then proceeded to describe me, etc., and the boy said, "I seen Mr. Bennett with *one* dog."

Yesterday Miss Nerney calculated that I had written 16,000 words of my new novel.[1]

Thursday, November 16th.

I came to town yesterday morning with Mrs. Lowndes, who had come to us on Monday afternoon for two nights. Two nights of excellent gossip and scandal. She was very nice about servants, war economy, etc. She said she had A1 knowledge that German supplies would run seriously out at the end of February.

Thursday, November 23rd.

In the afternoon, after some work, I found I had a chill on the stomach. I went with precautions to the Aldwych Theatre and got the last remaining circle seat for the first performance of *Aïda*. Theatre full. Goodish performance but offensive scenery that tried to be original and was only imitative and ridiculous. Oh! Russian ballet, what horrible sins you have caused.

Friday, November 24th.

I went to tea with H. G. [Wells] at St. James's Court. He told me his scheme for a whole series of new books, some being novels. He wants monarchy destroyed, of course, and to have a new religion (that there is one God—and apparently he can be what you like) without priests or churches. He thought very little of British high command at the front, had had difficulties with censor about his articles on the front, and meant to say what he thought in a book to be issued in January.

I was still suffering yesterday from my stomach chill, but I wrote 1000 words.

---

[1] This was *The Roll Call*, published in 1918. See p. 223.

I went up to the Omega workshops by appointment to see Roger Fry. Arrived as arranged at 2.30. I was told he was out. Then that he was at his studio, down Fitzroy Street. I went there and rang. He opened door. "Come and have lunch," he said. "I've had lunch, it's 2.30," I said. "How strange!" he said. "I thought it was only 1.15." Then as he went upstairs he cried out to a girl above: "Blank (her Xtian name), it's 2.30," as a great item of news. Fry expounded his theories. He said there was no original industrial art in England till he started, i.e. untraditional. He said lots of goodish things and was very persuasive and reasonable. Then he took me to the showrooms in Fitzroy Square, and I bought a few little things. I did not buy a fine still life by Duncan Grant. But I may, later. I gradually got to like a number of the things, especially the stuffs. He said manufacturing (English) firms roared with laughter at his suggestion that they should do business together. One firm quoted an impossible price when he asked them to make rugs to his design at his risk. But when a eulogistic article appeared in *The Times* they quoted a lower price, a reasonable one. He said that both French and German firms would take his stuff. I began to get more and more pleased with the stuff, and then I left with two parcels.

This morning I went to Carfax Gallery and bought a Sickert, "Coster Girl." Had some talk with the proprietor, who was highly intelligent, and stuck to it that Claude Phillips, though he couldn't write, had real taste. The boss thought Sickert the greatest artist of the age.

Saturday, November 25th.

The manager of the Carfax Gallery told me yesterday that some people were very antagonistic. One old gentleman in white spats said he had read in *Morning Post* a good account of Sargent drawings and he had come to see them. When he saw them he said that he regarded the show as a swindle—that it was robbery to charge 1*s.* for such an affair. Clifton gave him his 1*s.* back.

Thursday, November 30th.

It was only last week that I received a copy of the entirely new and revolutionary Instructions to Emergency Committees, which were issued on the 16th August last. Even then I only got one copy. I asked for half a dozen more and got one more.

Thus for three months the whole scheme has been changed and I, in charge of a district including several towns and 30 parishes, was entirely ignorant of it. So were the civilians concerned. I protested, but I got no explanation.

Sunday, December 3rd.

Central military representative for Essex has no copy of Scheme K, which is the present emergency scheme. He lent me his only copy. When he has to consider it in order to advise me on doubtful points I have to return it to him. It is printed. I have been able to get only one other copy. So the preparation of instructions for this division drags on. The matter is supposed to be urgent.

Thursday, December 7th.

Tuesday afternoon I read through what I have written of my new novel. Not so bad. Undoubtedly I have been refreshed and invigorated by reading Dreiser's *The Financier,* which absolutely held me. *The Titan,* which I am now reading, is not so good.

I came to London yesterday with M. Rebecca West, Gladys Wheeler, and H. G. Wells lunched with me at Romano's. Wells called my fob "gastric jewellery"! He offered to bet 2 to 1 that the war would be over by August next.

Friday, December 8th.

Dined at Thatched House with F. Rosher, Swinnerton, and Sir James Dunlop Smith, political secretary to the India Office. Among a number of interesting stories he told how he had found the largest ruby in the world (rather larger than the bowl of an ordinary liqueur glass), a historical stone, lost for 70 years, in a necklace of the Queen's.

Wednesday, December 13th.

Lieut. R., of a mobile Anti-Aircraft unit stationed at Thorpe, came for tea. He said he carried £15,000 worth of stores. He said that after big raid at Hull, end of last year about, when Mayor of Hull had been assured that Hull was one of the most heavily defended places, and a Zepp dropped 15 bombs in the town, the population afterwards mobbed officers, and A.A. officers coming into the town had to put on Tommies' clothes. Also that Naval Unit was telegraphed for and that when it came with full authorized special lights, the population, angry at the lights, assaulted it with stones and bottles and put half of it in hospital, and had ultimately to be kept off by the military. He outlined complex administrative system of unit, and showed how utterly and needlessly idiotic it was. He told me how he had been sent to some golf links with a big mobile gun, and had put gun into a good spot where it interfered with play on first hole, the officially indicated position being a bad one. The affair was urgent, as a raid was expected that night. He successfully repulsed various complainants from golf club; but next morning an infantry officer came specially down from War Office, with instructions (positive orders) that gun must be moved. R. gave reasons against. Infantry officer: "I don't know anything about artillery but that gun has got to be moved. It is my order to you." In order to fix gun in inferior official position, R. indented for railway sleepers to the tune of £127, and got them. Meanwhile the golf club professional had told him that it would be quite easy to modify the course.

Thursday, December 21st.

Ill ever since last entry.

I got up for lunch Tuesday and also yesterday. Today I was up for breakfast and have read through last finished chapter of new novel. But I can't yet write, except articles (for *Statesman*). During illness I have had excellent ideas for novel.

On Tuesday we had cable that Marguerite's sister, Gabrielle, had died at Pau.

Sunday, December 31st.

I finished the first part of my London novel this afternoon, 35,000 words. I wrote only 127,600 during the year. The totals of later years, however, cannot be compared fairly with totals of earlier years, as latterly I have not counted my journal.

We had 10 to Xmas dinner. I read *The Old Wives' Tale,* the first time I have read it through since I corrected the proofs 8 or 9 years ago, I think.

1917

Thursday, January 4th. London.

Came to town yesterday. Lunched with Wells and his two boys and Ross at the Reform. Ross told me, as regards inaccuracies in *Dict. National Biog.*, that he offered to look through the proofs of Wilde's biography, but proofs were never sent to him. He found 18 mistakes of fact in the biography.

Gardiner, editor *Daily News,* suggested that I should resume writing for *D.N.* I said I would resume only on similar conditions as before; namely that I had a regular commission for articles, to appear at regular intervals—I didn't mind what the intervals were.

After the immense public row between Lloyd George and Gardiner, the following lately occurred. T. P. O'Connor came up to Gardiner and said: "You may be interested in a piece of information which I have. It is not second-hand. I myself heard the words spoken. The other day Ll. George spoke of you in very friendly terms. He said you were not like the rest. Your difference of opinion was honest and he respected it. Yes, he spoke in the kindliest terms of you." A few days later another henchman of Ll. G. came up to Gardiner at the N.L. Club and said, "You may be interested to know that I heard Ll. George speak of you in the very friendliest terms the other day." And so on, as before. Thus is it sought to work the oracle.

Vedrenne wrote me, giving way and agreeing to pay £200 down on receipt of MS. of a play for Eadie, for option on it. He had said to Pinker, "I never have paid and I never will pay to read a play."

Friday, January 5th.

Wounded Allies' Committee in afternoon.

I read *Le Mystère de la Chambre Jaune* again. Not bad.

Evening I went to M.'s flat, and we dined at the Ristorante del Commercio, or some such name, in Frith St., very well. One of those family restaurants. Papa, stern, in charge, mamma pleasant, also in charge, a nice girl to help. Glimpse of kitchen with chef and a woman and a girl. Three children of papa and mamma messing about most of the time: girls of 7 or 8, in white silk with gilt and silvered diadems, and a smaller boy. This place was very agreeable.

This morning I called first on M. Then to see Lanchester, who described to me his scheme for tabulating information for Neville Chamberlain and Man-Service Board in the form of maps and charts. Very interesting. He also showed me a set of competition plans for use in my novel. Then to Carfax Gallery to pay a bill for a Sickert. Clifton said that Conder [1] was very casual. He would be out with Clifton towards evening and would say, "I've got no silk and I'd like to do a fan tonight," and he would go into any little draper's in a side street, the big shops being already closed, and buy a yard of silk of no matter what quality. He nearly always worked by candlelight.

Monday, January 8th. Comarques.

I came home on Friday afternoon, with Swinnerton. Walpole came the next day, and we had two uproarious evenings, too long and too smoky. Walpole insisted on my finding for him all Jacob Tonson's articles in *New Age*. [2] He spent all Sunday afternoon in reading them, and said that a selection from them ought to be published in volume. Swinnerton said that Chatto & Windus would be delighted to publish

---

[1] Charles Conder (1868-1909), the artist whose exquisite painting on fans gave him a particular vogue.

[2] "Jacob Tonson" was the pseudonym under which Bennett wrote his early articles for this periodical.

the volume, and I practically offered him the volume. Both of them left on Monday morning.

Saturday, January 13th. Comarques.

Wednesday evening I went into Westminster Cathedral and saw how to use it again in my novel. Very cold day. Nice warm cathedral. Ugly chapels, detail invisible. A non-R.C. parson or two squinting about. Noise of a charwoman washing floor. Exceedingly few people. Then at 10.10, either prime or tierce. A few performers came in, after a bell had rung, took their seats, and then the intoning begins, scarcely audible for a second or less. It "steals out." Words utterly incomprehensible. Outside, front of shop devoted to rosaries, crucifixes, etc.

Friday, January 19th. London.

Lunch at Reform today. Informed positively that Nivelle was to include all British Army in his command. It was said that he said of Haig: *"Il n'est pas assez souple. Il est trop orgueilleux."* This statement absolutely contradicted by Press Bureau tonight. Tonight in Piccadilly an immense red flare in sky, followed by a great explosion. Piccadilly rather excited. Mair informed on telephone at 10.30 that chemical works at Blackwall exploded and set fire to South Metropolitan Gasworks. "Thousands of wounded in hospital." We shall see if this is the fact.[1]

Mair and Willie Weir and George Whale dined with me tonight at Yacht Club. Very interesting. Mair said there was nothing in alarm of German invasion of Switzerland and that it had been deliberately got up by French authorities (who said Foch was at Besançon and actually began to dig trenches) in order to get Swiss securities out of Switzerland into France for purpose of helping to regulate exchange.

Mair promised to take me over London in airship.

Wednesday, January 24th. London, Yacht Club.

I came to London yesterday morning. Hard frost and cold travelling.

---

[1] This was the disastrous explosion at Silvertown when many workers were killed and injured.

Lunch with Pinker at Arts Club today about the whole question of cinematograph rights, which I regard as a swindle on the author. Constant fine snow showers.

Sunday, January 28th. Comarques.

On Thursday Wells and I dined at Reform. Tossed for bill and he lost. Then we went to Petit Riche basement restaurant and saw the Hayneses, the Lynds, and Rebecca West.

I came home on Friday morning. I am in unusually good form for work. In spite of radiators and fires, it is very difficult to keep the house warm. N.E. wind and frost.

Saturday, February 3rd. London, Yacht Club.

Went to London on Wednesday morning.

Wells and I lunched together again at Reform. He and Gardiner were in favour of communal feeding in case of starvation, as most efficient, beginning in schools. But Wells took submarine menace, like me, very calmly. On the other hand, Donald[1] and R. McKenna were much upset by it and gave dramatic figures. Afterwards I took Wells to Burlington Fine Arts Club to see English aquarelles, and he took me to call on Mrs. De Boer, and we took her to Roger Fry's at Omega workshops.

Monday, February 5th. Thorpe-le-Soken.

The announcement that U.S.A. had severed diplomatic relations with Germany caused really very little discussion here. It was discussed a little at lunch. Already the intensely misunderstanding and unjust attitude of M. and officers (some of them) to U.S.A. is changing. At tea, when Lieut. and Mrs. Tracy[2] came, it was discussed a little, and Mrs. Tracy well formulated for me the advantages of an "American peace," that is, an unbiased peace, which was received with silence not altogether hostile. Afterwards Clegg agreed with me as to the advantages of the

---

[1] Now Sir Robert Donald, editor of the *Daily Chronicle*, 1902–18.
[2] Louis Tracy, the author and journalist, had recently returned from America, where he had lectured extensively on the War.

"American peace." During the remainder of the evening nothing was said as to America.

Thursday, February 8th. London, Yacht Club.

Dined at Mme. Van der Velde's and sat at a spiritualistic séance with a clairvoyant named Peters, who brought his son, a youth in R.A.M.C., home for a few hours on leave. This son said there were 500 professed spiritualist soldiers at Aldershot. Theosophist. Peters (*père*), man of 45 or so. Short. Good forehead. Bald on top, dark hair at sides. Quick and nervous. Son of a barge owner. Present: Yeats, Mr. and Mrs. Jowett (barrister—she very beautiful), Roger Fry, hostess, and me. Peters handled objects brought by each of us. His greatest success, quite startling, was with the glass stopper of a bottle brought by Jowett. He described a man throwing himself *out* of something, down, with machinery behind him, and a big hotel or big building behind him. Something to do with water, across water. He kept repeating these phrases with variations. The stopper had belonged to the baronet (I forget his name) who threw himself off a launch, in response to a challenge from X., at 3 A.M. into the Thames, after a debauched party up river. All the passengers were more or less drunk. He was drowned.

He succeeded, with my toothpick, in getting me to the Potteries and into the office of the Staffordshire *Knot* or *Sentinel,* and described a man that might be either Goold or the editor of the *Sentinel,* and said that known or unknown to me, this man had greatly influenced me. He insisted on the word "Zola." "Zola." He said there was a message to tell me. I hadn't done my best work. I am morally sure he hadn't the least idea who I was. And even if he had, he didn't know the toothpick belonged to me, even if he knew it was I who had brought it, which he might conceivably have done as it was the last thing he picked up off the tray. I made full notes.

Friday, February 9th.

I wrote 1200 words of London novel.

Today George Moore and W. Sickert came to lunch. Sickert had swum that morning and skated. He had his skates with him—no over-coat. I said little. They talked. Moore was the man of letters. He said, of a Landor dialogue between Horne Tooke and Johnson, that it would not interest ordinary people, but that a man of letters might read it under his lamp at night with great amusement.

Sickert said that he cooked his own food and cooked it very well. Formerly he used to read between spells of painting during the day. Now he cooked. He would go over to the stove and say, "*Ça mijotte.*" They both used a lot of French and spoke it very well. Moore recited a French ballad which he had written about a *maquereau,* which I thought rather good. Then he recited Villon. Moore evidently wants to get into the theatre again. Unfortunately I had no encouragement for him. He has an idea for dramatizing *The Brook Kerith.* He is naïvely and harmlessly vain, and very agreeable. I enjoyed these men very much. 1500 words.

Saturday, February 10th. London, Yacht Club.

Continuing Moore and Sickert from yesterday. Moore seemed to have detached himself almost completely from the war. He said he didn't read newspapers now, as they only made him feel depressed and did him no good. He said several entirely foolish things, such as that he could not understand (very much emphasized) how any one could read a *war book.* To read about new war devices he could under-stand, but how any one could read a war book he could *not* understand. Sickert was much more reserved—he is much more normal.

Wednesday, February 14th. London, Yacht Club.

I met Dr. Shufflebotham (Stoke) and went with him to the Palladium (where the entertainment was awful). He told me one of the principal poison-gas factories was in Burslem. He said they had gradually learnt the effects of the gases on the Germans by the effect of the gases on their own workpeople, over *half* of whom had been on compensation during the past year. He told a funny tale of how in the early days there was a massed band Sunday fête (semi-religious) in Burslem Park, to which all the children in white came after Sunday school. Children began to cry. People said it was symptom of whooping cough. Then to cough. Further symptoms. Then adults began to cry and cough. Word went round at once, gas escaping from a factory. Every one fled from the park. Bandsmen dropped their instruments. Two of them met at gates. "Bill, where's thy bloody drum?" "It's where thy bloody cornet is, lad."

Tuesday, February 27th. London, Yacht Club.

We came to London yesterday morning. Stage Society in the afternoon. *Good Friday* by Masefield. A terribly dull and portentous thing in rhyme. I was most acutely bored. I found that all the élite said they liked the damned thing.

Shaw and Lee Matthews and I had tea together. I shifted Shaw a little in the end.

Last week I finished reading the Balzac vol. containing *La Recherche de l'Absolu* and *La Peau de Chagrin.* Both these are very fine indeed. The short stories, *Le Chef d'Œuvre, Inconnu,* and *Melinoth Reconcilé,* are good, the last the best. *Jesus Christ in Flanders* is negligible. On the whole a terrific volume.

Thursday, March 1st. London, Yacht Club.

Sharpe lunched with me at Reform Club. I seemed to be wandering about all day in search of ideas for novel. R.C. Cathedral. Lanchester's Bond St. shop, clubs. By about 6.30 I had got them all. A Lieut. Bayne (Gordon Highlanders, lost his left arm) dined with me and Shufflebotham at Café Royal—very well.

Shuff told me that when he went into factory for lachrymatory shells at Walthamstow the water poured out of his eyes and filled a jug.

Friday, March 2nd. London, Yacht Club.

I wrote about 1500 words of novel yesterday.

After dining alone at the Reform I went up to Roger Fry's newly constituted Omega Club in Fitzroy Square. Only about 2 chairs. The remainder of the seats are flattish canvas bags cast on floor near walls and specially made for this. An exhibition of kids' drawings round the walls. Strange crowd, including Mme. Van der Velde, Lytton Strachey, the other Strachey,[1] Yeats, Borenius, etc. They all seemed very intelligent.

Wednesday, March 7th. London, Yacht Club.

I returned home from London on Friday last, wrote large quantities of my London novel each day, wrote my Sardonyx article in odd moments, and came back to London again yesterday.

Lunched with Wells. The Webbs said that the new "business men" officials had upset all Whitehall. New ministers' habit of writing letters from home and getting answers at home and thus springing surprises on departments is also much resented.

I worked all afternoon at Y.C. Massingham, Ross, and I dined together. I was thus between two pacifists.

Massingham told a good story of an Australian who was asked his opinion as to the end of the war. The Australian said, "I think what my friend Fritz thinks. Fritz was my German prisoner—a very decent sort of chap. Fritz said, 'You'll win, but you'll all come home on one steamer.' "

This of course expressed Massingham's view beautifully, also Ross's.

Thursday, March 15th. London, Yacht Club.

H. L. Rothband,[2] the Manchester manufacturer, lunched with me yesterday at Reform, about his scheme for employment of disabled soldiers. Curious mixture of ingenuousness and acuteness. I missed the beginnings of a shindy between Spender and Massingham. Masterman brought this safely to an end by leaving the smoking-room with Massingham and sitting in the gallery. Spender was with Buckmaster.

I wrote another 1100 words of novel yesterday after another very bad night, and I was so exhausted in the afternoon that I could scarcely even walk.

---

[1] John St. Loe Strachey, editor of the *Spectator*.
[2] Sir Henry Lesser Rothband was originator of the scheme for the King's National Roll for Finding Employment for Disabled Sailors and Soldiers.

Penry Williams told me on Monday that he had his beagles with him at Bournemouth. They raided a butcher's shop. The dog-master asked butcher what the damage was. The butcher said £6. The dog-master said, "I'll toss you for it." They tossed and the butcher lost. This is a good sporting-military story.

Friday, March 16th. London, Yacht Club.

Another 1400 words yesterday morning of novel. Mair lunched with me at Reform and Davray joined us.

Mair said that Nivelle, in London this week, had been made C.-in-C. of all armies (French and English) on the western front, but that the appointment would of course not be published.

Afterwards we went to the Omega Club, and saw dancing by an alleged marvellous boy dancer. He did seem pretty fair for a kid. I asked if he was Russian and learnt that he had been discovered in Brondesbury and was entirely English.

Thursday, March 22nd. London, Yacht Club.

I had neuralgia a lot yesterday. Went to see M. in the morning. I curiously enjoyed going to A.B.C. in Piccadilly at noon for hot milk and a sandwich. Tonight, though, I have bought a first edition of an evening paper in order to read the morning's news over again. This is almost indispensable to a morning visit to an A.B.C.

I bought the new Conrad, *The Shadow-Line.* Good.

Friday, March 23rd. London, Yacht Club.

Today I began to find ideas for second part of my London novel, while spending most of the morning at barber's and in meditation in library of Reform Club. Much good political and military converse with Wells, Gardiner, and Massingham after lunch at Reform, and a solitary afternoon here.

I finished Conrad's *The Shadow-Line* last night. A short story disguised as a novel. Very good, but a certain anti-climax where the climax ought to be.

Saturday, March 24th. London, Yacht Club.

Dined with Sir W. Weir (Director of Air Supply), Major Weir (Flying Staff, W.O.) and Richmond, at Savoy, after spending ½ hour in the Angelica Kauffmann room at Weir's flat.

They began to try to startle me right off. Weir and Richmond said that the labour situation was acutely bad. Tyne strike not better. Men out at Barrow, and men out at 3 or 4 small factories that worked for Weir. The strikes were not officially countenanced by trades unions, the organization alien (U.S.A.) working through shop stewards, etc.

The Barrow men were stopped by men they knew a long way from their shops, and they obeyed the order to strike. The orders were mainly transmitted not by post but by motor bicycle. The Government knew all about it, as the trades unions had told them everything as fast as they learnt it.

After very long faces, both Weir and Richmond said that though it might be very awkward, it couldn't be permanently serious, as the men generally being honest and patriotic would not stand for it. Also that to catch hold of a few leaders (who were simply seditious) would do a lot to stop it. Then I was told of a new invention of a Rumanian, Constantinesco, for the transmission of power by means of an elastic fluid. This device is now actually in use in the machine guns of aeroplanes, but he said its applications were endless, and that it would revolutionize machinery. The Government will not at present let anything be published about it at all.

Weir—and all these Weirs are real experts—said Constantinesco was one of the great men, in his own line, of a century. Then they began on submarine question. Very serious. Weir said that if things went on as at present transport would be *vitally* affected in less than four months. Still, he believed in our victory in the field.

Talking about the labour question, they all greed that the margin of labour was sufficient; that is, that the Government could draw all the men it needed for the Army out of essential occupations and that the men left in the essential occupations could do all the work, provided they would *produce their maximum output,* which they don't and won't. All three were enthusiastic about the effort of France. W. Weir said that as regards aeroplane supply, the Germans got the best designs they could, and made a lot of it, telling the manufacturer meanwhile to use the field experience of his machines in thinking out a new and better design, but sticking to the execution of the original order. We were always trying after improvements, and Weir said that you can't "force" technical progress advantageously beyond a certain speed. The result was that while we always had easily the best machine in existence we never had enough. He intended that this should be remedied in May.

Monday, March 26th. Comarques.

Strange rumours on Saturday night. As that Ireland had revolted again and reserve batteries were being sent from Woolwich to Ireland by special trains. (Apparently quite untrue.) Also that five German cruisers were lying off Harwich. What the British fleet was doing meanwhile was not explained. Many troops were undoubtedly drafted into this district, and on Sunday morning Liverpool Street was a pandemonium of returning officers summoned by wire, necessitating special trains.

Friday, March 30th. London, Yacht Club.

I was wondering yesterday whether I ought not to keep a list of prophecies made to me.

Donald said that the Russians would make no offensive this year and that had it not been for the Revolution they would have made peace.

W.A.R.C. meeting, with funny written descriptions of rows between doctor and administrator and nurses at our Balkans Hospital.

Dined with M. at flat. Then to Ambassadors, but were too late for the ballet *Pomme d'Or*. Vansittart's French Revolution play, *Class,* was a pretty good idea spoilt by lack of invention and uncertain handling. Anatole France's *Man Who Married a Dumb Wife* served very well. Pierre Veber's *Gonzague* (with Morton), a common farce of intrigue, was a most ingeniously constructed affair. There is nobody in England (whether or not as bereft of genius as Veber is) who could construct a little farce so well. Nothing to it, but very agreeable to witness. Excellently produced and excellently played. This was the best evening I have had at the theatre for I don't know how long—perhaps during the war.

R. Donald said that he was getting some men to write messages to Russia for cabling, but he had to obtain Lloyd George's approval first. During the afternoon he sent me up a note to say he had obtained the approval and would I send in a 500-word message quickly.

Saturday, March 31st. Thorpe-le-Soken.

I came home yesterday morning. Beautiful day. Snowfall and a lot of rain this morning. As soon as the rain ceased at noon, the whole landscape began to steam, even before the sun had got fairly out.

Notice outside shop in the village this morning: "*A few potatoes. 2 lbs. each customer. No bags found.*"

Wednesday, April 11th. London, Yacht Club.

Last week I had an immense burst of work. I did not go to London. I wrote about 5000 words of my novel (including 2500 in one day), and finished penultimate chapter of it. On Monday I wrote *Daily News* article and more *Statesman* stuff. I slept badly the whole time, but a dinner at the Greys' on Saturday, where we met the ultra-blonde Danish dancer Karina and her husband Captain Janssen, did me good. Karina ran over Janssen in her auto and broke both his legs, and then married him. He looks after Karina so completely that he even cuts out leather for her shoes. She is very pretty and agreeable. I sat next to her and enjoyed it. Hard frost driving home.

Thursday, April 12th. London, Yacht Club.

Lunched with Davray and a Canadian officer (name forgotten) who knew 14 languages. He had been through the Russian Revolution and told me he didn't trust any of the parties.

T. Seccombe was to have lunched with me next Wednesday, but he made a mistake and came yesterday. He therefore joined us. He said that the pupils at the Royal Military College were now the most extraordinary crowd. Poets and novelists pullulated among them. He thought there might be 1 or 2 geniuses. He instanced Arthur Waugh's son, aged 18, who had written a remarkably realistic novel of school life (Sherborne).[1]

Webster and Swinnerton dined with me at Reform. Swinnerton showed me a letter from Walpole describing Russian Rev.; Walpole has written the official account of the Rev. Deaths 5000.

Thursday, April 19th. London, Yacht Club.

I dined with Sir W. and Lady Weir at Savoy. She was very agreeably dressed. Weir told me that sometimes delays in supplies of air machines were difficult to explain to public. He had ball bearings for aeroplanes on 3 ships from Norway. He asked for these to be convoyed. They were not convoyed. The Germans sank all of them. He had been to an Imperial War Conference and spoke very highly of Colonials, especially Smuts. I said Smuts's first speech on arriving was fine. It was about aeroplanes. He said that after 21 months' delay, housing for work people at Farnborough was at last being put up. Weir told me he had established the first regular commercial air service in the world (he thought) just lately: a daily service for his own use between London and Paris, 3 hours. 6 machines employed.

Friday, April 20th. London, Yacht Club.

Yesterday I began to think that the *tone* of the end of my novel wouldn't do. So I spent the day, exhausted, partly in dozing and reading, and 1½ hours at barber's, and generally thinking over the climax, which I ultimately got right. I dined with Wells at Reform. He had worked all day, and arrived only at 8.40. We had champagne. We tossed for the bill— he lost. This is the second time lately he has lost to me.

Tuesday, April 24th. London, Yacht Club.

Great creative week-end. I wrote over 3000 words of novel on Saturday and Sunday. This novel is to be called *The Roll Call.*

---

[1] This was *The Loom of Youth*, by Alec Waugh, published in 1917, with a preface by T. Seccombe.

I came to town this morning and lunched with Webbs. Webb told me that Lloyd George, contrary to the usual habit of ministers, would not deal with papers. He preferred to be talked to. Webb said that most ministers were followed about by dispatch boxes full of papers which they had to approve and initial. Sometimes hundreds of papers. He said there were several grades of keys; the highest would open all dispatch boxes. When he was at the Colonial Office he had a second-grade key, which would open some dispatch boxes but not all.

He said that ministers were still unable to get anything done as Ll. G. would not face the labour of deciding and giving authority. Mrs. Webb, who had just returned from a meeting of Reconstruction Committee, said that at one meeting recently at 4 P.M., just before the meeting started, the Marquess of Salisbury went to the mantelpiece and prayed aloud. She was talking to somebody else and could not hear what he said, but he was certainly praying aloud.

Webb told me that Russian sailors, fleet enclosed in ice, had put a lot of their officers through the ice, and the ships were therefore useless. Germans knew this and were preparing expedition accordingly. Talk of British and French naval officers going over to take charge, but these officers said they would prefer to take their own crews.

Wednesday, April 25th. London, Yacht Club.

I walked down past Buckingham Palace this morning. Two naval petty officers outside in full fig, and their women. A police superintendent (?) and a policeman at gates. Former said to latter, "We'd better be getting 'em in," and then to the sailors: "You decorations? Come on. Come along. Come on," curtly, as if they had done some deed suspicious, and not valorous. The sailors talked with their women for a few moments and then went obediently within the precincts. They were two roughish, short, thick-set chaps.

Called at Reform Club, where I spent 40 minutes with Wells and an American journalist-lecturer-professor named MacDonald, over here for the New York *Nation*. Wells was talking about the after-war exacerbationary reaction on nerves, which would cause rows, quarrels, etc. unless it was consciously kept well in hand, and MacDonald said that a year or so after the San Francisco earthquake prominent S.F. men would disappear; they were in sanatoria etc. Also lifelong friends, such as business partners, would quarrel over some trifle, each go to his solicitor, and never speak to one another again. He said that Gilbert Murray would not be a good Ambassador for U.S.A., as university influence was now over, there, and that the sources of opinion were the large and small towns of the Middle West. It was there that German and other pacifists worked with most success.

Monday, April 30th. Comarques.

Today, in accordance with time-table, I finished my novel *The Roll Call* at 4 P.M.

Friday, May 4th. London, Yacht Club.

I came to town on Tuesday meaning to take a few days' holiday after I had written my *Statesman* stuff. But Pinker had arranged for me to do the official War Savings article in 3 days for the *Strand* so that it could appear in their July number. So that I had to begin at once. And I had so much neuralgia yesterday that I couldn't do anything at all.

On Wednesday at the Reform I met the poet, Siegfried Sassoon, and considerably liked him.

Sunday, May 6th. Thorpe-le-Soken.

Returned here on Friday and met Bertie Sullivan in the train. Carrying F.O. mails over to Holland in the *Copenhagen,* he had been torpedoed by a submarine. He said 6 subms. waited for the boat, in 3 pairs. He was shaving. He seems to have kept pretty calm, but he said he couldn't get his boots on. "I was flurried," he said. Of 17 bags, he saved 16 and sank one. Result, after several days, a sort of lack of feeling in fingers. (It was March and he was not in rowboat for long.)

Yesterday, for the first time, and at my suggestion, we had no bread on the table at dinner. People who want it must ask for it from the sideboard. Wells gave me this tip. The value of these dodges is chiefly disciplinary. If the whole of the well-to-do classes practised them, the wheat problem would be trifling.

Wednesday, May 9th. London, Yacht Club.

On Sunday I had an idea for a short novel about an episode in the life of a French *cocotte*.[1] I thought I could tell practically everything about her existence without shocking the B.P. On Monday afternoon after doing my *Daily News* article I did my first water-colour of the season. In the garden. Rather goodish.

I came to London Tuesday. Lunched at Webbs'. Apropos of Squire's poem in current issue of *Statesman* the Webbs were both very funny, Mrs. Webb especially. She said: "Poetry means nothing to me. It confuses me. I always want to translate it back into prose."

Two quartets and a quintet before dinner at 8.45. Good male dinner, with champagne. During and after dinner, we had from Norton the finest exhibition of story-telling I ever heard. I was exhausted with laughing.

Later, W. Alcock[2] gave several parody treatments of *Three Blind Mice* according to Haydn, Chopin, Mendelssohn, and Grieg. Admirable. Werge and Hill played solos. I got to the Club at 1 A.M., and a half-dressed, half-asleep waiter let me in. This was one of the finest evenings I ever spent in my life.

Today Squire, Siegfried Sassoon lunched with me. Squire revealed himself more and more as being prim. He said he didn't like indecent jokes; didn't care for eating, either. Happily he likes drinking. Sassoon is a highly promising boy.

Friday, May 11th. London, Yacht Club.

Kindersley and Gardiner lunched with me at Reform, as K. wanted to meet G. K. talked very well. I shall tell him he ought to go into Parliament. I wrote part of another *Cosmopolitan* article in the morning.

---

[1] This was the origin of *The Pretty Lady*.
[2] Dr. Walter G. Alcock, the organist, and his wife Naomi were very old friends of Bennett.

After lunch it was funny to see H. G. Wells talking with an Indian ruler (I didn't catch his name) whom he was entertaining to lunch. He brought him to us. The ruler talked very sensibly, with a slight accent but extremely correctly. His burden was: "England cannot now throw us over by abandoning the monarchy. We need it."

Russian Exhibition and Tolstoy play with Marguerite at 5.30. I met George Moore on the way there, and he said that he had never made money out of his books worth talking about. £1500 or so out of *Esther Waters,* £1000 out of his latest, and so on. It seems that before I asked them to lunch he and Sickert had had a frightful row, which began by a newspaper scrap and ended by Sickert's inviting himself to dinner at George's and getting practically turned out. This was George's version. They had not met since till my luncheon. At that affair they were charming to each other.

Sunday, May 13th. Comarques, Thorpe-le-Soken.

Robert Ross gave a lunch at Automobile. Mr. and Mrs. Edmund Gosse, Eliz. Asquith, Mrs. Colefax, Captain Miller, and Dr. Borenius. I sat between Eliz. A. and Mrs. Colefax. Eliz. A. looks quite young. She seemed decent and hard, and socially extremely experienced. A tendency to phrase-making. Much deep ignorance of literature and even superficial ignorance, e.g. she didn't know that the French translations of Dostoievsky are incomplete and the English ones are complete, and read D. in French. She thought it easier to write a novel than a short story. She said she would send me a play of hers to read. It arrived today. I liked old Gosse again. He is anyhow educated.

Saturday, May 19th. London, Yacht Club.

I was looking out of the drawing-room window at M.'s flat yesterday morning when I saw two buses go along and then two more. And then, after about 5 minutes, 2 more. I said, "The bus strike is over!" It was. It had begun on Sunday.

Lunch at Reform. Wells came up here for tea. It was while talking to him that I had the idea of transferring the scene of my French *cocotte* novel from Paris to London, a vastly better idea, full of possibilities. H.G. certainly liked the idea.

Friday, May 25th. London, Yacht Club.

I returned to London Tuesday. Squire and Desmond MacCarthy[1] lunched with me at the Reform. At night after writing the Sardonyx article I went to Russian concert at Russian Exhibition, and it was very good. The pianissimos of the balalaika orchestra were marvellous, especially with music like Borodin's. On the other hand I had little use for Tchaikovsky's *Grand Trio* (A minor). Place pretty full.

But the chief thing yesterday was that I began on my novel about the French *cocotte,* with gusto.

Friday, June 1st. Thorpe-le-Soken.

Last Sunday my 50th birthday. Twelve people to dinner.

I went to London on Wednesday. Eliz. Asquith and J. C. Squire lunched with me at Ristorante del Commercio, Frith St. She certainly does amuse, but she is too professional over it, and she is a bad listener. Very neat.

She said that George V. really loved Mary and liked her much even while she was engaged to his brother. An absolutely conscientious monarch. She said that he had an immense regard and affection for her father, and that when it was a question of Asquith resigning, the King said, "If my Prime Minister resigns, I shall resign." Lately they were at Windsor and the King said, "I am so glad to have my Prime Minister back again with me."

Thursday, went to Philharmonic Hall to see the *Intolerance* film. A stupendous affair—I mean the Babylonian scenes. They were indeed staggering. But the modern story, though it contained some good rough satire on women social reformers, was very crude—even to an auto racing a train! A most fatiguing 3-hour affair.

Today lunch given by Davray to M. Helmer, an *avocat* of Colmar, in England to give lectures about Alsace-Lorraine. T. P. O'Connor, Massing-

---

[1] The present editor of *Life and Letters.*

ham, Gardiner, Spender, and 4 Frenchmen. T.P. began to Gardiner and me about his early youth. He evidently has a fancy for this sort of reminiscence. He said he had been the most trustful and easily deceived man imaginable. It was all very well, he said, but the connections of a simple man with women were apt to have "pecuniary endings."

Friday, June 8th. London, Yacht Club.

Walking about these streets about 10 to 10.30 when dusk is nearly over is a notable sensation; especially through Soho, with little cafés and co-op clubs and women and girls at shop doors. It is the heat that makes these things fine.

Afternoon, idea-finding for final section of first part of my *cocotte* novel.

Saturday, June 9th. Comarques.

Siegfried Sassoon lunched with me at the Reform yesterday. He expected some decoration for admittedly fine bombing work. Colonel had applied for it three times, but was finally told that as that particular push was a failure it could not be granted. Sassoon was uncertain about accepting a home billet if he got the offer of one. I advised him to accept it. He is evidently one of the reckless ones. He said his pals said he always gave the Germans every chance to pot him. He said he would like to go out once more and give them another chance to get him, and come home unscathed. He seemed jealous for the military reputation of poets. He said most of war was a tedious nuisance, but there were great moments, and he would like them again.

Thursday, June 14th. London, Yacht Club.

I came to London Tuesday, unwell. Lunch at Webb's. I spent the afternoon in writing *Observations*. Dined at the Reform with Clutton-Brock, who said that Wells was very rude to him about his very polite review of *God the Invisible King* in *Times Literary Supplement*.

Then I went slowly to Drury Lane to *Tristan* and arrived before the end of the 1st Act. I went to meet Turner, the *New Statesman* critic. Too much light on the stage at the crises, and horrible competition between the band and the singers; ugly costumes and scenery; and Rosina Buckman and Mullings both leviathans. A terrible sight. The second act was better, darker, and quieter. When King Mark began his monologue I departed. I thought the music was surviving pretty well.

On getting to Yacht Club from Richmond at 1.30 I had a telephone message from Marguerite to say that she and Anna were in the air raid [1] at Liverpool Street and unhurt. Today I found out that though the end of their train (11.38) was bombed, M. knew nothing of it, and Anna was only sure that she saw smoke "by the side of the train" behind her. Neither heard cries of wounded, nor broken glass or anything. M. heard 4 bombs or 5. Anna said she heard a noise and thought it was guns; then she saw a girl porter running and heard her cry "Oh" and thought it was an accident. When she realized that it was bombs she remembered nothing more till she "found herself" near underground lavatory, where people were taking refuge, with M. They were in different carriages and had lost each other. She saw people "crouching down" (near base of girders, apparently).

This morning I saw remains of a German aeroplane being motored up Piccadilly.

Thursday, June 21st. London, Yacht Club.

Atkins and Ross lunched with me yesterday here; and a very good lunch. I was startled to find Ross believing in the legend that the Germans had been cooking all their mortality figures since 1870. This shows how far a good brain can be deteriorated by a fixed idea. Whenever Ross talks about the war his whole face changes.

Friday, June 29th. London, Yacht Club.

No work yesterday. Lunched with Atkins at Reform and stayed there till 4.30. Afterwards I slept and read Dent's book on Mozart's operas, with profit. Dined with Marguerite at the Desmond MacCarthys', Wellington

---

[1] In the aeroplane raid on London of June 13, there were 157 killed and 432 injured. One of the planes was brought down.

Sq., but got to the Square too soon and idled round 2nd-hand shops and also listened to a Salvation Army street-corner show, which I think was the worst I ever did see. Four or five women and two men were the performers. It was ghastly in its melancholy, stupid, and perverse ugliness. One relatively pretty woman about 26, with the marks of pietistic obstinacy in her, sang a solo hymn in the most ridiculous way. Total audience, one boy.

Went to bed soon after 11, to read, for the first time, *Wuthering Heights*.

Friday, July 6th. Ludlow, Charlton Arms.

I came to Ludlow today. Fat female aristocratic in train. Dust cloak. Flower outside it. Jewel to fasten it. Many rings. Manicured. *Queen, Tatler*. Ethel M. Dell's latest novel. 3 cushions in a decided leather "envelope." Elaborate lunch-basket. Greedy. When ticket collectors came, she referred them, with an apprehensive gesture, to her maid, lest she might be bothered. Two of them knew of her maid. The third said roughly, "I suppose your maid has *your* ticket?" Her fear about being worried about anything was obvious. At Shrewsbury she held "envelope" while maid put cushions in it. Maid got her out of train and transferred her to Ludlow train. There was another and older and worse woman with an aged maid, in the same compartment. Very hard. She was met by a companion sort of girl at Birmingham.

Thursday, July 19th. London, Yacht Club.

I dined alone and Frank Shufflebotham, who had not been able to dine, came along here shortly after 10 P.M. He said that up to now £100,000,000 had been spent on gas, of which a large portion has been spent on experiments on animals such as guinea-pigs. He said that a certain firm had made £42,000 in 6 months clear profit on their gas factory with a capital of £1000. The Government put up the stills etc., which at the end of the war are to revert to the firm, and provided the whole of the raw material. This raw material for this one factory, in the shape of chemicals, has cost 2 millions in the last twelve months. I gathered that such factories exist up and down the country.

Friday, July 20th. London, Yacht Club.

Barrie came to lunch with me at Reform. 25 minutes late. He was very agreeable. He talked several times of "my boys." One is at the front.

Marguerite and I dined at a new restaurant, the Ivy, opposite Ambassador's Theatre. Very good. Then Brieux's *Les 3 Filles de M. Dupont*. It was much worse than I expected. Extremely crude throughout, and so false sometimes that I could not look at the stage. However, a great tract for those who need such things. Ethel Irving was very good, but she seemed to me to tear the big scene to pieces. She screamed hoarsely throughout it.

Wednesday, July 25th. London, Yacht Club.

Great raid over Felixstowe and Harwich on Sunday morning about 8.15. Heavier bombardment than we have ever heard before. For the first time the females fled to the cellar, and the temporary cook (who had been in a previous raid at Felixstowe) almost had hysterics. I was just beginning to shave, and so I did shave, but the row was disturbing. It ceased in a few minutes (during which over 40 people had been killed or injured). No firing nearer than 7 miles from us. The "air-raid warning" came through from the comic War Office about ½ an hour after the raid was over.

I came to London yesterday; lunched at Webb's, where was Glynne Williams, the new editor of the *Statesman*. Company *très sympathique*. Wrote my article in the afternoon, and went to dine at Barrie's with Thomas Hardy and wife. Barrie has an ugly little manservant and the finest view of London I ever saw. Mrs. Hardy a very nice woman, with a vibrating attractive voice. Hardy was very lively; talked like anything. Apropos of Chekhov he started a theory that some of Chekhov's tales were not justifiable because they told nothing unusual. He said a tale must be unusual and the people interesting. Of course he soon got involved in the meshes of applications and instances, but he kept his head and showed elasticity and common sense and came out on the whole well. He has all his faculties, unimpaired. Quite modest and without the slightest pose.

They both had very good and accurate appraisements of such different people as Shorter and Phillpotts.

Later in the evening Barrie brought along both Shaw and the Wellses by 'phone. Barrie was consistently very quiet, but told a few A1 stories. At dusk we viewed the view and the searchlights. Hardy, standing outside one of the windows, had to put a handkerchief on his head. I sneezed. Soon after Shaw and the Wellses came Hardy seemed to curl up. He had travelled to town that day and was evidently fatigued. He became quite silent. I then departed and told Barrie that Hardy ought to go to bed. He agreed. The spectacle of Wells and G.B.S. talking firmly and strongly about the war, in their comparative youth, in front of this aged, fatigued, and silent man—incomparably their superior as a creative artist—was very striking.

Thursday, July 26th. London, Yacht Club.

Headache yesterday after Hardy and cigarettes. Shufflebotham lunched with me at Reform, and then we had a Turkish bath, which with me last nearly 3 hours. Dined at the Reform with Massingham, who, like me, was going to the opera. He likes eating and drinking. Not much, but well. We had caviare, and we shared a trifle of champagne. Opera. I met Ernest Newman, very estimable and sound as usual. We agreed in our estimate of Beecham. He astonished me by saying that he liked a great deal in *Louise*. Apropos of Ravel he said, "No great man is ever idle"; which is very true. Apropos of Newman's liking *Louise*, Hardy said that he liked Lytton and that *Pelham* was a very able book. Both Hardy and Barrie expressed great admiration for Trollope, but they both expressed perhaps a little too much.

Friday, July 27th. London, Yacht Club.

American article yesterday morning.

Dined at flat and then with M. to *Marriage of Figaro*. Dramatically the last act is very poor in both scenes. Musically it is as good as the rest. Shaw grumbled much at the performance. The sentimental interest, as

Newman said to me, is the best part of the opera, and the Figaro music is not very surpassing. The sentimental songs were celestial.

Saturday, September 1st. Comarques.

I took a month's holiday, ending yesterday. We went to spend 2 days at the Schusters' during it, and I saw the first batch of the American Army from the windows of the Yacht Club during it.

Health not very good during it, but a distinct benefit as regards the outlook on work actually in progress. I made some advance in water-colours, and more still in monotypes. I didn't read a lot. Hardy's *Pair of Blue Eyes*, full of fine things and immensely sardonic. Murray on Euripides—formless, but gradually getting at something. Reminiscences of Tagore—good. *Duchesse de Langeais*, quite a major work, which thoroughly held me.

Friday, September 14th. Thorpe-le-Soken.

On Wednesday Shufflebotham carefully examined me at the club and decided that I must be X-rayed. He guaranteed that I had had appendi-citis several times without knowing it. He also insisted on a new visit to the oculist. All these things added to my gloom due to the sudden and long attack of neuralgia.

Thursday, September 20th. London, Yacht Club.

I began to write at 6:30 A.M. yesterday, and I had written a chapter by 12.15. Then X-ray séance at Harley Street (all the large front waiting-rooms of Harley St. with people reading old weeklies in them while waiting).

I lunched with Shufflebotham afterwards at Pagani's and had another séance, to watch the progress of the bismuth, at 5 P.M. Rain most of day, and I was walking about most of the day in the rain. Only spent 2d. on transport.

Friday, September 21st. London, Yacht Club.

Radiographed for the 3rd time yesterday, and nothing found wrong, except the common slight slowness of the work in the colon. Lunched with Davray and Weil (ex-member of the Reichstag). He was dining with Jaurés when Jaurés was killed in the restaurant.[1]

Monday, September 24th. London, Yacht Club.

Marguerite came to town this afternoon. I worked till 3.30 P.M., and then, seeing I could do more writing and could reflect just as well in train, I came up to town so as to save half a day tomorrow. I was unwell and without energy all day. Nevertheless I worked satisfactorily in the train. Then air raid.

I had a great subject for a water-colour on Saturday. I put my *enceinte* French Renaissance virgin (white) and the black *juju* that Molly Green brought from Nigeria for Marguerite, side by side, and called the picture "The Gods." A fine composition and a real subject. I started the sketch but couldn't finish it in the time. However, the subject will keep.

Wednesday, September 26th. London, Yacht Club.

A raid began precisely at the moment I left the Yacht Club. The buses seemed to quicken, the streets appreciably emptied. Most people hurried; I did; but a few strolled along. I was glad when I got to the Albany. Firing when there nearer, and everything was faintly lit up with flashes. I found that the Albany alley had been covered with thick glass thrown over from an explosion or a hit on the Academy on the previous night.[2]

Thursday, September 27th. London, Yacht Club.

Dined with M. at Waldorf. To get there, strange journeys in Tube. Very wet. Very poor women and children sitting on stairs (fear of raid). Also travelling in lift and liftman grumbling at them because no fear of raid, and they answering him back, and middle-class women

---

[1] The great French Socialist leader was assassinated on the eve of the outbreak of war, July 31, 1914.
[2] For about a week there were almost daily air raids over London. From September 24 to October 1 there were nearly 50 people killed.

saying to each other that if the poor couldn't keep to the regulations they ought to be forbidden the Tube as a shelter from raid.

S. said he had seen dreadful sights of very poor with babies in Tube on Monday. One young woman was in labour. He asked her if she was and she said that she was, and she had got up because she was told to go with the rest. He got her taken on a stretcher to a hospital. Proprietor of a restaurant where I lunched today with Swinnerton said that although his place was always full at night, he only had four people on Monday night and *not a single customer* on Tuesday night (fear of raids). He said also that at fish and vegetable markets he couldn't get what he wanted because supplies were not there, and that wholesalers had not taken supplies because they couldn't dispose of them, and that stuff was rotting. A raid was feared tonight, but evidently the German machines were turned back before reaching London.

Wednesday, October 10th. London, Yacht Club.

Dined with George Whale at the N.L.C. and in his great ugly sitting-room took what I wanted from his large collection of notes on war superstitions for my novel. His notes were extremely interesting.

Wells came in and slanged the Webbs as usual, and incidentally said: "My boom is over. I've had my boom. I'm yesterday." He said that in air raids he was afraid of going to pieces altogether; so if there was a balcony he stood on it. He had been through several raids at Southend. He said, "I get huffy and cross just as if——" but I can't remember his comparison.

Thursday, October 11th. London, Yacht Club.

Met Crane yesterday with Wells at Reform. He wouldn't talk at first, but afterwards talked excellently, till nearly 4 o'clock. He has spent several months in Russia every year for either 20 or 30 years. Also travelled through Asia sundry times and been U.S.A. Ambassador to China. Calm quiet man about 60. Very modest and yet knowing himself.

Rather sentimental about friendships and family relations, but very wise and balanced. He was pessimistic about Russia. Said Kerensky was a good young lawyer and nothing else. Related how K. had ordered a good place for the sister of his mistress in Imperial Theatre, and it was refused, and he had to give in.

He gave a very good account of the Rasputin régime and showed how complex the situation was and how a Rasputin could not be understood by Westerns. About the East, he showed how the boycott of Japan in China (unordered but complete and irresistible) had put a pause to Japan's scheme of conquest in China.

Friday, October 12th. London, Yacht Club.

Granville-Barker (2nd Lieut.) lunched with me here yesterday. He said he had to do with *liaisons* between British and U.S.A. Governments, and the latter said that they want, in addition to the official views, the views of the Independent Left. So he came to get mine. He had got Wells's and 2 or 3 other people's.

He said that the U.S.A. people were not greatly impressed by anonymous opinions. It was useless to say, "It is thought—" But if you said, "So-and-so thinks—" the thing carried weight.

Tuesday, October 16th. Comarques.

Went through all first two books of *cocotte* novel, and fairly well pleased with everything except last chapter or so. Today I tabulated all my information and ideas afresh.

Wednesday, October 24th. London, Yacht Club.

I finished a chapter of my novel this morn, and did packing. Tomorrow I go to Ireland at the request of G.O.C. Ireland, Intelligence Department.

Tuesday, November 6th. London, Yacht Club.

I returned from Dublin on Saturday exhausted; neuralgia. I spent

Sunday all alone between this and the Reform Clubs, and wrote my first Irish article complete.

In the evening I read a lot of Alec Waugh's *Loom of Youth* with great interest.

Sunday, November 18th. Thorpe.

I made the acquaintance of Lord Beaverbrook Thursday week. He and Ross lunched with me on Friday. At this second meeting he asked me to take him to Leicester Gallery, where I had mentioned there was a good etching of Rops. I did so, with Ross. He asked which was the etching, bought it (20 guineas), and gave it me on the spot.

This was at only our 2nd meeting. *Un peu brusqué.*

Wednesday, November 28th. London, Yacht Club.

I finished *Gulliver's Travels* on Sunday. The final episode is the best, and is indeed very fine; but all the difficulties of detail in describing horse life are evaded. The thing could have been done much more convincingly. On the other hand the comments of the horses on human character and manners are superb.

Sunday, December 9th. Comarques.

Better arrangements must be made for keeping this damned journal. On Thursday last I made my début at the Other Club,[1] to which I was elected without my knowledge. I sat next to F. E. Smith,[2] who is a live companion, inclined to recount his achievements, but interesting and informed. Duke of Marlborough in the chair—merely to propose the Royal health.

Sir Mark Sykes seemed the most interesting man there. He did a very original caricature of F. E. Smith and me. I heard he was the best amateur actor in England. He certainly has brains, and political brains. Lutyens amiably played the amusing fool. I greatly enjoyed the affair.

Turkish baths and a little dissipation have lately improved my health, and greatly improved my capacity for finding ideas and working.

---

[1] Carlton Club.
[2] Barrister, diplomat, later Earl of Birkenhead.

Tuesday, December 11th. London, Yacht Club.

Wrote an article yesterday for *Daily News* showing advisability of preparing peace terms and insisting—what few people seem to understand—that this can go on with ardent prosecution of war.

Wednesday, December 12th. London, Yacht Club.

Poetry recital at Mrs. Colefax's. Tea first; the usual crowds; but Spender and Garvin were there. Drawing-room nearly full. Miss McLeod, a woman with straight, thin, ruthless lips, read admirably 2 poems of Sassoon's. The best thing for me was "Hippopotamus" by T. S. Eliot. Had I been the house, this would have brought the house down. One of Miss McLeod's poems was pretty goodish too. Gosse, except for his opening speech—a bit long—made an excellent chairman. On the whole the affair was by no means so bad as I had feared. The Sitwell family was much in evidence, *tres cultivée.*

Thursday, December 13th. London, Yacht Club.

I was told the following at dinner last night. Two working men were in the Tube and began arguing whether a certain peculiarly dressed person in the same carriage was or was not the Archbishop of Canterbury. They bet. To settle it one of them went up to the person and said, "Please, sir, are you the Archbishop of Canterbury?" The reply was, "What the bloody hell has that got to do with you?" The workman went back to his mate and said: "No good, mate. The old cow won't give me a straight answer either way."

Friday, December 14th. London, Yacht Club.

During the evening F. E. Smith, Attorney-General, rang me up—how he got hold of me God knows—and said, "Will you go to the United States with me on Saturday morning?" He then spoke, low, some confidential remarks about his mission. I didn't catch them all and didn't get him to repeat them as I hadn't the slightest intention of going —especially for 2 months. He said, "Nominally you'll be my secretary, but only nominally, of course."

Although I like him as a companion I didn't see myself going to U.S.A. as F.E.'s secretary and boon companion. Still, he has considerable points.

Fog and mist, and a most damnable romantic London. I walked from Oxford Street to Piccadilly. Scarcely one of my "pretty ladies" about.

Saturday, December 15th. London, Yacht Club.

Dined with Benchers of Gray's Inn in hall, to meet Lloyd George and heads of Air Service. F. E. Smith in chair. A very "short," very ordinary dinner, and plenty of wine. I think Lord Halsbury made the greatest impression (aged 96-7) by his forceful way of saying that a man who made a bargain and didn't keep it was "a dirty scoundrel." Tim Healy and Garvin both quoted a good deal from all sorts of things. Ll. G. spoke for over an hour, too long, and said all sorts of platitudes for public consumption. His "set" effects were failures. But he had some great similes. Winston Churchill, after the principal speech, made an amiable tour of the tables. He wore all his military medals dangling on the lapel of his dress coat. (I suppose this is all right, but I had never seen it before except on the dress coat of the hall porter of this club.)

Sunday, December 16th. London, Yacht Club.

Dined at flat with M. and Richard [1] (who came home yesterday) and then to Barrie's *Dear Brutus,* where we had seats in the back row of the dress circle. A great success, and deserved. For a fanciful play the idea is A1, and it is worked out with much invention. As soon as I saw the scheme of the play I feared for the last act. However, the last act was very good. I enjoyed the play nearly throughout.

On coming away, vast jostling crowds in the streets, and the feel of a tremendous city in the dark.

Monday, December 17th. London, Yacht Club.

To Stage Society performance, where, owing to a misapprehension, we arrived an hour late.

---

[1] Richard Bennett, the nephew whom Arnold Bennett adopted, was at this time at school at Oundle.

Part of a ballet we partly saw from the upper circle, and it seemed very English and stiff and *voulu* and poor; but the old music was fine. Then I got the committee to take us into their box, and we saw Granville-Barker's play, *Vote by Ballot*. It contained any amount of witty and true dialogue, but it was not what I call a play. Theatre packed. All the usual crowd. Wives and mistresses of the same men all mixed up and friendly together.

Got to club at 9.40. Cut a lot of Chaucer pages, but I didn't read any because the glossary is all at the end.

Cut a lot of Rabelais pages. Read some of that and found it good. Also same in middle of night. Also Butler in middle of night. Rotten neuralgic night, but I feel a certain liveliness *ce matin*.

Tuesday, December 18th. London, Yacht Club.

To lunch at the Reform Club, where I joined Robert Ross, who had two young poets, Robert Graves and Philip —— (I forget his name and am not even sure if he is a poet). I was very pleased with both these youths. Lately I am more and more struck by the certainty, strength, and unconscious self-confidence of young men, so different from my middle-aged uncertainty and also my lack of physical confidence in my own body. In the afternoon 2¾ hours hard, in which I wrote 1200 words of *The Pretty Lady*.

Wednesday, December 19th. London, Yacht Club.

I was wakened out of my after-bath sleep by news of impending air raid. This news merely made me feel gloomy. I didn't mind missing dinner at flat, or anything—I was merely gloomy. As soon as I got out into Northumberland Avenue I heard guns. Motors and people rushing. Then guns very close. I began to run. I headed for Reform Club and abandoned idea of reaching the flat. Everybody ran. Girls ran.

However, I found that after the Turkish bath I couldn't run much in a heavy overcoat. So I walked. It seemed a long way. Guns momentarily ceased. So I didn't hurry, and felt relieved. But still prodigiously gloomy. I reached the club. Hall in darkness. No girls in coffee room.

The manservants manfully tackled the few diners. Nothing could be had out of kitchen, as kitchen under glass and deserted.

All clear at about 9.30.[1]

Thursday, December 20th. London, Yacht Club.

Swinnerton came to Yacht Club for tea, and stayed 80 minutes. He said that *Books and Persons* had sold 3400 and was still going steadily on.[2] He told me about his new novel of Barnet society and said he had consulted *Clayhanger* to see how I got over certain difficulties, but couldn't find out. I certainly couldn't tell him.

Saturday, December 22nd. Comarques.

Wells came for tea to Club on Thursday and talked about his very long novel, which he stated to be terrific indictment of the present state of England.

Sunday, December 23rd. Comarques.

Captain Hill and wife came last night. He related how after a long period (several weeks) of "special vigilance" he was sleeping in a blanket on the floor of the gardener's cottage at Thorpe Hall when a dispatch rider burst in just like a stage dispatch rider, at 3 A.M. The dispatch contained one word, which for Hill had no meaning. The rider couldn't tell him anything and only insisted on a signature in receipt, which of course Hill gave. Hill then got up and went to see another C.O. near. This C.O. had received the same message and also had not the least idea what it meant. Other C.O.'s were afterwards found to be in the same case.

Hill asked another C.O. to ring up the staff. C.O. said he daren't. So Hill did himself. He asked the telephone clerk what the message meant. The clerk replied that he knew but he daren't tell. Hill then told him to summon the brigade major. Clerk said he positively dare not. Hill

---

[1] Five aeroplanes bombed London, causing the death of 10 persons. There were over 70 injured.

[2] A collection of the Jacob Tonson articles. See pages 212–3.

insisted and took responsibility on himself. Brigade major came to telephone, using terrible language. It then appeared that the incomprehensible word was a code word signifying that the period of vigilance was over. Only no C.O. of unit had been previously informed of the significance of the word. The whole episode, with its middle-of-the-night business, absurd secrecy, etc., was thoroughly characteristic.

Tuesday, December 25th. Comarques.

War. Only about half a pint of methylated spirits left in the house. Marguerite decided to keep this in stock for an emergency of illness etc. Wise. So I can no longer make my own perfect tea at what hour I like in the morning. And this morning I had poor servant-made tea. However, there is a hope of my getting some other heating apparatus.

Je me suis recueilli somewhat yesterday for my novel, with difficulty. I re-read some of it in typescript and thought part was dullish and part interesting. Reading *Georgian Poetry 1916–1917* seemed to buck me up to raise the damn thing to a higher plane than it has yet reached save in odd places here and there.

Wednesday, December 26th. Comarques.

Only seven sat down to dinner last night, owing to difficulties of transport and engagements of officers for mess dinners. This is the smallest Xmas dinner we have had in this house. Soldiers were noisy outside during the day. Mason came for lunch and stayed till after nightfall. He rode off in falling snow, having made Richard a present of all the chemical reagents which he had ordered for him.

I read a lot, all I shall read, of Saintsbury's *History of the French Novel*. Very prolix, and bursting with subordinate sentences and clauses, but containing plenty of useful information; also it shows that he does understand something of the craft of novel-writing. His tracing of the development of the technique of the novel in the 17th cent. is interesting and, to me, quite new. The amount of this old man's reading is staggering.

Much bad music after dinner.

Thursday, December 27th. Comarques.

Dinner last night at 2/1st London R.G.A. at Bentley Huts. Caffery came and fetched us in a Ford car. About 30 people. Goodish dinner. I did nothing all the evening except sit in front of the stove. Solo whist and bridge partners, and much noisy dancing. After midnight the Ford car could not be started, and it never was started, though 6 men spent pretty nearly 2 hours on it, with blowpipes and things. M. and Olive slept at Steel and Caffery's lodgings. I came home in a G.S. wagon with 2 horses and 2 men, easy chair in wagon, rugs, eiderdown, and a rug like an extinguisher all over my head and face. Freezing hard, but I was quite warm. This journey took about 1½ hours. I made the two men happy and then had a hot bath and must have gone to sleep about 4.40. I slept till 8. I was thoroughly bored until it was discovered that the car wouldn't start. Thenceforward I was quite cheerful.

1918

Tuesday, January 1st. Comarques.

Much work on the novel these last two days. I wrote 2600 words yesterday. Last year I wrote 255,000 words. Not bad, considering the circumstances.

Wednesday, January 2nd. London, Yacht Club.

Came to London yesterday. George Paish's food-question lunch, arranged for yesterday, had been put off without warning me. So I lunched with Ross at Reform. Afterwards, Turkish bath with Masterman, who said that the shine of the present Honours List would be nothing to that of the List when Ll. George quitted the premiership. He would have everything to wipe up, then.

On reaching the club I read the Book of Esther in the Eversley Bible, which I have newly bought. A good Eastern story, exceedingly ingenuous, all based on copulation.

Thursday, January 3rd. London, Yacht Club.

Lane told me a British bomb had descended through the roof of his house and wrecked his library, but the damage was only £46. More Bible reading here this evening. I Kings makes excellent reading. But the way David ordered executions before he died, and Solomon upon his ascension, is rather startling.

Monday, January 7th. Comarques.

Sundry officers, including Saunders Jacob and Cummings, dined on Saturday night, and the delight of these two in singing more or less at sight good and bad songs from the *Scottish Students' Song Book,* to my bad accompaniment, was most extraordinary. Last night Richard was talking about being set to learn 40 lines of *L'Allegro* in 45 minutes prep and to write essays in ten minutes. What a fool of a master! It appears that this master once said in class, "Your Hall Caines, Arnold Bennetts, and H. G. Wellses will pass away and be forgotten. Classics will remain." I couldn't find my Milton, but on my offering a reward of 6*d*. Richard found it. I re-read some of *Paradise Lost* and thought it very fine and interesting. The remarks of Adam and the angel about the relations of man and wife have not yet been beaten for sense.

Tuesday, January 8th. Comarques.

Another chapter of *The Pretty Lady* yesterday. Too much smoking, ostensibly to provide Richard with tobacco ash for chemical experiments.

I have read 100 pages or so of the Hammonds' *Town Labourer.* There is undoubtedly a pleasure in reading recitals of horrible injustice and tyranny.

Wednesday, January 9th. Comarques.

I didn't like reading the child-labour chapter in the Hammonds' *Town Labourer.* It exceeded the limits in its physicalness. I wish I had read it before I wrote the child chapter in *Clayhanger* to which the Hammonds refer. I could have made that chapter even more appalling than it is. But at that date probably all the materials had not been collected, as the Hammonds have since collected them.

Friday, January 11th. Comarques.

Marguerite bought a pig at the end of the year. It was a small one, but we have been eating this damned animal ever since, in all forms except ham, which has not yet arrived. Brawn every morning for break-fast. Yesterday I struck at pig's feet for lunch and had mutton instead;

they are neither satisfying nor digestible, and one of the biggest frauds that ever came out of kitchens. All this is a war measure, and justifiable. I now no longer care whether I have sugar in my tea or not. We each have our receptacle containing the week's sugar, and use it how we like. It follows us about, wherever we happen to be taking anything that is likely to need sugar. My natural prudence makes me more sparing of mine than I need be. Another effect of war is that there is a difficulty in getting stamped envelopes at the P.O. The other day the postmaster, by a great effort and as a proof of his goodwill, got me £1 worth, which won't go far.

It occurred to me how the war must affect men of 70, who have nothing to look forward to. The war has ruined their end, and they cannot have much hope.

Sunday, January 13th. Comarques.

I outlined in the bath this morning an idea of a play about a man being offered a title and his wife insisting on his accepting it against his will.[1] Spender told me that such a man had once asked him for advice in just such a problem, and he had advised the man to suppress his scruples and accept the title. Ross said that this would be a good idea for a play, and it is.

Tuesday, January 15th. London, Yacht Club.

We came to London this morning, dog, Richard, cook, M., and me. Lunch at Webb's. Then I hurried back to Reform Club to join after lunch the Writers' Group. A peace campaign on foot—i.e. peace with German people. Spender, as usual, had the most information to give, and it seemed very well founded. After dinner to *Sleeping Partners* at St. Martin's. Adapted from Sacha Guitry. Slow at first, but very adroit and amusing indeed as it progressed. Seymour Hicks had all the jam and was marvellously good. We all really enjoyed it. I met Lucas in the entr'acte and he took me round to see Hicks, whom I instantly liked and decided to ask to lunch.

---

[1] This was *The Title*, produced at the Royalty Theatre, July 20, 1918.

Sunday, January 20th. Comarques.

I went to the Leicester to see the Dyson war-drawings and ended by buying a Brabazon gouache. I was hoping the sight of pictures would stimulate my novel-cerebration, but it did not. However, yesterday, after a sleeping draught, I was in form again and wrote over 2000 words, a complete chapter.

Heard at the Reform on Thursday afternoon on very good authority that a telegram recalling Haig and appointing Allenby in his place had been drafted and was to have been sent on Wednesday, but was withheld for further discussion on Thursday.

Monday, January 21st. Comarques.

M. has now joined a Y.M.C.A. canteen for soldiers coming home on leave, near Waterloo Station. The hours were from 10.30 to 3 P.M., no interval for lunch. She came home and said that "any fool could do the work" and that it was "easy and interesting." She was going to undertake 4 hours on Tuesdays, Thursdays, and Saturdays, going to town on Monday afternoons, thus leaving only Sundays for Comarques. However, I stopped this. She really began as a formal helper on Saturday. She was put on to washing-up. She had a nice girl of 15 as colleague, very smart. It seems they had to work at really top speed all the time, in order to cope with the demand. This was for 3½ hours—11 to 2.30 or so. No interval of any kind for lunch, even a sandwich, not 5 minutes. A cup of coffee brought to them, from which they snatched sips. (No breakfast before starting. No dinner in the evening, owing to concert.) Standing all the time. There is no doubt that she and all the other women think this rather fine, but still she admitted that it was thoroughly bad organization. Women do like this exhausting kind of work. It wears them out and then they think they have done something grand.

Tuesday, January 22nd. Comarques.

Miss Nerney found I had written already 75,000 words of my novel, which was to be its total length. And there are probably 5000 more words to write.

I read Balzac's *Une Double Famille*. Very good, but the plot by no means clear at the end. In fact, though I have now read the thing probably 3 times, I don't really know what happened in the interval before the epilogue. Still, his leaving out is very fine and effective as a rule.

London, Yacht Club.

Came to London this morn. Great outcry at the Reform about a new rule against having guests to lunch. I was asked to draft a protest and I did so. Just as I was going away Gardiner introduced me to Col. Repington, now celebrated for having thrown up his *Times* job as a protest against attacks on the General Staff. He has very large eyes and must be a strange old man. He said, when I said that the matter with the war cabinet was that it was not *English,* "Yes, did you ever know a Celt to win a war?"

Thursday, January 24th. London, Yacht Club.

Rumours from two sources of food riots, either in Camden Town or in Highgate, or both; quelled by the military. I gravely doubt the last detail.

Monday, January 28th. Comarques.

Today at lunch-time I finished my novel *The Pretty Lady*—about 80,000 words. The close seemed to me to be rather ingenious, well executed, and effective. But for years past I have ceased to try to judge the value of a novel until it has been published for a year or two—I mean one of my own. I thought *The Old Wives' Tale* was dull when I had finished it.

Wednesday, January 30th. London, Yacht Club.

I came to London yesterday morning. No posts and no newspapers at either Thorpe or Colchester, so that my first news was obtained in London of the "great" air-raid. Lunched with Runciman and Buckmaster in order to get particulars of any Liberal party programme there might be. Runciman talked very well, and with firmness. He complained of the Liberal press. His programme had evidently not been put together; and he admitted that any anti-government concerted action by Liberals (such as he himself directed) was done without either the approval or the help of Asquith. Yet he would insist that Asquith was the actual, veritable leader of the Liberal party!

Then Turkish bath with Masterman and Walpole. Walpole very young, strong, happy, and optimistic. He said he enjoyed himself all the time. Masterman very gloomy and cynical, and prophesying the most terrible things. He said he hadn't had a happy day for 19–20 years, and that the only thing that really bucked him up was winning an election. In fact he was a sad spectacle. The Galsworthys and a Mrs. Bainbridge came to dinner at the flat.

Air-raid maroon warning at about 10 P.M. We went down into the bank basement, which is well heated, and stayed till 12.30 A.M. Marguerite and the cook knitting. I noticed that John [Galsworthy] was just as chivalrous to the cook as to any of the other women. He even gave her a chocolate. The time passed quickly, even on hard chairs. From time to time I went out. The red warning with "Take cover" on it shone steadily at the intersection of Oxford St. and Tottenham Court Rd. But people were walking about. Infrequent guns. Then the G.'s ventured to depart.

Thursday, January 31st. London, Yacht Club.

Collecting ideas for my article on the future of the Liberal party. Then to show of the Senefelder Club at the Leicester Galleries. There was a lithograph of Forain, "Conseil Juridique," which put everything else in the show clean off the map. I couldn't think of anything that I had ever seen more perfect. 28 guineas; so I didn't buy it. A loud-voiced old man in very sporting costume, and deaf, came in with a fairly young woman, who called him alternatively Claudie and Sir Claude. It was Claude de Crespigny, the sportsman. Many of these chaps have very loud voices. He said 2*s.* 6*d.* was too high a price for entrance, had never known entrance to a gallery to be more than 1*s.* He was mollified when he learnt that 2*s.* 6*d.* paid for two. He had come to see a painting by Laura Knight of a prize-fighter. As soon as he saw it he shouted: "I think they ought to give you your money back. It's not like —— at all. He hasn't got those muscles on him—never had. And look at his legs. And look at the size of the ring. It's not 8 feet square." However, the woman soothed him, and in the end he seemed to be quite a decent sort of chap.

Lunch at Marlborough Club. The first I saw at the Marlborough was the Duke of Marlborough. I like this chap—also he said he was very interested in my articles and agreed with them. I liked him the first time I saw him. Ex-King Manoel was there, lunching like nobody at all with two military officers. Then to Reform Club to meet Wells, who was very angry with the insular commercial machinations of the aeroplane m'facturers, who, he says, are greatly over-represented on the Civil Air Transport Committee, of which he is a member. He told me the latest theory is that the first floor of a well-built house is safer than the basement in an air-raid, owing to the new heavy delayed-action bombs which go through everything and burst only when they can't travel any further.

Wednesday, February 6th. London, Yacht Club.

Gardiner and Massingham at club in afternoon were extremely gloomy, but Spender preserved his even temper as usual. So did E. M'Kenna keep cheerful. I heard various interesting things, but can't remember them, except that U.S.A. has 400,000 men in France now, but frankly admitted its present inability or absence of military genius to organize a *fighting machine* at present. It is to be hoped that it will improve. It seems as if Ll. George had got his way as to a united command in west.

Friday, February 8th. London, Yacht Club.

I seemed to do nothing yesterday morning except call on M. and write letters and just reflect for a few minutes on the first article of my 2nd series for the *Cosmopolitan*. Lunch at the Reform with Ross and Chalmers Mitchell. Mitchell, aged 53, with his grey hairs, stuck to it that he had found a sound definition of poetry. I forget what it was. I told him he ought to know better at his age than to imagine that poetry could be defined. Hedley LeBas told me that my amateur article outlining a policy for the Liberal party had made a deep impression on Gulland, the chief whip, who said it was the best article on the subject he had seen for years, and he "should show it to Asquith." Majestic and impressive phrase. "Show it to Asquith."

Saturday, February 9th. London, Yacht Club.

I heard that all merchant vessels leaving Egypt were agog as they left to know whether they would be escorted by Japanese or British men-of-war. If by Japanese they were happy, as the Japanese had never lost a ship. If by British, they became very gloomy.

Buckmaster told me that Lady Buchanan[1] told him last night at dinner more and more astounding stories of Petrograd. After a debauch, heaps of dead, wounded and drunken lying together—literally in heaps. In order to get some people out of a mixed lot in a cellar, the cellar was flooded. No result, except that the water froze, and will remain frozen till the spring. Two regiments of women and one of young men alone defended the Winter Palace. When it was taken the women were captured, tortured, and raped. Some killed themselves; some escaped to tell. Massingham said that a friend of his had seen men burnt alive in kerosene tubs on the Nevsky Prospect.

Monday, February 11th. London, Yacht Club.

I came up a day earlier in order to meet Grey[2] at Spender's, as one of the "Writers' Group." The "Writers' Group" now consists of George Paish, A. G. Gardiner, J. A. Spender, J. A. Hobson, Graham Wallas, Lowes Dickinson, Gilbert Murray, Hartley Withers, Leonard Hobhouse and myself. We lunched first at Café Royal, the name of which had rather startled Gardiner & Co., at the start. At Spender's there were

---

[1] Wife of Sir George Buchanan, British Ambassador at Petrograd.
[2] Viscount Grey of Fallodon.

also invited M'Kenna, Runciman and Buckmaster. Webb and Henderson had been invited to lunch with us. They came also.

Grey looked younger than I had expected. Hair scarcely grey. Trousers too wide. He played with a pencil-case half the time. He looked well, and spoke easily, clearly and well. We all sat in chairs in Spender's study in Sloane Street, surrounded by Spender's water-colours, some of which were very good. Grey said that both Italy and Rumania had not been asked to come in. They suggested coming in, and gave their terms, which in the main we had to agree to, in order to prevent them being inimically neutral, or, as regards Rumania, going over to the other side. He said that agreement with Russia, as regards giving her Constantinople, was result of Turkey, after promising to be neutral, wantonly attacking her ports. He explained why none of the principal Governments *dared* make peace—they could offer nothing to their peoples to show for the war.

Paish made it absolutely clear that unless men could go back to field *this* autumn there would be famine in 1920—spring. There seemed to be no light at all until M'Kenna, who came late, said that the only hope was a new attempt at an international labour conference. He said he was quite sure international labour could agree on something reasonable, and that if they did, the hands of Governments would be forced. M'Kenna was valuable in insisting that the idea of us trying to make peace now on the assumption that we had won was idiotic. He said that if we held out till 1920 we could have everything we wanted. He showed how tenacious Germany had always been in all her wars and that even the labour terms of peace gave no help to pacifist Germans. All were agreed that this government must be overthrown.

Wednesday, February 20th. London, Yacht Club.

We now ask nearly every one whom we ask to dinner to bring some food. On Saturday I finished off the proofs of *The Pretty Lady*. I can now see things that I have left out of that novel. Nevertheless the story held me well as I read it again—a good test.

Thursday, February 21st. London, Yacht Club.

I lunched with Rosher to meet Kennedy Jones at Thatched House Club. He is a Glasgow man, aged 52, with pale eyes, and when talking he screws them up a little and looks far away as if cogitating on the most difficult and interesting aspects of what he is discussing. During the lunch he said that *he* was really the parent of the new journalism, because he was the journalist—and it was he who had gone to Northcliffe with the idea of buying the *Evening News*. This I fairly believed. He also drew out of his pocket a cutting from a Bristol newspaper about 7 ins. long of a speech of his. He said this showed what attention his remarks had in the press. He spoke humorously but was serious behind the humour, or he would not have pulled the thing out of his pocket at all. I laughed and said it proved nothing, because he could do what he liked with any newspaper. He laughed and said I was cynical.

He related stories of how American newspaper owners stole men from each other and how Hearst had stolen X. from Pulitzer, and Northcliffe had stolen him from Hearst, in each case after being specially requested not to do so. He said Northcliffe had taken on Wells for the *Mail* because he felt that "new ideas" were coming and he wanted to be able to say when they did come that he had favoured them etc.

K.J. struck me as a powerful and ruthless man, but I wouldn't have any of his ruthlessness. When he was firm, I was firmer. In spite of the superior knowledge of which he boasts he has already lost 2 bets to Rosher about the war. I wouldn't like to be one of his men, but he was interesting enough to meet.

Wednesday, March 13th. London, Yacht Club.

The Writers' Group entertained Asquith at the Reform last night, and there was a very good dinner and plenty of various wines. Twelve people. Asquith looked very well. He came in a smoking jacket and a good soft silk shirt, but his overcoat and soft hat were ridiculous. Only Spender, of the hosts, was in evening dress. Asquith ate and drank and laughed well. He has a good "contained" laugh at implications. He showed no signs of decay. He was surrounded by first-class men, some very first class, but easily held his place as chief man. He did not talk a lot in the discussion, but he talked well and showed a complete grasp of the subject, which was the respective virtues of a conscription of wealth and a heavier income-tax to meet after-war budget. It was admirably carried on by George Paish, Sidney Webb, Hartley Withers, Graham Wallas, and J. A. Hobson. Withers (anti-conscription) was beaten, indeed yielded at the end. The conclusion was that super-tax should be *much* more steeply graded and that as much of national debt should be paid off by conscription of wealth as would enable income-tax to stay at 5s. in the £.

Apropos of taxation Spender told a funny story. He said a Frenchman (official) in England had recently asked him for details of our income- and super-tax. Spender gave them, but the Frenchman would not believe them. He could not credit the high rates, and demanded documentary proofs. When he got them and was convinced he exclaimed, *"Mais c'est l'anarchie!"* which incidentally shows how anarchy can be confused with its most striking opposite.

Friday, March 15th. London, Yacht Club.

Rumours all day of peace offers. Clemenceau and the whole Versailles conference in London for pow-wow, and so on.

Monday, March 18th. London, Yacht Club.

On Saturday we went to Oundle to stay with the Sandersons [1] for the week-end, and I greatly enjoyed it—especially Sanderson's company. He is a great modernist, with a fruity sense of humour and much personal power. Food excellent, Mrs. Sanderson being a *maîtresse-femme*. On Saturday night we attended a school debate on the subject, "Is enough as good as a feast?" Not brilliant, but one or two boys had a pretty turn for sarcasm. On Sunday, the first morning Church of England service I ever (I think) attended in my life. In the afternoon two masters gave us the *Kreutzer Sonata*—just that. The piano part was played by Brewster, the mathematical master, very well. Applause not

---

[1] F. W. Sanderson, headmaster of Oundle School.

allowed. Then S. and I and Chadwick (apparently running the library etc.) went to the library and art rooms, and I aroused the sympathy of S. by inveighing against there being reproductions of only old masters on view. He knows nothing about painting, but he was at once very anxious for me to send him a list of very modern painters. I also objected to the prominence given on the walls to mere large photos of cathedrals. Chadwick agreed. This will be altered. I looked at my watch. 8.10! "I shall catch it," said S. He hurried off to the waiting supper. I liked Sanderson very much indeed.

Sunday, March 24th. Comarques.

The great German offensive began on Thursday and yesterday. After various delays due to exhaustion and neuralgia I began my new play. I wrote the first scene from 5 to 7 P.M. The most magnificent weather of late that the English mind can imagine.

Tuesday, March 26th.

Brothers McKenna at Reform Club on bad war news. They came in together. I said, "The brothers," and they sat down with me, and asked if I'd been to any newspaper offices to get news. "My God! It's awful," said Ernest, in a quiet, disgusted, intensely pessimistic tone. I referred to Spender's 2 articles that day. Ernest said Spender was a good man, kept his nerve—but Reginald looked at the first article, saw one line, and said: "Now I need read nothing but that. The man who will say that——" etc. Ernest said: "There's only one thing to do. Call Parliament together at once and get more men." Reginald repeated this after him. They had evidently been long talking together and had exactly the same ideas on everything. "Robertson was right. Jellicoe was right," said Reggie oracularly. "Robertson is on the beach. Jellicoe is on the beach. In order to be on the beach you only have to be absolutely right."

Wednesday, March 27th. London, Yacht Club.

Lunch at Webb's. Webb said his wife couldn't sleep on account of the war news, and he had to exaggerate his usual tranquil optimism in order to keep the household together. It was one of the rare human touches I have noticed in the said household. However, they were soon off on to the misdeeds of the Reconstruction Committee. I was told that the whole of the staff on the Department of Information had resigned when Beaverbrook was appointed minister over them, refusing to serve under "that ignorant man." They won and were transferred to the Foreign Office—one more instance of the hand-to-mouthism of Ll. George. Went to Reform Club to see papers. Massingham was so gloomy he could scarcely speak. The brothers McKenna came in, intensely pessimistic. I was rather ashamed of them. Spender's two articles in the *Westminster* were A1 for fortitude and wisdom. I think more and more highly of this man. Then to flat to dine. Electricity not working there. Gloom of candles. M. very gloomy about the war. This sort of thing always makes me cheerful.

Sibyl Colefax gave a very good description of the "all clear" signal in a few words at dinner. She said she was walking with her husband in the streets towards the end of a raid. Everything was quite silent. Then the searchlights began winking the "all clear" all about the sky. Then the sound of the "all clear" bugles was heard. Then the footsteps of a man. Then the footsteps of ten people, of twenty, of a hundred. The town was alive again.

April 4th.

Lloyd George's introduction of Man Power Bill, for conscripting Ireland and raising military age etc. Policeman looks at card outside. Then you go up on a lift. Through an outer room with one or two journalists, hat pegs, etc. Then an inner room, with two Morse instruments tapping, and then into Gallery, at entrance of which your ticket is looked at again by an official (very friendly with all reporters, and doing their little errands etc.) in evening dress with large insignia on his breast.

Two rows of seats with narrow desk all round. A few standing at either corner, including Spender, Gardiner, and me. Reporters passing in and out all the time, crushing past; a horrible lack of space. No light in House of Commons except through glass roof. No repose in Press

Gallery. Sharp corner of elaborate wood-carving against which you knock your head if you sit or lean in corners. Glimpse of Ladies' Gallery above, with glimpse of a smart woman, past first youth, with complexion *soigné* but going. Looking from left, I could just see Ll. G., Churchill, Bonar Law, Cecil, Balfour, etc., on right. House full. 12 or so standing, between cross benches. (Gallery opposite full. Side galleries half full.) Two M.P.'s wearing hats. As the M.P.'s left, they bowed awkwardly to Speaker in getting up if in front rows or on reaching central space if not; and on coming in they bowed either on rising or on reaching open space. Speaker under a canopy. Cheap effects of Ll. G. looking round as if challenging; trick of dropping his voice for last, rather important word of sentence. Unpleasant Nonconformist voice.

He did not know his case, and having made a muddle, deliberately left the muddle. Truisms about values and will-to-win cheered. Proposal to conscript Ireland cheered loudly a long time by Tories. No applause as he sat down. The whole thing a vast make-believe, with an audience of which a large part was obviously quite unintelligent and content with the usual hollow rot. Ll. G.'s oratorical effects very poor— like a Lyceum melodrama. Asquith with long hair very dignified, at home, and persuasive.

Wednesday, April 10th. London, Yacht Club.

Too much occupied and preoccupied with the British defeats, the Government proposals for increasing the army, the publication of *The Pretty Lady,* political journalism, the gardening and household difficulties, chill on the entrails, neuralgia, insomnia, Marguerite's illness, the nightly rehearsals in the small drawing-room of a play for a Red Cross performance at Clacton, and my new play—to be bothered with this journal or with notes of any kind. However, I did at last, in spite of all distractions, get my play going, and it *is* going.

Meeting of British War Memorial Committee this afternoon. Beaverbrook arrived. He told me that he liked *The Pretty Lady* better than any other book of mine, and better than any other modern book. As regards sales I hear that it is "doing very nicely."

Maurice Baring and F. Swinnerton dined with me tonight at Yacht Club. After F.S. had gone, Maurice grew communicative about the war. Knows Haig. Thinks him a real personality, with decision, grit, and power of command. Never rattled. A good soldier, but not a genius. Henry Wilson a wind-bag. He spoke in the *highest* terms of Trenchard, chief of Air Service; also very highly of Cox, chief of Intelligence. He said that Gough and others protested against having to take over extra front, as ordered by war cabinet. Gough's front was under-manned and under-gunned. No reserves in France. Depots empty. Ll. G. always refused to look at facts, but liked ideas, grandiose etc., for new stunt. Gave particulars of how Northcliffe had announced months ago that Robertson would be attacked and have to go; ditto in regard to Spring-Rice. Cabinet did not believe in German offensive. Soldiers did.

Haig told cabinet long ago facts as to inferiority in man-power and expected them to be frightened out of their lives. They were not, as they did not believe in offensive. He expected an attack on Haig next. He didn't think we should lose war—we could hold on and Germans would crack. He said that Haig had no desire to conceal the facts as to lack of troops and spoke freely of them and permitted others to do so. Unfortunately, of course, one can't print the facts, although the Germans probably knew them pretty well.

Thursday, April 11th. London, Yacht Club.

I went to see Beaverbrook this morning to ascertain, in view of the fact that I am to write for *Lloyd's Weekly News,* whether he was going to buy the paper, and if so whether he meant to change the politics. He said he wasn't going to buy it. Before this Beaverbrook asked me to accept the directorship of British propaganda in France. After objecting, I said I would think it over and let him know. He said no one could know French psychology better than I do—this conclusion he drew from reading *The Pretty Lady!* Rothermere was in the room before we began business, walking about, sitting down, standing up. He wanted a holiday. I told him it would pay him to take one. He said he couldn't. "Here's this great united Air Force of 170,000 men just come into existence. I can't leave the baby."

Tuesday, April 16th. Comarques.

On Sunday I wrote to Beaverbrook agreeing to his request that I should enter Ministry of Information in order to direct British propaganda in France.

Friday, April 19th. London, Yacht Club.

Lunch at Reform, where Spender was exceedingly good and Davray exceedingly emotional. In the afternoon I wrote a preface for the catalogue of Paul Nash's exhibition. I dined with the Nicholsons at the Café Royal grill. Lutyens and Mrs. Stuart-Wortley were there, the latter nervous and quiet, the former full of puns and tiny jokes, but agreeable and ready to stand being teased. Then I saw Nicholson privately as to his proposed work for Memorial Committee and his situation in the army. Before going to bed I wrote a report on this for the committee. A day! Last night the new Military Service Act became law, and I am now legally, at nearly 51 years, in the Army Reserve. I saw Dennis Eadie yesterday going from his rehearsal at the Haymarket to his lunch at the Carlton and had a few words with him. The matter was not mentioned, but he was evidently preoccupied by his impending military obligations.

Friday, April 26th. London, Yacht Club.

On Wednesday night I had Professor Henry S. Canby (English literature) of Yale after dinner at the Reform. Wells joined in. A young man, probably about 30. He made one or two shrewd remarks and liked *Candide*.

Sunday, April 28th. Comarques.

Today I finished the second act of my new *Honours* play,[1] after two sleepless nights. I read a lot of *A Dreary Story* of Chekhov in the night.

---

[1] *The Title.*

I had read it once or twice before. It now seems to me quite fresh, full of new powers and beauties, and one of the finest things I ever did read.

Mair told me about painted girls in the Registry department. I had myself noticed some others, with studiously considered gait, in the corridors. Mair said that one of the Registry girls met him in tube train. She smiled. He acknowledged. Then taking out her meat card, she leaned over and showed it to him, exclaiming, "What about that for a meat card?" The idea was that he should thus learn her name. Mair said that he advised her to use her coupons with care and handed the card back.

Wednesday, May 1st. London, Yacht Club.

I came to London yesterday and interviewed Beaverbrook and Roderick Jones [1] at Ministry of Information and arranged that I should begin as head of British propaganda in France next week.

Thursday, May 2nd. London, Yacht Club.

Cravath said, apropos of an Englishman named Broughton who had lived 25 years in the U.S.A. without losing his spots, that Cravath's youngest daughter, on seeing Broughton on board a British ship on voyage to England, said to her father, "Poppa, I always used to think that Mr. Broughton was affected, but now I see he's only an Englishman."

Yesterday I had lunch with Ross and a flying officer friend of his, Beverly Robinson, who had escaped from Germany after 2½ years' imprisonment. Robinson's account of the escape was not exciting. His account of prison insolence by the brothers Niemeyer *was*: ordering officers to kneel after stripping them in the presence of soldiers etc. He told me he'd got most of the books he wanted and had formed a library of 500 books. But he could not get *Books and Persons*. It was stopped by the censor. I couldn't think why until he reminded me that it contained a couple of pages about German colonies. This is a really remark-

---

[1] Sir Roderick Jones, chairman of Reuter's and in 1918 appointed director of propaganda.

able instance of German thoroughness. He tried to get them to tear out the two pages and then give him the book, but they wouldn't. He said they were intensely easy to deceive. He would hear *nothing* of their starving. He said he had got an excellent meal at a railway buffet for 4 marks.

Friday, May 10th. London, Yacht Club.

I finished my play *The Title* on Wednesday, but in order to do so I had to knock myself up and also to inform people with whom I had appointments in London that I was laid aside with a chill. I wrote the last act in four days' actual work.

Then yesterday I came to London to take up my duties as head of the French section of the propaganda department of the Ministry of Information. On the whole the first day was rather a lark. It began with a lunch to Allied journalists, where I sat between *Le Journal* and *Le Petit Parisien* and had the *Débats* opposite. I didn't like my room, nor my staff being on different floors from me.

Night: Dinner of the Other Club. I made the acquaintance of Smuts. He has a peculiar accent (foreign) and puts his hand on your knee constantly while talking to you. A man of principles, and a fine man; but I doubt if he is the great man some of us thought. He was quite serene about the approaching end of the war.

Saturday, May 11th. London, Yacht Club.

Dined at F. E. Smith's. An enormous house, considering it isn't a special house, but only at the corner of a row (32, Grosvenor Gardens). The library is even equal to his boastings about it, but he would continually refer to prices. What astonished me was that he does not keep even really valuable books (from £100 to £2000 apiece) under glass. He was greatly amusing over incidents of his American trip and especially as to how he and his brother Harold, in one of the dryest States, Nebraska, made the professor of rhetoric at some university drunk—although this professor was the origin of the dryness. They drank to the great orators and then to the stars of American literature. At the end the professor said, of F.E., "The most brilliant man I ever met," and later, to friends, he said of F.E., "He is a *whale*."

Tuesday, May 14th. London, Yacht Club.

Did 4 hours' hard work at the Ministry. People kept coming into my room on various excuses, but just to look at me. Miss Nerney began to work there yesterday. I have now abandoned literature until I am chucked out of the job, or the job ends, or I am called to a better one. But I do journalism, and a damned nuisance it is. Two articles this week. Three next week.

Friday, May 31st. London, Yacht Club.

Other Club dinner last night. Justice Darling came after his day in court over the Billing-Maude Allen case. He has poor literary views. Kept insisting that *Salome* was nasty etc. *I* said it was only poor. A thin little man, rather clever and agreeable. He has a hell of a job on and knows it. Beaverbrook made £85 in bets over the distance of Château-Thierry from Paris. Smuts presided. I sat next to him.

Tuesday, June 4th. London, Yacht Club.

In arranging for the King to attend Westminster Abbey on France's Day I thought I had set in motion a great thing to my credit. It was not so. I was misled. I took things for granted, made mistakes on them, and the whole affair had to be cancelled. Religion was at the bottom of the trouble. Hence the trouble. At the last moment I was asked to write the British contribution to the first daily joint wireless messages sent out to the world by Britain, France, and Italy together. I wrote it between 6 and 7.

Wednesday, June 12th. London, Yacht Club.

Usual hour home Saturday afternoon, and usual early train back here on Monday morning. I have now somewhat lessened the strain of writing articles and doing other extra-office odd work by the discovery that a lot of the extra-office can be done at odd times intra-office.

Last night, dinner inaugurating the Groupe Inter-Universitaire Franco-Anglais, at Pagani's. A big gathering—in the chair Guéritte, with his hearing-apparatus. A most charming man, though he did call on me for a speech after I'd signed to him that I wouldn't speak. All the speeches in English. Several Frenchmen spoke English very well. This organization is based on a smaller organization of which the rules were: no subscriptions; no chairman; no toasts; no speeches—the idea being simply the interchange colloquially of opinions. On the whole I thought last night's affair wasn't so bad—for sense. I met Denison Ross (now Sir), head of the School of Oriental Languages. A wild, very interesting person.

Friday, June 14th. London, Yacht Club.

Wednesday night. Dinner of the Writers' Group. Gilbert Murray read his draft of a Liberal manifesto for us to sign. It was a superb piece of really sound and elegant writing and was generally approved.

Tuesday, July 2nd. London, Yacht Club.

Last Friday, for Ministry, I saw Generals Macdonogh and Macready (first visit to War Office) and Albert Thomas.[1] I finished up at William Weir's and saw Richmond and two brothers and two wives. Saturday I learnt at home that Lockyer was called up for medical exam. Last night I dined with Beaverbrook, the Edwin Montagus and Diana Manners being of the party at the Savoy. Dinner arranged for 9 P.M. At 9.15, Montagu and I, having waited, began. The rest arrived at 9.20. When the conversation turned on Diana being the original of Queen in *The Pretty Lady* my attitude was apparently so harsh that Beaverbrook changed the subject. We afterwards went 5 in a taxi to B.'s rooms at Hyde Park Hotel. After a time Diana and I sat on window-sill of B.'s bedroom, looking at the really superb night view over the park. One small light burning in the bedroom. B.'s pyjamas second-rate. Some miscellaneous talk about life and women. After they had all gone but

---

[1] The French Socialist politician.

me B. asked me what I thought of Diana. I told him I thought she was unhappy, through idleness. He said he liked her greatly.

Friday, July 5th. London, Yacht Club.

11th anniversary of our wedding yesterday. We dined at the Café Royal. Raymond Needham [1] came and lunched with me at Yacht Club and told me much about Lord Beaverbrook and much as to his own private affairs. On Wednesday night Eadie came to the flat and read two acts of *The Title* very well. The first act, though I thought consistently good, seemed a hell of a length.

I lost my food card.

Tuesday, July 16th. London, Yacht Club.

Far too busy with ministerial work, articles, or official dinners and rehearsals of *The Title* to be able to keep up any diarizing at all. I went to the dinner to the Canadian journalists at the Savoy on Friday last, Beaverbrook the host. Lloyd George sat at the end of one table and Borden, the P.M. of Canada, at the end of another, and I heard of smaller P.M.'s of various territories in Canada.

Yesterday Beaverbrook asked me to take control of another department at the ministry in addition to my own. I temporized.

Dinner to American professors last night.

Thursday, July 18th. London, Yacht Club.

Minute from war cabinet yesterday censuring me for my most successful pro-France article in the *Observer* on Sunday. It had been used on Monday by *Daily Mail* as an axe to hit the Government with about "baleful secrecy." Lord B. was furious and asked me to write a pungent letter in reply, which he signed. By evening Ll. G. had apologized and promised to have a new minute of the cabinet prepared.

---

[1] Raymond Needham, K.C., was at that time private secretary to the Ministry of Information.

Tuesday, July 23rd. London, Yacht Club.

I went home on Saturday afternoon, after witnessing dress rehearsal of *The Title* on Friday night at the Royalty. On Sunday morning I received five telegrams, from which I gathered that the play had quite succeeded with the first-night audience. I came to town yesterday and found that the first-night success had been really immense. Eadie asked me to go and see the 3rd act last night. M. and I went, and he and his wife were there. He admitted that the Sampson Straight scene went better last night than on the first night. There is really nothing wrong with it except that, like anything else, it could be improved. So I agreed to improve it for him.

Friday, July 26th. London, Yacht Club.

Major David Davies asked Massingham, Gardiner, Gooch, J. Douglas, and McCardy to lunch yesterday at the Carlton, about his League of Nations Association. Coal-owner. Said to be worth £3,000,000. Very simple-minded. Spoke of "some one named Mrs. Humphrey Ward," "some one who is called 'Q.'," etc. But he has faith.

At night I went with Needham to *Le Coq d'Or*. We were too close to the trombones. The only music of Rimsky's that I ever liked. I thought the tale rotten and the spectacle 2nd-rate. Still, I enjoyed the whole.

Tuesday, July 30th. London, Yacht Club.

Back home Saturday afternoon. Thoroughly unwell. I went to bed after dinner and arose for lunch on Sunday. Some tennis. Some spelling-game. 200 pages of George Moore's indecency, *A Story-Teller's Holiday*—very good.

Friday, October 4th. London, Yacht Club.

This journal broke down through pressure of work and neuralgia. I have lost priceless things by this slackness.

The French section at the Ministry of Information began to buck up in July and August. I got a special grant of £100,000 out of the Treasury and the appointment of Lord Lytton as British commissioner of propaganda in Paris. Roderick Jones recommended this man strongly, and I accepted him blindly on the importance of his name to French society. He left yesterday on his mission.

M. and I and Richard went for a holiday to Cleveden on Sept. 10th. Richard stayed 7 days, and we 16, we being held up by the railway strike. In the end I got a car down from London. On my return I found myself appointed at the M. of I. to the post of director of propaganda (vice Sir R. Jones), together with general supervision and co-ordination of all departments of the ministry, i.e. deputy minister. This is the most marvellous, disconcerting, and romantic thing that ever happened to me. At any rate, whatever happens, I, an artist, shall have had the experience. It would be enormous fun except for the responsibility and the 3 A.M. worryings.

Tuesday, October 8th. London, Yacht Club.

At night, having been reproached about not visiting the artistes at the Royalty, I went there, and saw bits of the play and all the artistes except Joan Carey. They seemed very well pleased with everything. A poor house. Nigel Playfair told me he was trying to get the Lyric Opera House at Hammersmith for what is wrongly called a repertory theatre. He had got the rent promised, but one of the London ring of managers had made a bid over his head without even having seen the theatre, just in order to keep the ring closed. Playfair didn't know whether he would get the place after all. I told him if he did I might collect £2000 for him.[1]

Thursday, October 10th. London, Yacht Club.

At the Ministry yesterday I found out that the meetings of the Turkish committee were being held at the offices of the British-American Tobacco Co. I at once wrote to the minister and told him that I meant to revoke his order to that effect.

---

[1] When the plan was further matured Arnold Bennett became one of the directors of the Lyric Theatre, Hammersmith.

Saturday, October 12th. London, Yacht Club.

Dinner of Writers' Group last night at Reform, at which it was decided to drop our 3-months-debated manifesto entirely as being quite absurd in present circumstances. A wise decision, my God! Spender spoke about the poverty of Germany and of a great struggle between inhabitants of 2-room tenements in poorer quarters and the police. The police laid down that it was unsanitary for people to sleep in a room where cooking was done. This, of course, would have put the whole family into one room to sleep. They could not enforce the decree practically. Then they had kitchens constructed in new tenements in such a manner, so full of corners, that beds could not be put into them! He also spoke of seeing a highly-respectable-looking long row of tenements in Munich, as to which a guide friend said to him: "You see those houses. There isn't a w.c. in the whole row. When the tenants want a w.c. they go to that beer-hall there and have a drink in order to use a w.c." Ellery Sedgwick, of the *Atlantic Monthly,* was at the dinner. I talked privately to him afterwards and walked with him back to the Ritz and gave him my ideas on most of the big political personages. I was just in the humour for being highly indiscreet, and I was indiscreet. He said seriously to me at the end, "You may like to know that I accept your judgment absolutely." Every now and then in the rain he would stand still in order to put an important question.

Tuesday, October 15th. London, Yacht Club.

Reflection upon the German answer to Wilson's reply to their request for an armistice made me think the end of the war was getting very near and that the whole policy of the M. of Information would have to be swung round. I drafted a minute before catching train; Mair added to it a little, and when I showed it to Beaverbrook in the evening he said he would use it as a minute to the cabinet. For me there was already an air of unreality in the work of the ministry and especially about our scheme for re-organizing it.

Saturday, October 19th. London, Yacht Club.

I heard through Mair from Buchan, who was in the F.O., that Germany had capitulated to all Wilson's terms and that the Kaiser had abdicated. This was the F.O. information. Strange. It proved not to be true. A day later, Milner was being interviewed in the *Evening Standard* (or was it the *P.M.G.?*) to the effect that all Germany was not militaristic—in a word, to the effect that some mercy ought to be shown, lest Bolshevism should appear in Germany and spread everywhere. It was a move to save the Kaiser, instigated by cold feet in the F.O., the cabinet, and elsewhere. And afterwards Mair told me that the F.O. had intimated to Wilson that his terms would not quite do.

Beaverbrook away from Ministry all this week. Rothermere gave a dinner in my honour at the Marlborough Club last night. He chose his company in the most extraordinary way. Australian Hughes, a good talker, sheer brass, but a good slashing talker; very deaf, with an apparatus looking like a rather large kodak closed, on the table, and a flex from it to his ear. Henry Dalziel, a bluff person, not without a certain attractiveness. Hulton, Andrew Caird, manager of the *Daily Mail,* bluff and decent and crude, but clever. He told me everything I already knew about propaganda after dinner. Churchill, Blumenfeld, somewhat quiet. F. E. Smith came very late and said little. Churchill talked the best. I like Rothermere. He told me he wanted to sell all his papers except the *Sunday Pictorial*. He said he had worked hard since he was 14, and if a man had succeeded and chose to slave as hard as ever after 50, it merely proved that that man didn't understand life. He was turned 50.

This morning Major Holt came to me from Beaverbrook and said that B.'s doctor has advised him to resign, but he hadn't yet taken his decision. Of course this meant that he *had* taken his decision. B. is certainly unwell with glands, but equally certainly ill health is not his full reason for resigning. I propose now to write to him and say that I shall resign.

Wednesday and Thursday nights I slept at the flat.

Wednesday, October 23rd. London, Yacht Club.

When Northcliffe returned from America and was appointed head of enemy propaganda, he kept the title of the organization he had controlled in the U.S.A., namely British War Mission, and he still uses this for his Crewe House organization.

Some time ago he approached the Ministry of Information and the War Aims Committee to form a committee to co-ordinate policy in regard to propaganda. An excellent idea. This committee, however, was called the Policy Committee of the British War Mission, which in itself was a bit thick, seeing that the M. of I. is a far more important organization than the enemy propaganda show. When the Germans began to be defeated, Northcliffe called the committee together to draw up peace terms to be used as groundwork of propaganda. Mysteriously, all the govt. departments began to be represented in this committee, including Reggie Hall, a very great man in his secret service business for the Admiralty, but, I should have thought, unsuited to draw up peace terms. Including also a number of absolute duds.

This committee drew up its Allied peace terms and submitted them to the war cabinet. The war cabinet said it was very busy and couldn't consider them and turned them over to Balfour to pass. Balfour passed them. Reggie Hall then suggested a serious alteration, namely that the non-return of the German colonies to Germany should be removed from the "negotiable" to the "absolute" group of conditions. (Quite right!) These terms of peace will form the basis of all our propaganda. This is a really good story and shows Northcliffe's lust for power very well, for of course he lords it over the committee.

I have slept at the flat since end of last week. Very exciting and rather uncomfortable, with a mad servant aged 70 in the place. Saturday night: *As You Were* at the Pavilion. A few fair jokes (verbal). As a whole, terribly mediocre. Every scene turned on adultery, or mere copulation. Even in the primeval forest scene, an adultery among gorillas was shown. This revue is the greatest success in London at present and is taking about £3000 a week. In bed all day Sunday with neuralgia. Poured with rain all day. It now appears that Beaverbrook, more and more ill, will resign. Confabs daily between me, Snagge, Mair, A. J. Bennett, and Needham. Reconstruction within the ministry going steadily on.

Thursday, October 24th. London, Yacht Club.

I had to lunch at Savoy yesterday with Davray to meet Painlevé, Steeg, and another French politician and Wickham Steed. Painlevé came only for a quarter of an hour, as he had to lunch with Ll. G. Steeg, *rébarbatif,* and as I knew his connection with Malery, I at once didn't like him. Davray, however, said afterwards that he was quite all right and *extrêmement constructif.* He looked rather like a fairly strong Nonconformist preacher. Steed did not impress me as a strong or a first-class man. He talked a great deal too much about foreign politics and really didn't say much that we don't all know without saying. He may be a nervous man. Tall, very thin, silly beard. He certainly didn't appear as an original thinker at all. Around this cascade of words, the fearful din of the restaurant. I did manage to get Painlevé off politics and on to personal, concrete things such as his impression of Ll. George. The usual awful ignorance of the Irish situation.

Sunday, October 27. London, Yacht Club.

Interview with Masterman on Friday apropos of his "Literature and Art" department at ministry being broken up. He had a bad cold and was gloomy. He resented the provisional arrangements having been made through his 2nd in command and not through him—though he had been greatly away, ill. Still, at the bottom of his heart he wasn't really worrying, because his own place and salary were secured, and this, of course, was bound to affect him. Considering that he had been a cabinet minister early in the war and that I, politically a nobody, was now his superior, he behaved excellently in an extremely trying situation. So did I.

The sensual appeal is now really very marked everywhere, in both speech and action, on the stage. Adultery everywhere pictured as desirable, and copulation generally ditto. Actresses play courtesan parts (small ones, often without words but with gestures) with gusto.

Tuesday, October 29th. London, Yacht Club.

News of Austrian separate demand for armistice yesterday afternoon. I heard a newsman in Oxford Street cry: *"Evenin' News.* Last edition. All abaht it. Tonight's and tomorrow night's too. Only one German left."

Meeting of Nationals in the morning, at which I preside. About 30 present. Masterman insisted on the dangerousness of our handling and spreading documentary peace terms which the government had approved but would not publicly approve and certainly would not publish. Suppose these came out. He called them trinitrotoluol. He didn't seem to see that this was one of the essential, primary risks that a Ministry of Information must take.

Wednesday, October 30th. London, Yacht Club.

I was summoned to Beaverbrook yesterday. He was in bed, bandaged, depressed, having been told by the doctor in the morning that he had septic poisoning. When Lady B. and Needham had left the room, he began to smoke and to talk intimately, and said: "You know, Arnold, my life has been all crises. I was worth 5 millions when I was 27. And now this is a new crisis, and it's the worst." However, he cheered up. Bonar Law came in and was very courteous and cautious to me. He said his sister had been a very great and constant admirer of mine, but since *The Pretty Lady* she had done with me.

Beaverbrook's resignation in the papers. I got instructions to carry on.

Thursday, October 31st. London, Yacht Club.

Beaverbrook was as bright as anything yesterday. He was up, laughing, and had had news of a quack doctor who had cured some one with the same disease as he has. (Nobody, however, knew what the disease was.)

Dined with M. at Barrie's and saw his Lutyens room. Good, short dinner. He told me that he didn't smoke till 23 and that he wrote *My Lady Nicotine* before he had ever smoked. He said when he first came to London, he dined on 2d. a day (four halfpenny buns or scones) for a year, eating them in the street, and ate little else. He wrote about two articles a day and sold about one in six. He found at the end of the year that he needn't have been so economical, but he was afraid of the rainy day. He said it took a long time for him to see that there was any material in Scotland. He wrote *An Auld Licht Wedding* and sold it and thought he had exhausted Scotland. Next few articles he didn't sell, and then an editor said, "We liked your Scotch stuff." So he wrote *An Auld Licht Funeral*. And so on.

He told us that he had had Asquith and Birrell to dinner the other night and had arranged with Asquith's daughter-in-law and another female friend that they should dress up as housemaids and serve the dinner. They did so. The daughter-in-law wore a black wig. Neither Birrell nor Asquith recognized the women. But after dinner, in the drawing-room, Asquith said, "One of those maids is extraordinarily like my daughter-in-law." Barrie told this practical joke with great restraint and humour.

Wednesday, November 6th. London, Yacht Club.

On Monday at lunch at the Reform I learnt the details of the secret history of Northcliffe's encyclical to the newspapers of the world about the proper peace terms with Germany. According to C.M. the idea of the letter was not N.'s at all, but C.M. got Campbell Stuart to persuade him to do it. Stuart took N. out to lunch for that purpose. The thing was written by C.M., but the style being too good, it was re-written down to some resemblance of Northcliffe's supposed style. Northcliffe then signed it and immediately went off to Paris (where, as Beaverbrook told me last night at dinner, Lloyd George took good care not to see him at all), to be near the scene of the armistice negotiations.

Monday night dined alone with M. at flat and came home to club in pouring rain, because M. said Fifi wouldn't sleep anywhere but in the bedroom, and I said I could not sleep with the dog there.

Thursday, November 7th. London, Yacht Club.

Yesterday afternoon I arranged with Alistair Tayler that he should join the Board (Playfair and I being the others) of the Hammersmith Lyric Theatre enterprise, and that I should be the chairman.

Friday, November 8th. London, Yacht Club.

Yesterday afternoon my secretary was twice rung up by officials at the War Office to know if the war was over—that is, if the armistice was signed. The rumours were immense and numerous.

Yesterday Lillah McCarthy made a determined effort to get my play *Instinct* out of me, after a refusal. But I put her on to Pinker, and she failed. By 10.15 she had already rung me up three times.

Tuesday, November 12th. London, Yacht Club.

In Sunday's papers we saw the abdication of the Kaiser. Returned to town yesterday morning. In Lower Regent Street first news that armistice was signed—a paper boy calling out in a subdued tone. 10.45. Maroons went off at 11, and excited the populace.

A large portion of the ministry staff got very excited. Buchan came in to shake hands. Girls very excited. I had to calm them. Lunch at Wellington Club. We had driven through large crowds part way up the Mall and were then turned off from Buckingham Palace.

Raining now. An excellent thing to damp hysteria and Bolshevism. Great struggling to cross Piccadilly Circus twice. No buses. (It was rumoured that tubes stopped. I believe they were stopped for a time.) It stopped raining. Then cold mire in streets. Vehicles passed, festooned with shouting human beings. Others, dark, with only one or two occupants. Much light in Piccadilly up to Ritz corner, and in Piccadilly Circus. It seemed most brilliant. Some theatres had lights on their façades too. The enterprising Trocadero had hung a row of temporary lights under one of its porticoes. Shouting. But nothing terrible or memorable. Yet this morning Brayley, my valet, said to me the usual phrases: "You wondered where the people came from. You could walk on their heads at Charing Cross, and you couldn't cross Picc. Circus at all." When he came in with my tea I said, "Well, Brayley, it's all over." He smiled and said something. That was all our conversation about the end of the war. Characteristic.

Last night I thought of lonely soldiers in that crowd. No one to talk to. But fear of death lifted from them.

Thursday, November 14th. London, Yacht Club.

I dined at flat on Tuesday night (Pinker there) and slept there; so I didn't see anything of the "doings." But there was a bonfire in Piccadilly Circus, kept alive by theatre boards and boards off motor-buses. Girls are still very prominent in the "doings." Swinnerton told me that the staidest girl they had suddenly put on a soldier's hat and overcoat and went promenading in them.

Was told that the scene at the Carlton on Monday night was remarkable. Any quantity of broken glasses, tables overturned, and people standing on tables, and fashionable females with their hair down. On Tuesday night I noticed that all the principal restaurants had commissionaires in front of doors scrutinizing people who wished to enter and keeping out (apparently) all who had not reserved tables. Last night a cabby told me he would go westwards but not towards Piccadilly Circus, as he did not know what would happen to him.

The feature of last night was girls with bunches of streamers which they flicked in your face as you passed.

Friday, November 15th. London, Yacht Club.

My resignation from ministry took effect yesterday. Buchan, the liquidator, came down to see me and was very explanatory and apologetic. The behaviour of the Cabinet to me was, of course, scandalous. But they have treated many others similarly; so I was not surprised. The only notice I got was a Roneo'd [mimeographed] copy of the war cabinet minute. I was never consulted in any way.

Luncheon to Robert Donald at Connaught Rooms. 400 there to honour him because he had not sold himself to the new proprietors of the *Chronicle*. The toastmaster in a red coat was the cream of the show. He had a terrifically bland manner, especially with his supplicating hands. And having prayed silence for toast of King he rushed madly right round the room and played "God save the K." on the piano.

At night, dinner to American editors of trade journals at Savoy. Smuts in the chair. Nothing special except that Smuts claimed some German colonies for British dependencies.

Afterwards, Snagge and Kindersley and I went to ball-room. Packed with dancers. Coon band. A few couples sitting on stairs. A few drinks. Some women in a great state of sexual excitement. Others not. The dancing custom of pressing the abdomens of the partners together is really very remarkable indeed and shows an immense change in manners if not in customs. The whole affair was a fine incitement to fornication.

Tuesday, November 19th. London, Yacht Club.

I went to Wells's alone for the week-end. Second time I have gone away alone because M. could not leave her dogs. Five guests at the Wellses'.

Thursday, November 21st. London, Yacht Club.

Attending ministry about an hour a day, and yet I seem to have no time to think out plays. I had tea with Max[1] yesterday. He wanted to compare my desire to express myself and make money with the political desire to get titles, but he failed.

Saturday, November 23rd. London, Yacht Club.

My article in the *D.N.* which ended by blaming Liberal leadership, on Thursday, must have caused some commotion, seeing that Asquith himself wrote me a polite letter of self-justification. Most Liberals are delighted with the article, and Asquith said he was in general agreement with it.

Tuesday, November 26th. London, Yacht Club.

Week-end at Beaverbrook's, Cherkley Court. Good, except not enough food, B. not being interested in food.

I read B.'s printed account of the conspiracy that overthrew Asquith in Dec. 1916. It was exceedingly well written and showed great judgment of men and some sense of historical values. In fact it was remarkable and heightened my originally high opinion of Beaverbrook. The War Office and Ll. G. both came badly out of the account, especially the former. B.'s

---

[1] Lord Beaverbrook.

own share in the affair is kept very modestly in the background. He seemed almost inclined to publish it in the *Daily Express*. I advised him against this.

Tuesday, December 10th. London, Yacht Club.

Week-end at Dr. F. Keeble's at Weybridge. Lillah McCarthy also there.[1] In spite of my neuralgia we had a great week-end, full of good and not too serious conversation. I promised to write her a play on the subject of Judith, if a firm contract was made at once.[2] In fact I constructed the play on the spot, after having read Judith myself and having heard it read by Keeble. (Some difficulty in getting an Apocrypha.)

Saturday, December 14th. London, Yacht Club.

Interview with Lillah McCarthy and Drinkwater at Adelphi Terrace at 12.45. I promised to write *Judith* by the end of January, and they promised to produce *Don Juan* also. In the afternoon Captain Basil Dean came to see me about his London theatrical scheme. He said he could get and control £20,000. I definitely promised to write a play for *him*, too. This, with Goodall's, Vedrenne's, and Lillah's, makes 4 plays!

We dined at the Galsworthys', Grove Lodge, Hampstead, and the Masefields were there. Mrs. M. and I got on excellently. Masefield gloomyish, and very precise in diction. Fine voice. Diction of a public speaker. Galsworthy very nice. Ada Galsworthy adorable.

Sunday, December 15th. London, Yacht Club.

I began the scheming of my play *Judith* yesterday. At his request I went and had tea with Weir yesterday. He wanted me to put a speech into order for him which he is going to deliver at Manchester on Friday and in which he will define the proper British air policy for the future. He told me some interesting things. He said that the great difficulty in long-distance flying now was not mechanical but navigational. A big machine had started for India from London on Friday and, coming into

---

[1] Lillah McCarthy was divorced from Granville-Barker in 1918. She married Professor Keeble in 1920.
[2] *Judith* was produced at the Kingsway Theatre, April 30, 1919.

a storm, had come down in France. He said that the commander, a general, was a first-class pilot etc., but if he had been a really 1st-class expert in navigation, such as they did possess, he would never have come down. Weir said that he had been up in a "flying boat" weighing 17½ tons, carrying 9 passengers and a ton of goods, that travelled at 118 miles an hour and carried petrol for 1000 miles. He said that the flight to the United States would occur between March 15th and April 15th. On politics he was extremely grave and bitter.

Thursday, December 19th. London, Yacht Club.

I met a Captain Griffin (from Walsall) at Reform yesterday, with Shufflebotham. He had been wounded 9 times, I think; prisoner in Germany. Was reported dead. After he returned to life, his solicitor, among other bills, forwarded the following: "To memorial service (fully choral), 3 guineas."

Friday, December 20th. London, Yacht Club.

Welcome to Sir Douglas Haig and 4 carriages full of generals yesterday. Vast crowds in front of Reform Club. Girls at windows opposite covered their shoulders in the cold with national flags. Reform full of women, boys, and kids. In ground-floor room, east, grave members standing on tableclothed tables in front of windows (me too) and in front a dame covering the throats of two small boys. All front windows of club occupied by women. Roadway kept by very few police. Roadway sprinkled with gravel. Cheering in distance. Handkerchiefs taken out. One or two mounted policemen on fine horses. Then a sort of herald in a long hat. Handkerchief-waving; cheering, louder and louder. Then the four carriages, 3 in 1st carriage and 4 each in the other 3. Generals wore no overcoats. One or two bowed and smiled. Gone in a moment, and we all jumped down and turned away. Such was the welcome to Haig and Co.

THE JOURNAL

1919-1920

1919

Saturday, January 11th. Comarques.

Having given up all the work except *Observations* for the *New States-man* I came to Comarques on Saturday last, 4th inst., with the intention of writing *Judith,* the play for Lillah McCarthy, and finishing it before 7th February. I began it on Sunday, 5th inst., and tonight, 11th, I fin-ished the first act.

Last year, in spite of the fact that I was engaged officially at the M. of nformation for 7 or 8 months, I wrote 165,700 words of my own stuff.

Tuesday, January 28th. Comarques.

I finished *Judith* yesterday at 7.30, having written it in twenty-three days. I had several very slight headaches, but no dyspepsia worth a damn. Nervous dyspepsia did give indications of attacking me, but the mys-terious and expensive tablets which I got kept me in excellent order.

Saturday, February 8th. Comarques.

Judith was delivered yesterday week. On Tuesday Marguerite met Lillah McCarthy, who nearly fell on my neck in the street, from enthusiasm about the play. Eaton also wrote to me that he was "violently enthusiastic" about it.

These two and old Drinkwater came to dinner at the new flat on Tues-day last. Drinkwater said nothing good or bad as to the play until late in the evening, when I asked him.

He then said indifferently that he liked it, but didn't care much for the last act, or words to that effect.

Sunday, February 16th. Comarques.

I am chiefly occupied with the stage. I give a considerable amount of time to the Lyric, Hammersmith, where money has been lost in my absence, owing to the lavish expenditure. And I am also being drawn into the production part of *Judith*. Lillah McC., Drinkwater, Eaton, and I had a séance of nearly three hours on Tuesday about the cast.

I finished Professor Arthur Keith's *The Human Body* (Home University Library). A thoroughly sound little book, rottenly written, even to bad syntax. It is strange that these experts, such as Keith and Sidney Webb, do not take the trouble to be efficient in their first business, the vehicle of expression.

Monday, March 3rd. Comarques.

On the 1st I began my book on women,[1] but I only wrote about 100 words. I meant to go on with it yesterday, but couldn't. After muddling about nearly all day I began at 5 P.M. and wrote 600 good words before dinner. The book is now really begun.

Wednesday, March 5th. London, Yacht Club.

We came to London yesterday. M. went to Newcastle to stay with the Shufflebothams. Swinnerton, Playfair, and A. E. W. Mason dined with me at the Garrick. Mason told us some of his secret service adventures in Mexico. He was very good as a *raconteur,* and evidently has a great gift for secret service, though he said he began as an amateur.

Mason said that practically all the German spies and many of the Zeppelin men carried a packet of obscene photographs on their persons. I fully expected he would laugh at the reputation of the German Secret Service for efficiency, and he did. I felt sure the German temperament is not a good secret service temperament. Too gullible and talkative. Mason

---

[1] *Our Women: Chapters in the Sex Discord,* published in 1920.

said their secret service was merely expensive. Money chucked away idiotically.

Saturday, March 15th. Comarques.

I went to London on Tuesday after a solitary week-end here in which I earned £300 in two days, by hard work.

Tuesday night M. and I attended the first rehearsal of *Judith*. It was in Eaton's room at the Royalty. The Royalty was in process of reparation, and there was an almost continuous slapping noise of whitewashers in the room above.

Later rehearsals were held in the Ampthill Room at the Connaught Rooms. Happily, the leading lady, Lillah, is easy to deal with. Eaton knows immensely more about producing than I do, but I was able to convince him that his plans for the murder in the second act were all wrong and that my original plans were all right. I also changed Lillah's conception of her acting of it. In fact the murder scene will be the author's own.

March 27th. 17 Berkeley St., London.

The 285th and last performance of *The Title* occurred on Saturday last at the Royalty. A good house. The provincial tour which began some weeks ago was a failure for the first fortnight.

While I was being shaved at the Reform on Tuesday, Henry Norman came in and waited. He read me a letter from his wife, who is inspecting the fronts to make a record for the Imperial War Museum. He told me other things not in the letter as that Englishwomen are still looking after French *permissionaires* at the railway stations and that French-women do nothing in this line and even try to prevent the Englishwomen from getting lodgings in the towns. I regard Englishwomen as silly for doing it. It seems that the French soldier is very rough when drunk or half drunk. One woman had coffee thrown in her face three times. Another was stabbed and killed. The English psychology is very queer in these things.

Friday, April 11th. Comarques.

Richard, M., and I went to Eastbourne last Saturday for the first production of *Judith* (Devonshire Park Theatre).

Lillah McCarthy behaved well, considering her double anxiety of manager and star—both as it were making a fresh start in life. Lillah had there Dr. Keeble (her fiancé), her mother, her sister, and a niece and nephew, offspring of another sister (or brother). All these were all over the theatre all the time. She protested that all the creative producing work had been done by me, M., and her. I had to put this right.

Evidently Lillah is used to authors who will stand no damned nonsense. She got rather excited after both 2nd and 1st performances, because Bagoas's rushing forth and killing a spying woman detracted from her kissing Holofernes, and she had to be soothed. Her tent costume frightened one of the lessees of the theatre. Above a line drawn about ½ inch or 1 inch above the *mont de Vénus* she wore nothing except a 4-in. band of black velvet round the body hiding the breasts and a similar perpendicular band of velvet starting from between the breasts and going down to the skirt and so hiding the navel. Two thin shoulder straps held this contrivance in position. Bracelets and rings, of course. The skirt was slit everywhere and showed the legs up to the top of the thigh when she laid down there at Holofernes's feet. She looked a magnificent picture thus, but a police prosecution would not have surprised me at all. She gave an exceedingly fine performance—as good as could be wished for. The house was very full for the first night. (Capacity about 115–120.)

I refused the persistent calls for author and sat with Lillah's maid in Lillah's dressing-room until the calls had finished. Terrible silly mishaps occurred with the sack containing Holofernes's head in the 3rd act, despite the most precise instructions to the crowd. Further instructions to the crowd and similar mishaps on the 2nd night.

I took supper 3 nights running, and survived it.

Sunday, May 4th. Comarques.

I never before took so much interest in the production of a play of mine. *Judith* was produced at the Kingsway Theatre, London, last Wednesday, 30th April. It certainly bewildered people. Numerous comic touches were quite lost in the 1st act. In the 2nd act Lillah McCarthy had put down her dress as low as it was at the first night at Eastbourne (after raising it for later performances at Eastbourne and for dress rehearsals in London). The end of Act II might have been spoilt by an untimely descent of the curtain 10 seconds too soon. The performance as a whole was excellent. The disinterested applause was fair. The interested friendly applause was too insistent. House held over £150, the highest first night the Kingsway ever had, I think. The ordinary first-night public was *dérouté*. Common people seemed thoroughly interested and well pleased.

The press criticisms next day were without exception unfavourable. The Sunday criticisms that I have seen were not bad, though there was much exception taken to Lillah's nudity in Act II. In general the press quite failed to comprehend the play and said the most ridiculous things about it, showing immense stupidity.

Thursday, May 8th. London, Yacht Club.

Came to London on Tuesday after a week-end in which I did nothing but get up to date with my things. Saw *Judith* on Tuesday night. The news that Hardy was enthusiastic about the play gave me more satisfaction than anything that has happened to me for a long time.

Wednesday, May 14th. London, Yacht Club.

Constant insomnia. Doing nothing except the series of articles about women, which I shall be immensely relieved to finish. Then a year of plays. Seeing Rickards weekly.

The receipts of *Judith* were just under £900 last week, the first complete week. Marguerite began to be less sure about its success. I know that there is too much psychological realism in the play to please a large section of the public. On Monday night the receipts fell to £56. This was a bombshell, especially for Marguerite. We knew after this that the play must be regarded as a failure.

Friday, May 30th. London, Yacht Club.

A political dinner having been put off, I found myself aimless, but I also found Siegfried Sassoon, Osbert Sitwell, and Robert Nichols, and went with them to the Russian ballet. Promenade.

H.G.'s *The Undying Fire* came along. The machinery of it is bad and unconvincing, but the stuff is good. I hope to finish my damnable, pedestrian, fair-minded, sagacious woman book on Monday.

Monday, June 2nd. Comarques.

Today at 4.30 I finished my book about women. I haven't yet come to any conclusion as to its value. I now have 3 plays to write in the next nine months, all commissioned; and fortunately I have nothing else.

Thursday, June 5th. London, Yacht Club.

Dined at Osbert Sitwell's. A pert parlourmaid and a good-looking young male servant. Good dinner. Fish before soup. Present, W. H. Davies, Lytton Strachey, Woolf, Nichols, S. Sassoon, Aldous Huxley, Atkin (a very young caricaturist), W. J. Turner, and Herbert Read (a very young poet). The faces of Woolf, Atkin, and Read were particularly charming in their ingenuousness. Davies I liked. He had walked all the way from Tottenham Court Road to Swan Walk. A house with much better pictures and bric-à-brac than furniture. In fact there was scarcely any of what I call furniture. But lots of very modern pictures, of which I liked a number. Bright walls and bright cloths and bright glass everywhere. A fine Rowlandson drawing. Osbert is young. He is already a very good host. I enjoyed this evening, though I knew I should have indigestion after the creamy sweet, and I have got it.

I dined with Garvin tonight at the Café Royal. Knoblock also there. Garvin said: "I said to Ll. George, 'The 19th century was the century of the vote. The 20th century will be the century of profit.' He was rather struck by that. I'd given him something portable."

Wednesday, June 18th. London, Yacht Club.

Basil Dean and Alec Rea [1] came to tea here, and I was very pleased with

---

[1] The backer and chairman of the Liverpool Repertory Theatre.

them and their general attitude. They proposed to try out *Sacred and Profane Love* at Liverpool on September 15th and to open at Aldwych about October 1st.

Basil Dean told a good rehearsal story. He said that they rehearsed Shaw's *Pygmalion* for 9 weeks at His Majesty's and that in the middle Mrs. Pat Campbell went away for two weeks on her honeymoon. When she returned she merely said by way of explanation, "George (her new husband)[1] is a golden man." There was some trouble about her rendering. When she had altered it she said to Shaw, "Is that better?" Shaw said, "No, it isn't. I don't want any of your flamboyant creatures, I want a simple human ordinary creation such as I have drawn." He was getting shirty. Mrs. P. C. was taken aback. She replied, however, "You are a terrible man, Mr. Shaw. One day you'll eat a beefsteak, and then God help all women." It is said that Shaw blushed.

Thursday, June 19th. London, Yacht Club.

Masterman and I got Barrie to lunch at Reform Club. He remained very quiet for nearly 2 hours and then began to talk about the cricket team that he used to organize. For about 10 minutes he was brilliant.

Tuesday, July 1st. George St., Hanover Sq.

Peace with Germany was signed on Saturday.

Wednesday, July 9th. George St., Hanover Sq.

Official religious celebrations took place last Sunday. Official pagan celebrations will take place on Saturday, 19th, but the chief interest of an enlightened public has been the lawn tennis championships and the transatlantic voyage of R34. My chief interest has been my new play, of which I started the actual writing on Thursday; and the process of getting fixed in this flat—interminable. However, the play is so interesting that I don't mind sleepless hours in the night, as I can think about it and see part of it.

Tuesday, July 22nd. Comarques.

Marguerite came home yesterday from the peace celebrations on Satur-

---

[1] George F. M. Cornwallis-West.

day. She said, *"Tu n'as pas idée.* The air was positively *warm* with the *frénésie* of the reception of the procession." The only thing that happened at Thorpe was that the village mob threw an adulterer into the mill pond because he'd attacked the woman's husband. They would have lowered him into a well, but they couldn't find a rope.

Massingham and Masterman came for the week-end. Leslie Green was the fourth. Much fine wine. Much tennis on Saturday. Masterman showed great gifts at tennis and didn't use them. He was beaten. Characteristic. He said he had an article to write urgently. He didn't write a line. But he was a perfectly delightful companion. And when Massingham read the first act of my play aloud, Masterman grasped all the points and difficulties with astounding quickness.

Massingham worked hard and wrote an article on prohibition in America. He showed an all-round highly sensitive appreciation in all the arts. Masterman left on Sunday night, and Massingham yesterday.

Wednesday, July 23rd. Comarques.

Adding to her descriptions of peace procession last Saturday, Marguerite said that many women cried during the clapping and cheering. On the other hand the emotion of some women (better classes) in windows seemed forced and unnatural, or hysterical.

Way gave reminiscences of marching in Palestine and Asia Minor. Horses without drink for 3 days. One well 50 to 70 feet deep, one canvas bucket only could be lowered at a time, ½ of water spilled at each raising. Each horse required about 8 buckets; they were simply mad for water. They had no camels, when camels would have made things much easier. A camel can go without water for 5 days. They averaged 12 miles a day for 37 days in one march.

Friday, August 1st. Comarques.

I spent an evening with Walpole last week and we went to the Russian ballet, *Three-Cornered Hat*. After the hysterical laudation of *The Times* I feared for this ballet, and I didn't, in fact, care so much for it. Monotonous and noisy. But I might like it much better later on. This has occurred more than once before. I remember when I found *Carnival* tedious. Hughie introduced me to one Bruce, a tall diplomat, young and agreeable.

He suggested we should go and see Karsavina afterwards. I said I was too ill, and I was. But I might have been warned by Hughie that Bruce was Karsavina's husband.

Last Saturday with Leslie Green to the finals of the Frinton lawn tennis tournament. I had a longish talk with Mrs. Lambert Chambers, who in her talk, herself, and her play, fulfilled my hopes of the truly classic player. I liked her.

August 15th–20th.

Motor tour with Beaverbrook to Aberdeen.

I only saw Max afraid or out of feather once, and that was when we landed in a poor hotel at Perth on Sunday afternoon for the night. He could not stick it. We went on to Aberdeen.

We travelled up to the rate of 75 m.p.h. Passed a racing Mercedes at 69½ and somewhere near Forfar on the way to Sterling, killed 3 partridges on the wind-screen out of a covey that was picking in the middle of the road and failed to get up quick enough.

Max's interest in the Border—chieftain robbers and their keeps and methods—was very noticeable. He returned to the subject again and again.

He told me that some one said of him: "He began at   [1] and   wasn't big enough. He left Montreal because Montreal wasn't big enough. He went to London and London wasn't big enough, and when he gets to hell he'll be too big for hell."

At Perth, dining, we met Lord Dewar. Excessively rich, but won't spend money. He said sorrowfully that he would have to spend 7 hours in the train the next day in order to get to Harrogate. The idea of having a car had not apparently occurred to him.

Max gave me the history of the last 15 years of his father's life, beginning with the old man's phrase when he retired from the pastorate at the age of 70, "The evening mists are gathering"—meaning that doubts had come to him about the reliability of the doctrines he had been preaching.

---

[1] So in Bennett's manuscript. Probably the place is Halifax.

He died at 85, and in his last years he spent 55,000 dollars of Max's money. It is a great subject for a novel.

August 26th. Dublin.

At 7.30 the bookstalls were opening at Euston. The girls thereof all read either the *Mirror* or the *Sketch* at once, in their spare intervals. The *Daily Express* was sold out at 7.45 A.M.

Nothing special on journey. I thought of 14 titles for Edyth Goodall play. On the steamer an Irishman from New Zealand, who hadn't been home for 21 years, told me at great length how his luggage had not reached the boat. He simply, however, had not looked after it. When I left him he seized on to another man and treated him the same as me, but at greater length still. A feckless fool. Had wasted his passage over. In N.Z. he had caught enteric through letting an enteric patient drink cough-medicine out of the bottle, his bottle.

We arrived at 6 P.M.

August 27th. Dublin.

Horse Show. Lady jumpers who jumped better than the men. Irish faces of nearly all the girls in the Grand Stand. A certain chic. Many good-looking men. Motor-car enclosure full of cars all higgledy-piggledy. *God Save the King* when H.E. (French) came and left, and very feeble cheering of the same. The women won the jumping competitions easily. It seems a few of them go round and round Ireland, jumping; but this is the first time they have been allowed to jump at Dublin Show.

August 29th. Dublin.

Hired a taxi for 3 hours and went with O'Connor and Bodkin[1] to search quays in pouring cold rain. I bought four pictures, two lacquer tables, and 3 fine Victorian vases. I went to bed at 5 P.M. and got up at 7 to go to Bodkin's. Good dinner. Goodish talking. Especially from old Miss Purser[2] who had known Marie Bashkirtsev intimately and now, at

---

[1] Sir James O'Connor, the prominent Irish lawyer; and Dr. Thomas Bodkin, writer on art, and in 1927 appointed Director of National Gallery of Ireland.

[2] Olive Purser was the first woman student to obtain a scholarship after the admission of women to Dublin University.

75, owns a stained-glass factory in Dublin and bosses it herself. Bodkin is acquiring fine pictures for songs. Fancy getting a Diaz in Belfast for a song. He has a magnificent Bloemaert, and Domenico Feti. And he knows a deuce of a lot. He saved me from buying an alleged oil painting in the style of Poussin by suspecting that it was merely painted on an engraving. The dealer, who was quite honest, took the backing to pieces and we all examined it, and it *was* painted on an engraving. Last night's was a mixed dinner—I really believe the first I have been to in Dublin.

August 30th. Dublin.

Yesterday I went to see George Russell (Æ.) in the morning at Plunkett House—3rd floor, editorial offices of *The Homestead*. Susan Mitchell there as sub-editor. Russell very untidy. Longish beard. Gleaming glasses. He said he could not stand the dullness of the walls. So he had given 4 afternoons to painting the whole of them with figures and landscapes.

Russell said he had said to Yeats that Moore's *Hail and Farewell* was the finest biography Yeats would ever have.

Later, to the Phœnix Park races. Very Parisian in general looks, this meeting. I spent most of the time with the wife of Boss Croker. About 44. The most beautiful woman at the meeting. Of Cherokee descent, and very proud of it and full of interest in Cherokee music and history. Her tips, however, were no good. Boss Croker moved about, indifferently benevolent.

August 31st. Dublin.

Yesterday morning with O'Connor and Bodkin to National Gallery, where James Stephens is registrar. A little thin man, untidy, strange accent, with a continuous flow of ideas and fancies. He said *The O.W. Tale* was "it," but *The Pretty Lady* was "itter," and he put it at the top of all modern fiction. (On the other hand, a society journalist at the races in the afternoon said to some one, who told me, that Elinor Glyn would have given the story "a more human touch.") Stephens seemed to me to be a stronger man than I had thought. He said that anybody who re-wrote Doyle's detective stories from the standpoint of psycho-analysis would make a vast fortune. He gave me further tips about plots in Irish literature. Then we saw a few pictures in the Gallery, and then off somewhere else to see young Clarke's stained glass. Then lunch at Dolphin, and O'C. and I joined X. and wife and friend for Phœnix Park. X. is a solicitor, with 7 children, goes racing, lives very well, keeps his mother, and hires autos on contract. O'Connor said he made £1600 a year. The mystery of how Irish people cut the dash they do is very deep. They must be improvident. Racing a gay sight. Vast crowds. Much money lost, as the starting prices are an organized swindle. In one race there were two horses at even money. However, nobody cares. Got home at 6 and slept. *Soirée tranquille.*

September 2nd. Midland Adelphi Hotel, Liverpool.

Came here from Dublin yesterday. Pouring rain. Packed steamer. Couldn't move on it except with greatest difficulty. People placidly getting soaked through while being ill. I felt sure my luggage would reach Liverpool with me. It didn't. Great melancholy. Fruitless expeditions by hotel people to lost luggage office. At 9 P.M. I strolled up there myself, and the trunk came in at that identical moment. It was like a miracle.

On Sunday we drove over Wicklow mountains and things to Glendalough; ancient ecclesiastic city. Much of the scenery was superb. I drank 1½ bott. of stout, which gravely incommoded me. Yesterday I sat in wet boots after leaving the boat, 12.30 A.M. to 9.30 P.M. No alternative. Yet did not catch cold.

September 4th. Liverpool.

At 6 I went down to the pier head and witnessed the departure of a liner, the *Canada*. Boats of all sorts, rafts. Passengers all packed on starboard rails. Crowsnest. Going and coming over gangway seemed as if it would never cease. Absurd tiny fluttering of handkerchiefs. Then drawing in of hawsers. Bell ringing. Band: *Auld Lang Syne.* She slipped away. No perceptible movement of propellers, but the helm moved. She just grazed floating outposts of landing-stage. A tug joined her and closed her. Many other steamers made much smoke, obscuring her and the distance. She seemed to stop in mid-stream a few hundred yards down, the tug hugging her starboard bow. People said she would wait there till midnight. It was a moving sight.

September 6th. Liverpool.

W. G. Fay came to dine with me last night. He entered the hotel and then the restaurant with almost as much modesty and diffidence as if he had never had any experience at all. He said he was not interested in money and had kept all his simple habits. He told me how he and his brother had started a theatre in Liverpool with £5 capital each which they previously had to work for and save. They took a hall and made the seating themselves. He said his father was a civil servant and he was to have been one, but he failed at the prelim. and hated it. During his first theatrical enterprise he worked as an electrician in Dublin from 8 to 6. Then worked on his theatre from 8 to 11, and then would go and talk to Yeats or Martin or Russell till 2 or 3 A.M. He said the opposition to the *Playboy* was indirectly due to the opposition to *The Well of the Saints*. The opposition to the latter made Synge say, "I'll write something that *will* make 'em sit up." He wrote the *Playboy* and it *did* make 'em sit up. He said that at the first night not a word could be heard after the first three minutes. All had to be in dumb show. Later he had policemen to chuck out the worst rowdies. Then the theatre was empty. But he kept open, playing to £2 or £3 a week. He stopped all newspaper advertisements and hoarding advts. and kept on. He used to invite the audience to collect in the first row of the stalls. He lost many of his friends and has never got some of them back. After 6 months the newspapers asked for seats. He said they must pay. They said they wanted his advts. back. He said they would have the advts. on condition that they didn't say in the paper that his theatre was empty. He would let them slang his plays and his players, but not say that his theatre was empty. Then the hoarding people came and made peace. He won out. It seems that Yeats, Lady G.,[1] and Synge were directors at this time.

---

[1] Lady Augusta Gregory, writer of poems, plays, and stories and one of the active movers in the Irish literary revival.

This man was a hero and never shows. He is full of creative ideas about the theatre. Afterwards we went down to the theatre, and later we went with Olive Brook (lead in *Over Sunday*) and Clift (business manager), and I saw these people eat supper at their hotel, the Stork, where you could get drink afterwards.

This morning I went with Iris to choose a *jeune fille* costume for the first act.

Friday, September 19th. Comarques.

Sacred and Profane Love was produced at the Playhouse, Liverpool, last Monday 15th, at 7.30. The audience laughed when Iris Hoey called out "I cannot bear it" as the hero was playing the piano. True, the playing was appallingly bad. This ruined the first act, Sc. 1. Act 1 Sc. 2 went perfectly. The hold of the play on the audience gradually increased, and at the close an emphatic success was undeniable. I took a call because I had to. Then I had to take a second call. A thing I never did before.

1920

January 6th.

At Garrick last night Mair told us that he was absolutely sure that Shaw had not been an ascetic. Also he said that, in reply to an American criticism to the effect that when talking about love G.B.S. did not know what he was talking about, G.B.S. wrote to the paper to say that few people could possess greater practical experience as amorists than he possessed. This found us very startled and Anthony Hope incredulous, but Mair reiterated that he was quite sure.

As to Shaw's amorism. It occurs to me that only a practical man would have written the 1st act of *Man and Superman*.

January 11th.

Symphony concert yesterday at Queen's Hall with Sassoon and E. M. Forster. Henry Wood having a chill, Frank Bridge conducted in his place at a few hours' notice. After Schubert C major symphony, much applause at such good conducting at such short notice. Members of the orchestra applauded their conductor, and there was general mutual applause. Sassoon said: "I often wish when all these mutual compliments are going on they'd give the composer a show. Instead of pointing to the orchestra, why doesn't the conductor hold up the score and show it to the audience?"

At night Olympia, Victory Circus, with M. and the two Sitwells. Circus part, fair. Performing seal the best. Why can all performing seals do balancing feats infinitely better than Cinquevalli himself could ever have done?

March 9th. London.

I went with Swinnerton on a month's holiday to Portugal on Jan. 29 and returned last Wednesday, March 3rd. While I was away, *Sacred and Profane Love* finished its London run at the Aldwych of just over a hundred performances. Still, I made quite a lot of money out of that play. On Feby. 2nd, *Sacred and Profane Love* started its American career under Frohman & Co. with Elsie Ferguson as "attraction" in Pennsylvania and went on to Baltimore for 2nd week, and the receipts for first fortnight were 25,000 dollars. On the same day, Feby. 2nd, a spring provincial tour (21 weeks) of *Milestones* started at Oxford.

W. R. Hearst newspapers asked me if I would go to Russia to interview leaders and examine Soviet system for them. I said I would go for 2000 dollars a week, plus all expenses, and a journalist-courier with me to see to all formalities. They said this was prohibitive and offered alternative to send me in tow of the Allied Commission going out to Petrograd at £200 a week to include expenses. I refused.

I also got the idea for my next novel (on the old age of Max's [1] father, as related to me by Max himself) fairly complete, and I read *Le Curé de Campagne* for the death-bed scene at the end. I shall have a great death-bed scene at the end of my novel, and I want to stage it with the utmost magnificence. I got a tip or two from Balzac, but he is not at his best in this book and can be bettered.

Lately we have seen 3 revivals. *Arms and the Man* seemed better than it did 25 years ago. Very fine. Shaw's title to be the modern Molière not so rocky as I had thought. On the other hand *Pygmalion* is on the whole poor. Most of the characterization is quite rotten, and wilfully made so for the sake of art and eloquence. The last act is foozled. Mrs. Campbell was superb. There is still nobody else to touch her. Last night *The Admirable Crichton*. Excellent. I liked it better than when I first saw it, much better.

---

[1] Lord Beaverbrook. See pages 289–90.

Wednesday, March 10th. London.

In search of ideas for island play, I spent yesterday morning in walking about and went to the stores and bought things in 4 departments. A wonderful and delightful way of spending time and money. Better than most theatres. It is surprising that rich or fairly rich people don't consciously practise. "Let's go and spend £100 somewhere." Or even only £10 or £5. I think this sort of activity does stimulate creative ideas.

Philippe and Hélène Berthelot came for dinner last night. Also Massingham and Legros. Berthelot said that he read from 11 to midnight. Then worked from 12 to 3, writing out his telegrams, and got up at 7.30. He had done this for six years—I think he said without a break. He talked exceedingly well, indeed perfectly, rather in the manner of Cambon. All his judgments seemed to be quite detached and fair. But you could see he was the official, crafty, urbane, and also good-natured. He told several funny stories, two pathetic ones, quoted *mots,* quoted poetry; and poured my best champagne into a tumbler of water; didn't smoke; and left at 10.30, having given us a most finished entertainment.

On the other hand, he never once showed the slightest curiosity about anything whatever outside his own sphere of action—not the slightest. He had a great notion of Ll. George's agility of mind and quickness to grasp new ideas. He said that among the big men at the Conference, Clemenceau was the only one who thought only of his country. (True, I imagine. But I wish he had thought of it differently.) He was politely fierce against Hoover, while recognizing his value. Of Wilson he said that during the war he had all his immense correspondence from persons unknown to him classified regionally etc., and got local people to report on the senders, and thus arrived at a notion of what public opinion was in each district, and suited his political arguments to that district, and thus in the end managed to bring the U.S.A. into the war. I thought this rather good, but Berthelot despised it, and implied that a truly great man would convert the state of public opinion by means within his own mind, not employing machinery.

As a fact, Berthelot has little use for public opinion. He said, *"On peut toujours s'asseoir dessus."* He said that Wilson had got on by failing at everything: the bar, university, New Jersey, etc.; and that some people *did* get on like that: which is true. His judgment on the man's double quality—idealistic, and yet ruthless in affairs—was excellent. But he didn't seem to realize that this judgment doesn't dispose of the Americans and of their future predominance. You can understand the secret disdain of such a highly-cultured, broad-minded, efficient, conscientious, and industrious man, descendant of a great father and the finest civilization, for the crudeness and mental slovenliness of representatives of the U.S.A. and even of England. And he gave us a great show.

Saturday, March 13th, 1920.

Players and Authors.

I saw on a bus an advertisement of a play called *Come Out of the Kitchen*. Above the title was the name in very prominent characters of Miss Gertrude Elliott. Below the title was a line in characters so tiny that I could not decipher them. However, the bus stopped. I went close, and read the name of Alice Duer Miller. It may be, and on the other hand it may not, that Miss Alice Duer Miller has a clause in her play contracts, as I have in mine, obliging the theatrical manager producing the play to print the name of the author in all advertising matter. In either case, the appearance of Miss Alice Duer Miller's name on that particular advertisement was as nearly perfectly futile as makes no matter, for not one person in a thousand would read it or perhaps notice it at all. There can be no doubt that in Great Britain the name of Miss Gertrude Elliott has incomparably more advertising value than that of Miss Alice Duer Miller. But even so the disproportion between the types of the two names was excessive.

I am not, however, among those playwrights who kick angrily against the great importance given to players in theatrical advertising. Theatrical advertising is mainly under the control of players, who are human. If it were under the control of authors, players would not have much of a show, authors being equally human. And there is a good reason for the players' advantage; the public is more interested in players than in authors. It sees players; it likes them, loves them, worships them. Players feast the eye. Authors are seldom seen; discreet authors never. And when authors are seen they amount to nothing at all as a spectacle. I once lately "appeared" against my will, after a first performance. Some said maliciously that the unwillingness was unreal. This was nothing. But one reporter stated that I was wearing a blue shirt—naughty fabrication which I felt compelled to contradict. Nevertheless, although I fully admit the superior advertising value of players' names—Barrie himself has never got more than even with his interpreters in size of type—I do not think that players are more important than authors to the success of a play.

A good play may and sometimes does triumph over bad players; but the greatest player cannot make the public go to see a play that it doesn't want to see—at any rate in sufficient numbers to put money into the purse of the manager. Some managers are, if possible, more human than either actors or authors. They print their own names larger than anybody else's. Nay, they sometimes entirely suppress all other names. This is not business; for the public assuredly has no whit of interest in theatrical managers. It is merely megalomania. I have thought of inserting a clause in my contracts to the effect that my name shall be printed at least half as large as that of any player. This would coincide fairly well with my idea of a good subtle joke.

Monday, March 15th, 1920.

Women's Education in 1920.

The daughter of a rich friend of mine came to see us yesterday. Her age is sixteen, and she is at a French "finishing school" in Mayfair. This school, which moved over here from Paris during the war and will shortly move back again, counts among the most fashionable establishments of the kind, and is I suppose an example of the best and costliest that the rich have managed to get organized for the education of their daughters in the medieval year of 1920. It has twenty-eight pupils. Miranda told us that there were no rules. I discovered, however, that there was at any rate one. Namely, that pupils, out alone, may not acknowledge salutes from male acquaintances in the street. I asked Miranda whether, if I met her, she would cut me. She replied that she would not. Mistresses and pupils rise at about 8.30 A.M., but Miranda rises an hour earlier in order to practise the piano, of which she is very fond. She "learns" nothing but music and French. Nothing. She shares a bedroom with three other girls. All the pupils are English; but only French may be spoken in the presence of mistresses, who nevertheless are beloved. I should say that such a school would "finish" any girl, unless she happened to have a very powerful and unfinishable personality. The Renaissance seems nearly due.

Tuesday, March 16th, 1920.

Style.

"The King and Queen were present at a first night in a London theatre last evening for the initial time in their reign." I take this from the dramatic criticism, *not* of a provincial but of a London daily. It is quite a first-rate example of bad English. The culprit, whose name is well known to myself and other members of the London literary police force, evidently thought that it would be inelegant to use the same word twice in two lines; so he substituted "initial" for "first" in the second line. The affair must have cost him considerable cerebration, and no doubt he was rather pleased with the elegance of the result. Perhaps he had never reflected that words express ideas, and that, therefore, if a precise idea recurs, the precise word for that idea ought to recur. The idea expressed by the word "first" is precise enough, and no other English word means what "first" means. Certainly "initial" does not mean "first." Still, the man meant well. His misfortune was that, having picked up a good notion without examining it, he imagined that repetition was inelegant in itself. Repetition is only wrong when it is unintentional, and, when, being horrid to the ear, it is reasonably and honestly avoidable. On the other hand, repetition, used with tact and courage, may achieve not merely elegance but positive brilliance. What a phrase, "the initial time"!

Thursday, March 18th. London.

Saturday. Knoblock's play *Mumsee,* Little Theatre. After the first night he cut off the last (fourth) act entirely. Which leaves the play ending in a raw stump. It is astounding how people can do these things, with apparently no sense of the fact that they are butchers.

Yesterday I had my first dancing lesson.

Today I lunched with Newman Flower. He knew Hardy's mother. His mother lived in the original thatched cottage. She said to Flower that she couldn't understand how Americans would give her as much as £1 for a straw pulled from the roof-thatch.

Friday, March 19th. London.

Yesterday morning, after careering in the park after play ideas and catching them, I went to Neville Lewis's show and bought a small picture of a woman suckling a child (portrait of Madame Litvinov) for 15 guineas. Clifton, with whom I had a talk, told me of the times when a Johns could be bought for 10 guineas—and damned few buyers. He said he had once sold a very large pastel of Johns's for 10 guineas to a woman and had never heard of it since.

I heard yesterday that the first week's receipts of *Sacred and Profane Love* in New York were over 16,700 dollars. This easily bangs *Milestones* and all my other records. My royalties on that week exceed £350. My faith in the theatre as a means of artistic expression was, of course, instantly re-established. It would be.

Sunday, March 21st. London.

Yesterday morning I wrote the first scene of 2nd act of the play which for the present I am calling *Caspo*.[1] It turned out more vivacious than I had expected, but then I took the precaution of inspiring myself with the spirit of Italian comedy *dell' arte,* and I used one or two more of its jokes. The success (apparent, anyhow) of *S. & P. Love* in New York gives me hopes of one of my other plays being soon produced there. I find the elation caused by a 16,000-dollar week in New York wears off in about 24 hours, but it faintly reappears at intervals.

At night to Coliseum to see Barrie's *The Truth about the Russian*

---

[1] It was subsequently rechristened *The Bright Island*, produced in 1921.

Dancers. I bought the last two stalls on Wednesday. The stalls only filled up towards 9.30—proof absolute of what made those particular people buy those seats. Much of the piece is very amusing and well imagined. But Karsavina has no atmosphere in which really to exist.

Thursday, March 25th. London.

I went down to see E. last night about her affairs and especially about the efforts being made by the landlady to turn her out of her house. I had a strong impression of the acute misery caused to people by the shortage of houses. It seems that agents have notices fixed on their doors: "No unfurnished houses or flats of any description to let under £160 a year." I also had a strong impression of the misery among demobilized girls, many of whom can get neither work to do nor rooms to sleep in. City people, it appears, instantly turn down any application from a W.A.A.C. or W.R.E.N. etc. City people are always very imitative. I went and came back in a bus, between 8.30 and 11. I suppose that few of the people in the buses thought that their lives were hard, but I thought so.

Wednesday, March 31st. Comarques.

On Sunday, performance by the Stage Society at Hammersmith of Ashley Dukes's translation of Georg Kaiser's *From Morn to Midnight.* This play, though mostly ineffective and very mad, improved as it went on. It had ideas. It showed how all English and French dramatists are in a rut. Its last scene, saving of souls at a Salvation Army meeting, was strikingly good.

Monday, Gilbert Miller and Stanley Bell lunched with me. I wanted to talk about Miller's projected block of flats; but they wanted to talk and did talk about a dramatization of *The Card* and *The Regent,* for which they guaranteed me as many lightning changes of scene as I might demand.

Sunday, April 11th. Comarques.

P. J. came on Friday for a week-end of painting with me. But the weather has gravely interfered with it. He was in heavy artillery during the war. He said the staff orders of the British Army so far as he knew them were uniformly bad—always full of errors and negligences which had to be corrected on the telephone so far as possible, though any attempt to correct from below was always much resented (and often revenged) from above. He instanced a celebrated international footballer who was a staff captain and hopelessly stupid throughout. His indictment was most calm but most sweeping. On the other hand, he highly praised the staff work of both the Australian and the Canadian armies, which he always found efficient, correct, and as simple as possible. He said these staffs went solely for essentials and had a horror of filling up the useless forms which ravaged the British armies. He said, e.g. the heavies in which he was never had any horses or mules, but nevertheless had to fill up forms 3 times a day (among countless other forms) giving a return of horses and mules.

I read the *Mémoires d'une Chanteuse,* attributed to Wilhelmine Schröder-Devrient (in French). I don't think it is hers, but it has very powerful passages, is informed by a comprehensible philosophy and wisdom of life, and must have been written by an individual with some individuality. But, except at the close, it is obviously "composed" in general form, so as to lead on from one outrageous scene to a scene still more outrageous. It is a masterpiece in its way, but very *cru,* as a German work ought to be. The French translation is funny in places. The word *aphrodisiaque* is constantly used as if it meant a contraceptive device.

Wednesday, April 14th. Comarques.

I went to London today. Stores and other things before lunch. At the Reform I saw Spender for the first time since his return from Egypt. He goes to my (and the King's) tailors, and if his attire was not always the perfection of quietude, he would have to be called a dandy. When you see him in a tight corner in debate, and ultimately flooring everybody— which I have never known him fail to do—you perceive that he is a man capable of passion—though always restrained passion. I lunched with Swinnerton and Wells. I told H. G. that he ought to spend some of the profits of *The Outline of History* on new clothes. He said *The Outline of History* was ruining him—in income tax.

I had no tea, but read Emerson's essays instead. The essay on History is very noble.

Monday, April 19th. Comarques.

Frank Swinnerton came for the week-end, and I got endless gossip literary. Among other things he told me that Robert Nichols seriously advanced the proposition that his new sonnets were better than Shakespeare's. On Saturday we went to Bertie Sullivan's for tea, and went down among the yachts again. Sullivan told me that I could get a 100-ton trading ketch all transformed and well finished into a yacht for £3500, and that it would cost less than £1000 a year to run. Considering that I could make more than £1000 a year out of it in articles, and that also I could do all my ordinary writing on board, I determined to have it. Robert Nichols gave me Henry James's copy of the Fowler translation of Lucian in 4 vols. Looking through these volumes in bed last night, I found that the only part of which the leaves were cut was the Dialogues of Courtesans. Swinnerton and I agreed this morning that it was a very pretty problem whether these leaves were cut by Henry James or by Robert. Swinnerton left this morning in lovely weather.

Tuesday, April 20th. Comarques.

Yesterday I wrote the explanatory matter for the play *Caspo*, and today I almost decided to call it *The Bright Island*. Also I reflected and decided upon the theme and general plot of my next play (for Eadie). Tonight, drawn thereto by a reference to Rossetti's sonnet, *The Last Days of My Life*, in Blunt's diaries,[1] I read the same. Exceeding fine. Also a number of other sonnets in *The House of Life*. Also some Francis Thompson, chiefly about girls' love. These things gave me the idea that I might conclude my next play with something very fine about love.

---

[1] *My Diaries, 1888–1914*, by Wilfred Scawen Blunt.

Thursday, April 29th. London.

I came to London on Tuesday and went to the dentist, who threatened me with wholesale extractions, as several teeth were exuding pus.

Wednesday morning I had 90 minutes' business with Pinker and Eric at their office, after Pinker's return from America. He enlarged on the importance of the film business in the U.S.A. He said that all the big theatrical people were in the film business. Further that my play would not have been produced if the film had not been bought, and that it was very difficult to get any play produced without the concurrence of the film people, who regarded the play production as an advertisement for the film. They gave big prices when circumstances were favourable.

Wednesday, May 5th. London.

I went for week-end to Beaverbrook's on Saturday and returned on Monday. Max has now two crazes—playing tennis all day and sleeping at night in the garden. He gave me the full history of his relations with his father as material for my next "big" novel. (But I'm afraid I shall have to write a little one first.) He also promised to tell me stories of "deals" as material for short stories. Especially Strathcona's [1] life in England.

He had a series of Mutt and Jeff cartoons in which Ll. G. and Bonar Law were Mutt and Jeff, and Ll. G. was always playing tricks on B. Law. He said that in the end Law asked him to stop this and he stopped it. Ll. G. expressed earnest curiosity to see these things, and so Max asked him and Mrs. Ll. G. to come to Cherkley with several other ministers to see them on his private screen, and Max got an orchestra, which cost him £25. Ll. G. saw the whole lot. Max said it was an ordeal for him (Ll. G.) and that Mrs. Ll. G. was very subdued during the rest of the evening. Practically the whole Bonar Law family came down in batches while I was there. All perfectly delightful,—papa, 2 girls, and 2 boys.

Monday night: *Mary Rose,* Barrie's new play at the Haymarket. Tedious. The papers for the most part hailed this work as a great masterpiece.

---

[1] Baron Strathcona, the former Donald A. Smith, was, like Lord Beaverbrook, a Canadian.

Last night, *The Skin Game,* Galsworthy's new play at the St. Martin's. This play may be a melodrama, but it is a very good one indeed and it holds you absolutely. It is very well acted. It is a tale, an incident, whose effect depends on a coincidence, and it has no general significance. The writing and the observation are excellent. After this show we went to Lillah and Fred Keeble's reception after their marriage. Lillah most beautiful. Lady Wyndham was there; aged. I thought, "Lillah will be like that one day." But perhaps she never will be like that. The usual crowd.

Monday, May 10th. Comarques.

I spent the week-end in doing gratis work for other people. Alterations and additions to *The Beggar's Opera* for Hammersmith, a prospectus for the *New Statesman,* and a descriptive sketch of H. G. Wells for W. Rothenstein's new book of drawings. I also finished the proofs of *Body and Soul.*

I read Atkins' and Ionides' *A Floating Home* all through. It is a very good book indeed. Some of my illustrations to it are fair and some are merely awful. I read most of Aldous Huxley's *Leda.* The first poem in it is the best modern poem I have read for years. This last week I have read Ernest Newman's book on Gluck.[1] It is a youthful work, published 25 years ago, and written in style very much less sure than his present style, but it is the goods.

Saturday, May 15th. Comarques.

Wednesday I went down to Bournemouth to see Rickards, and I returned on Thursday. Glimpses, through Rickards, into a vast world of sickness and tragedy—a whole world complete in itself and looking on angrily and resentfully and longingly at our world. The fact is that Rickards has stood very admirably this trial of being all of a sudden cut off from our world and all that he so extremely *savoured* (rather than *enjoyed*) therein. So has Mina Rickards. He grumbles terribly, but he has stood it, and his judgment has remained sane. On Thursday night we

---

[1] *Gluck and the Opera,* by Ernest Newman, published in 1895.

took Richmond to see Sacha Guitry and wife in *La Prise de Berg-op-Zoom*. Episodically very amusing. But nothing whatever in the play. Sacha is really a better actor than an author. He is really very good. Yvonne Printemps young and fairish. It was rather pathetic to see the once young and worshipped Suzanne d'Avril playing the small and purely farcical part of the *ouvreuse* in the 2nd act. *L'assistance était très snob*. I took pleasure in pointing out to sundry acquaintances in the foyer that what we were seeing was really nothing in particular and that the whole season, artistically, depended on Lucien Guitry's interpretation of his son's clever 2nd-rate boulevard plays. The acting generally, however, and the production, were without question superior to English ditto.

I got some books on St. Paul and began to read them.

Saturday, May 29th. Comarques.

Thursday was my 53rd birthday, and I had rheumatism all day.

James Douglas was in the strangers' room of the Garrick lunching a boy. Afterwards he introduced me to this boy, who proved to be the celebrated Colonel Lawrence.

Saturday, June 19th. Comarques.

I came here for the summer yesterday evening. A fortnight yesterday Basil Dean refused *The Bright Island* and forfeited his £200 "caution money." Yesterday it was accepted with enthusiasm by the Lyric, Hammersmith, which theatre had refused *Sacred and Profane Love,* which Dean subsequently accepted with enthusiasm.

Saturday, July 3rd. Comarques.

In spite of queer health and much loss of time, a period of hard work is setting in. I have got more into the habit of getting up about 5.30. This is a great advantage. I wrote the opening scene of my new play on Thursday.

Yesterday I went to London and, with Lasky and Pinker at lunch, made a contract with Lasky for a film. Lasky asked me to go and stay with him in the cinema city in California and offered to pay my fare both ways. I have to deliver this film in 6 months. I have to deliver a 100,000-word novel in about 7 months, and a series of, say, six short stories before the end of April anyhow.

Monday, July 5th. Comarques.

Edgar Selwyn here for the week-end. Edgar gave me some good tips about screen writing. He said: You haven't got to write for London, you have to write for Thorpe. I added to this and said: You have to write for a Thorpe man who can't hear and who can only read simple words. I see that any projected revolution in the film can only be done gradually.

Edgar told me that the rents of N.Y. theatres ran from 40 to 70 thousand dollars p.a., and that the Morosco was 45,000. I already knew how much the Morosco holds. It held 16,000 dollars a week for *Sacred and Profane Love.* Edgar read 2 acts of *The Bright Island* while he was here, and I doubt if he saw anything in it at all. He said that political plays always failed in the U.S.A. and that you could not interest the U.S.A. people even in politics themselves, to say nothing of plays about politics. I don't believe either of these statements.

Speaking of the labour question in the U.S.A., Edgar said that for the big labour meetings the streets were always choked with cars—and not Fords either. It is obvious, of course, that if there are 12 million cars in use in the U.S.A. a vast number of working men must possess cars. It means one to less than every nine of the total population, men, women, and children.

Monday, July 12th. Comarques.

I finished the second act of Eadie's play [1] yesterday afternoon at 7, having written 1500 words of dialogue in 3½ hours. This is work. I was extremely exhausted. I took my Sunday today. Drove to Clacton this morning, but had no interest in it. Weather full of heavy thundershowers with

---

[1] *The Love Match*, produced in 1922.

hurriedly hot interludes of tropical sunshine—reminding one of Conrad's equatorial landscapes. Beneath all my work and occupations, I have been getting information as to yacht for sale. This is really interesting. I must have a yacht rather bigger than I ought to have. This will give me the new interest and anxiety which I want.

Monday, July 19th. Comarques.

I finished Conrad's *The Rescue* yesterday. It is better than some of his recent things, but it has dull passages. Also the motivation, especially of the Malay minds, is obscure. But some of the situations are fine. The opening reads so stiffly that it might have been written a long time ago, when Conrad was learning to write. I at last got *Flatland* the other day, price 30*s*. It is quite up to its reputation. The author only fails towards the end, when he tries to do sustained conversations. He can't do convincing dialogue. He is fine at exposition, irony, and genuine creative imagination; but he cannot do the picturesque; he can't "reconstitute" a scene as a whole.

Monday, August 2nd. Comarques.

Having begun my play, now called *The Love Match,* on 1st July, I finished it on 31st ditto. The stuff in it is all right, I think. But I should not be at all surprised if Eadie declines to take up the option for which he has paid £200.

Yesterday evening I finished *La Chartreuse de Parme* and immediately began *Le Rouge et le Noir,* of which I have already read over fifty pages (8 A.M.). The *Chartreuse* is very great. It is only in reading such parts as the escape from prison that one sees that the technique of the novel has advanced. This part is not fully imagined; it is very well imagined up to a point, and very well invented; but the physical acts of escape are not as well rendered as Stendhal probably intended them to be. However, the wit, the power, the variety, the grace, the naturalness, and the continuous distinction of this book will want some beating. In reading Conrad lately, I sometimes had a sense of effort. Not so with this, which

I have now read three times. The opening of *Le Rouge et le Noir* has the air of being *très ingénue,* but after 20 pages you see *avec qui vous avez à faire.*

Friday, August 6th. S. W. Hotel, Southampton.

I came down here on Wednesday with Bertie Sullivan in a hired Rolls-Royce from London to buy a yacht. Bad weather. We lunched at Alton on Wednesday, and then went on and inspected the much-vaunted *Julia* schooner. £5000 odd. No good. Ruled right out. (All yacht yards are closed this week up to Thursday, in spite of the fact that it is Cowes week and any racer might want repairs in a hurry.) Yesterday morning we tried to see the *Hinemoa,* but couldn't, in spite of appointment. At 11 A.M. we went to Cowes and I saw *The Wanderer,* ketch, 88 tons, and decided to buy her if I could get her at my price, £2500, including a motor launch and two dinghies. By 9 P.M. I had got her at my price subject to inventory and survey. I reckoned she will cost £1500 to put right below.

Saturday, August 7th. Royal York Hotel, Brighton.

On Thursday I saw two of the finest yachts afloat. *Iolanda,* which I have often admired at Cannes. The other yacht was the Duke of Westminster's *Belem,* lying in the Medina near to *The Wanderer.* A converted French merchantman. Fantastic luxury, but real taste. I got some ideas from it for *The Wanderer.* A lovely ship. Allen said the Duke had spent. well over £100,000 on her and that £35,000 would buy her; which probably meant £25,000. The wages bill must be £700 a month. She appears to be used for only about a week or so a year. This is a social crime.

I think I should fancy more than any of these boats the *Shenandoah,* a 3-masted schooner, with a big beam; she floated on the water like a duck and looked superb. When we went out from the Supermarine Yard in a launch to inspect the motor launch that goes with *The Wanderer,* we went close by the *Shenandoah,* and it was sickening to think she wasn't mine.

Friday, August 27th. Comarques.

Yesterday afternoon I received the second and final part of the survey of *The Wanderer,* and it was thoroughly unsatisfactory, so that I was obliged to refuse the yacht. The first part had been pretty good, especially for a 60-year-old boat.

I read *Erewhon* again. The nature descriptions are as good as anything. The best *Erewhon* parts are the criminality of ill health and the musical banks. The "machines" part is not nearly so good. The form of the book is very clumsy, and the philosophic theories ought to have been worked more ingeniously into a narrative of picturesque events. It is much inferior to *Gulliver* as a whole, but the finest parts seem to make it a classic.

During the last two or three weeks I seem to have done nothing, but still I have done something. Idled with Swinnerton at Clacton and Frinton. Finished my sketch of Rickards for the Rickards book. Got into final order all the matter for the first annual volume of *Things That Have Interested Me* and evolved the idea and structure of my film. Also I have played a lot of tennis and can now play four sets in an afternoon without dropping down dead. Croquet has also improved. But still no water-colours at all since Portugal. I expect I shan't do any now this season.

Friday, September 3rd. River Black Water, on board the Yacht Zoraida.[1]

On Sunday morning I had a telegram from Pauline Smith that Rickards had died at Bournemouth early that morning. Tubercular meningitis.

Gilbert Miller was at Comarques for the week-end. I made some progress in intimacy with him. He left on Monday morning, and André Gide and nephew came in the afternoon for one night. I had great book talks with Gide. I had to leave at 8 A.M. Tuesday to go to R.'s funeral.

---

[1] Lent to Arnold Bennett by Herbert Sullivan.

Wednesday, September 8th. Brightlingsea, on board the Zoraida.

We left Harwich about 9.30 yesterday, but there was no wind till after lunch, so that instead of going to Burnham as intended, we came in here. Flat calm this morning at 7 A.M. Ronald, mate, slept ashore, and came aboard in a fisherman's boat. The 3 men in the boat went to a small smack close by, pumped her, and then went somewhere else, two of them rowing face to stern and standing up. Smacks' sails everywhere being set, rattle of running rigging and anchor chains; small boats moving everywhere; riding lights extinguished etc., etc. A yacht towed out by a Gvt. steamer.

Sunday, September 26th. Glasgow.

We drove in Richmond's open car yesterday up W. side of Loch Lomond and past Lochearnhead and home by Stirling. About 135 miles. Driving rain and mist nearly all day, so that we saw Scotland in a characteristic aspect. After dinner at the hotel 10 P.M. we went out to view the streets. Renfield Street and Sauchiehall Street crowded with people, largely young. Many picture palaces. In quiet side streets off Renfield Street and Sauchiehall Street I noticed large knots of men. It took me some time to find out what they were doing. The largest group was a thick ring, in the middle a man about 32 was quickly selling tracts. His speech was finished. He had some scrap with a man in the crowd, but apologized and said he had no intention of being discourteous. At last I discovered that he was an advocate of birth-control. He must have been doing pretty well out of it.

In a smaller group a man was advocating something about franchise. He argued with his little audience, whose nearest faces were within a foot of his own. A few others craned their necks to listen. The social tone of the argument was admirable. These street phenomena seemed to show how Scotchmen like argument. Not one woman in these little crowds. Presently two pairs of tall policemen from different directions converged on the two groups and very quietly and persuasively broke them up.

Waiter in coffee-room at hotel didn't know that *riz de veau* meant sweetbread, in fact asserted that it didn't. It often happens that waiters don't know at all what they are selling and don't care. They ought to be told in detail every day.

Saturday, October 2nd. Durham.

Left Edinburgh yesterday at 10.20 and missed the fast connection at Newcastle for Durham. Newcastle is a vast, dirty, and dishevelled station. It doesn't seem to belong to anybody in particular. Enormous *ennui* of the casual local train to Durham. A few "first seasons" (I thought) in our compartment: men well accustomed to the boredom of travelling in slow trains. I went to sleep and only awoke as we were entering Durham. At station the stationmaster asked me if I was the Earl of Darnley. Presently the Earl of Darnley arrived with wife. He is in fact rather like me but older and bigger. We stuck our luggage on a cart for the hotel and went direct to the cathedral.

This cathedral comes up to expectations. It is not a homogeneous whole, but many of the parts are magnificent. The verger who guided us was dignified and very funny at times without knowing it. Still, he told us a lot. It is a gigantic affair, this cathedral, and I regret that the view from the north side shows up so acutely the disparity of the towers. The view from the river is all that Turner & Co. made it out to be.

Thursday, October 7th. London.

Monday night, *The Romantic Young Lady,* from the Spanish, Royalty Theatre. A pretty fancy, but feeble and lacking consistent invention. Tuesday, Shufflebotham came to dinner and told me his troubles. Swinnerton was also here with his troubles. Still, much gaiety. Last night, *The Whiteheaded Boy,* at the Ambassadors with Maire O'Neill, Sarah Allgood, and Arthur Sinclair. On the whole a very good thing, superlatively well acted by the principals. Maire O'Neill and Sinclair together were most richly humorous.

Saturday, October 9th. London.

Yesterday afternoon I went down to Cambridge to stay a night with Rivers[1] and see to Richard's induction into Clare College. Train full of undergrads and relatives. Tea at Rivers's. Then by "backs" to Clare where I saw Richard's rooms.

I dined with Rivers in St. John's hall. A "short" dinner, too short, and professors etc. rather dull. Too cautious; too pedagogic. Another professor there, agriculture. I forget his name. His chief interest seemed to be the history of the barley plant. Went on with him to Rivers's, where there was another psychologist (psycho-analyst) who had just been on a visit to Freud. Freud speaks English perfectly. Talks little. Gets the "patient" to analyse himself. Was told afterwards that a good psycho-analyst would charge 300 guineas for a case, which might employ one hundred hours. I went to bed hungry, and woke up so hungry at 3.15 that at about 5 I got up and searched for cake and found it. Three undergrads to breakfast, besides Richard. But among them only Davison (poet) talked. He *did* talk well. Rivers's delightful personality! Richard's work seems to be arranged so that he has no afternoons for sport. Laboratory every afternoon, including Saturday. Cambridge was most beautiful. We went into King's College Chapel and heard choir practice.

Thursday, October 14th. London.

Yesterday afternoon while I was correcting proofs Robert Nichols burst in, much disturbed about his own gloominess. After tea he began telling me about ragging at Winchester in his time—presumably about a dozen years ago. He said that he and two other kids were often put up side by side against a wall, and the game was to throw boots between their heads. He was thus frequently hit in the face. Another dodge was to fill a canister with ordinary gas, and light it at a little hole in the top, put it under a cane chair, and put the boy with his behind naked on the chair. The heat was not unbearable, but the affair always finished with an explosion, and waiting for this expected explosion *was*

---

[1] W. H. R. Rivers, noted psychologist and anthropologist, author of the classic work on *The Todas*.

nearly unbearable. And so on. And so on. He said that there had been several attempts at suicide and one suicide.

Monday, October 18th. London.

Coal strike began today, but accepted with a notable calm. I worked every day on my novel last week.[1] Beaverbrook and Masterman came for lunch on Friday. Max in great conversational form and histrionically effusive about inner history of the cabinet.

Tuesday, October 19th. London.

At Siegfried Sassoon's suggestion we went last night to Flonzaley Quartet's chamber concert. Haydn, Beethoven, Schumann. I made notes of it for a chapter in my new novel. Seemed thin, and too small for the hall. Anyhow I was bored. Ottoline Morrell was there. Distinguished features. In fact a personality. She left with us after the Beethoven. Siegfried, delighted with the music, would not leave till the end.

Thursday, October 21st. London.

Rivers came to lunch at the Reform on Tuesday. He and Shufflebotham were talking about miners' eye-diseases etc., and Rivers said that the danger factor on the nervous system had never been taken properly into account. Shufflebotham said that he had been preaching it for years. Shuff said that you could always distinguish miners from potters on their way to early morning work. Miners had an apprehensive look. Potters would whistle on the way to work, miners never. It appears that some one has just pointed out in *The Times* that if you put the mines in order of frequency of accidents and also in order of majorities for strikes, the two lists coincide! All this, of course, so far as the miners are concerned, is chiefly subconscious. Shuff said that of course boys voted for strikes. They had not had time to become accustomed to the danger, and the instinctive reactions were very strong.

I got frightened about the opening of my novel, *Mr. Prohack,* yesterday. But on reading it through I thought it wasn't so bad.

---

[1] *Mr. Prohack,* published in 1922.

Saturday, October 23rd. London.

George Sampson came to lunch at Reform on Thursday. Sassoon, with Jascha Heifetz, violinist, and his pianist. Something distinguished about Heifetz. Very young. A gold collar-pin and a pearl scarf-pin. I went with those three to a concert of Josef Hofmann at 3 P.M. They said he was the finest pianist in the world and that there was no good second. This is his reputation in America. (They are both—Heifetz and his accompanist—markedly Americanized.) Hofmann certainly played magnificently, but the programme was not a good one. I thought of asking the three to come along for tea, but decided not to, in view of my interest in my novel.

Yesterday M. and I lunched with F. Swinnerton at Café Royal to meet the St. John Ervines. This was quite excellent. I dined with Reeves Smith at the Savoy to meet Sharper Knowlson, and Dr. S. Knowlson decidedly better than his writing.

Sunday, October 24th. London.

Reading Repington's diary (*The First World War*). It is an inexcusable violation of confidences, but emphatically it is "the goods."

Four orators in Hyde Park. One: a sort of imitation working man, old, on political themes. Good crowd. Extremely dull. Two: an oriental preaching Islamism in fluent English with exaggerated r's. Extremely dull. Three: a young man preaching I don't know what, though I listened several times. Monotonous gestures. Extremely dull. Four: an evangelistic scene. A little man with a big nose, and a group of attendants including 5 or 6 dull women. Bad singing of bad hymns. Extremely dull. Still, he did say: "When I lived in the country and worked on my farm the girl came out and shouted (very loud), '*Mr. Way!*' '*What?*' '*Dinner.*' Ah! That was a good moment. But God's dinner is better than that. On the farm I wanted a fresh dinner every day. God's dinner lasts for ever," etc.

Wednesday, October 27th. London.

I finished the fifth chapter of *Mr. Prohack* yesterday morning and corrected all the proofs of the E. A. Rickards book in the afternoon—and they wanted a lot of correcting. When they were done I suddenly realized that I was exhausted and that the top of my head was coming off. Jascha Heifetz concert at Queen's Hall. M.'s one idea as soon as the concert had begun was to depart again. I thought Heifetz was a marvellous performer, with a lovely tone, but his interpretation of César Franck's sonata did not excite me.

Friday, October 29th. London.

Haidée Wright, Vernon, and the Alec Reas for dinner. Haidée very like the 3rd act of *Milestones* and exactly like the 2nd act. Depressed and captious about the world generally, though much pleased with an alleged *renaissance* which she has observed in English acting. A strong, "vibrant" (as they say) personality, always interesting. You can see all the time why Haidée Wright is a great actress. Something is always oozing out of her. She is very shy and nervous and diffident, yet well aware, somewhere within herself, that she is a person of considerable importance in the artistic world.

Sunday, October 31st. London.

Friday night, Olive, Marguerite, Legros, and I went to the Hammersmith Palais de Dance. It was the first time I had ever danced in public. However, there was no ordeal about it. I even danced with M., who knows less about dancing than I do. Intense respectability of the whole place. The instructresses had a certain *chic*.

Yesterday I went with M. to Dickens & Jones' new shop, just opposite in Regent St., and was much pleased with the ribbon department. I was as usual struck by the felinity of the women customers with the *vendeuses*. These latter, I suppose, get into a habit of diplomacy and forbearance. They need it, by God! One phrase that girls must have been taught is, "Are you having attention, Madam?" The dress department head (a decent, worn, diplomatic sort) showed enormous tact, after we had put her to a certain amount of trouble about a dress which we had not the slightest intention of buying, by saying, "Perhaps you would like to call and see it again on Monday."

Tuesday, November 2nd. London.

I concocted a film plot yesterday evening in the streets between 5.15 and 7.15, after spending most of the day in worrying about the proposals and cast for a revival of *Milestones*. I first heard of this affair on Wednesday last from Eric Pinker on the phone. He had just heard of it, but negotiations had previously been going on between Eadie and Bright (on behalf of Knoblock). I refused to agree to Eadie's being the producer and wanted to cable to Knoblock. Miss Nerney, however, learnt on the phone from Bright that Knoblock had left no address and that Bright had a power of attorney and that Bright agreed to Eadie's being the producer. So I agreed.

On Friday evening Eaton came to see me and assured me that Eadie would produce it all right, which I much doubted. He also showed me a copy of his letter to Eadie, in which he indicated that there would be no trouble about the casting and that I should only have to be formally consulted. On Monday I learnt from the Pinkers, on going to see them, that Bright and Vaughan had fully discussed the cast on Friday. Why they didn't ask me to join in I don't know. I then got Eric Pinker to send to Vaughan for the cast, and he brought it up to me here yesterday at 3 P.M. The only "name" in it was Eadie's, with possibly Harben's. I told him to say that I insisted on Haidée Wright for Gertrude. I said that a failure of this revival would damage the play for ten years, that the bulk of the players were unused to London, and that everything centred round the star, whereas there never has been a star in *Milestones;* and I wanted some balance to the star in the shape of a first-rate actress in the most important woman's part. I said that Haidée W. had a good figure and could make up for the first act at least as young as Eadie, and that she was perfect for the other acts.

The *Star* rang me up yesterday and asked me to review Mrs. Asquith's book for Friday. I wondered about the reason of this move till I saw the *Evening News* with an enormous announcement that Churchill was going to review it for the *Daily Mail*. Evidently the papers are going to make a tremendous feature of it. I refused.

Wednesday, November 3rd. London.

Macbeth last night at the Aldwych with the American actor Hackett and Mrs. Patrick Campbell. He has good diction. Mediocre as a whole and largely bad. Mrs. Pat inaudible. Witches appalling. Music ditto, besides being much too slow and besides being played in darkness.

November 8th. London.

Difference between London and provinces. I have several times noticed in provincial theatres and music-halls that the men in the audience do not stand still when the national anthem is played. They do not even take off their hats (or caps). In West End theatres the observance of the protocol is still absolutely strict.

Thursday, November 11th. London.

Last night Bertie Sullivan and I gave a dinner to Harry Preston. Tom Marlowe (*Daily Mail*), Seymour Hicks, and Reeves Smith (Savoy Hotel) also present. Hicks told a number of fine stories, and a few really great; but Tom Marlowe told the best one. Harry Preston was very flattered and quiet. Hicks is a great wit. His flashes are almost continuous. When we were talking about black puddings and the constituents thereof and then got on to chitterlings, lights, etc., he said, "All this ought to be in the Christmas number of *The Lancet.*"

Wednesday, November 17th. London.

On Monday, MacAlarney of Famous Players called to discuss my project for a film. On the whole he warmly approved it. He showed excellent understanding of the characterization and the psychological implications thereof (no—it was not Monday, but one day last week). I was to have proceeded with the film yesterday, but could do little owing to lassitude and engagements. I did a bit, and this morning in a very brilliant hour in the streets I did a whole chunk. In fact all the first part.

Sunday, November 21st. London.

Dress rehearsals of *Milestones* on Thursday–Friday. The first performance last night. I took Bertie Sullivan and Legros. Much real enthusiasm. But by last night I had got tired of the play and went home gloomy. I introduced Legros to English clubs yesterday, and he was immensely struck. *"Quelle vie charmante!"* he said at the Garrick, where all the members chaff each other.

Wednesday, November 24th. London.

At work on film all morning. Lunched with Pinker and Swinnerton at Reform, and then I got information from Shufflebotham about the nursing home for my film. Barrie, Elgar, Massingham, Hy. Head, and Sassoon to dinner, and Rivers came afterwards. Massingham had forgotten the date, had to be rung up, and arrived 45 minutes late. Large quantities of interesting things were said at this dinner. Some of the fellows stopped till 12.25. I smoked too much. But I have survived it all right. Barrie said he never went out at all except to dine with me once a year. Elgar is fine, though in fact they all were.

Tuesday, November 30th. London.

Friday I went to Brightlingsea to see the yacht again, and I made further arrangements for changes therein.

I read Lawrence's new novel, *The Lost Girl*. It would be absolutely great if it had a clear central theme and comprehensible construction. It doesn't end; it stops. But it is very fine indeed, the work of a genius. It held me. I read it in less than 24 hours.

Saturday, December 4th. London.

Today I began to work on the film and other things, though short of sleep. I took M. this afternoon to see the Japanese prints at the B.M.[1] and was more impressed than the first time even. Of course the mummies held M. on her way through their rooms. She is obsessed when she

---

[1] The British Museum.

sees them by the fact that they once lived, loved, etc. To be just, she showed just as much interest in the Greek sculpture. We were struck anew by the immense size and grandioseness of the B.M. It is a very efficient affair. Crowds of people, especially girls, most of them uncomprehending. Experts giving popular lectures.

Wednesday, December 8th. London.

Last night reception at Edith Sitwell's and Helen Rootham's. Two small rooms very full of smoke and people. But not dull. I have never been bored there.

Yesterday at the Reform I was told that Shaw said that he had received a film offer of £10,000 per original film, he to furnish two films a year. I gathered that he was going to accept it.

Friday, December 10th. London.

Wednesday night, first performance of the Swedish ballet at the Palace. This affair was very good. Particularly the *El Greco,* the *Nuit de Saint Jean,* and the *Vierges Folles.* Yet a number of idiots in the press yesterday morning treated it with cold condescension and said that Russian ballet had spoilt us for anything third-rate! The *El Greco* was a wonderful reconstitution and thoroughly well done.

Saturday, December 11th. London.

Yesterday lunch with Thomas Vaughan, partner in God knows how many theatres, M., and Gilbert Miller also. This lunch must have cost Tommy £10. The beefsteak was a failure.

Last night a dinner, organized by Albert Rutherston, to Nigel Playfair, to mark his departure to the U.S.A. to produce *The Beggar's Opera* there. Milne was in the chair and made a brilliant sort of speech full of jokes, proposing Nigel's health. The speeches were too few and too short, and after them there was an anticlimax.

This morning at 12.30 I finished the writing of my first film. I have temporarily called it *The Wedding Dress.* It has taken 25 days, out of

which I was ill on 7 days and did nothing whatever. I should estimate
that the MS. is about 10,000 words.

Sunday, December 19th. London.

The last few days, having delivered the film, I have read through the
first instalment of the novel, *Mr. Prohack,* and been inspiring myself
for the next instalment. I read George Moore's play which he sent me
in the edition de luxe, *The Coming of Gabrielle.* The idea is very
ancient and the plot very clumsy, but there are very bright distinguished
things in the dialogue, which is highly readable without being at all
fireworky.

I gave permission to the Everyman Theatre to do *The Honeymoon.*
They did not consult me in any way about casting, scenery, production.
The first word I had from the theatre was 2 tickets for the first night.
I returned them. In the first place I had a curious absence of all desire
to go, and in the second place I thought it was like their darned cheek
to ignore me entirely until the first night. The thing has been played
in Manchester and Harrogate before the London production tomorrow.
I only knew of this from the papers.

Tuesday, December 21st. London.

Last night, Helen Rootham's friend, the Serbian, Milrénovic, came to
see me. He arrived at 9.40 and left at 11.40. Previously M. and I dined
alone. He said he had lived in London six years without knowing any
one, and had thought, within himself, about religion. He seemed rather
profound: full of fine ideas of which perhaps about the hundredth part
will be realized in about a century. I told him practically how to begin
to realize his dreams.

On Sunday night Legros dined here, and then he and I went to the
Stage Society show at Hammersmith. H. O. Meredith's *The Forerunner*
was one of the feeblest things I ever saw on the stage. Then Franklin
Dyall introduced me to the author. I said to him, "You have written a
highly curious play." Later I said, "You have written a damned curious
play." This was the best I could do.

Christmas Day, 1920. London.

Two thoroughly bad nights, full of the church clock. Still I wrote over 4000 words of my novel in 3 days, with lots of preoccupations.

This afternoon I finished *L'Immoraliste*. It is a better novel than I had thought, full of emotion wherever the wife comes in. No such novel could be published in English. It is philosophical, realistic, and even homosexual. Construction a bit confused, but it is a book. I now want something else to read.

Sunday, December 26th. London.

I gave my Xmas dinner last night at Claridge's. M., Legros, and Lorna Lewis, who told me she was 20½ and Welsh. A vast crowd; the two lounges added to the restaurant. Many family parties. Impossible not to contrast this show with the financial crisis now existing. A crude contrast, of course. But interesting to think of the apprehensions in the minds of many hosts there. Crackers, paper caps, and much throwing of paper missiles.

Thursday, December 30th. London.

In spite of much fatigue after Xmas night I did some work on my novel in the afternoon. Yesterday I lunched (alone) and dined at home and wrote 2100 words, also of my novel. After dinner I went out to be polite to the members of the *Milestones* company. Eadie was very gloomy. Stella Jesse, Ada Barton, and 2 others were the gayest. Stella asked me whether I could tell her what old gentlemen with long beards did with their beards when they took a bath.

The front-of-the-house manager displayed the usual illogical optimism in face of a poor house. The night was awful and the audience thin and chilly (according to Eadie). Perhaps that accounted for the atmosphere of the dressing-rooms. I think that Harben was the only realist in the assembly.

INDEX

INDEX

NOTE: Wherever possible, the Index includes some brief explanatory reference to the names, titles, etc., mentioned in the text.